THE SUCCESS OF OPEN SOURCE

STEVEN WEBER

The Success of Open Source

HARVARD UNIVERSITY PRESS

Cambridge, Massachusetts, and London, England

Library of Congress Cataloging-in-Publication Data

Weber, Steven, 1961–
The success of open source / Steven Weber.
p.   cm.
Includes bibliographical references and index.
ISBN 0-674-01292-5 (alk. paper)
1. Open source software.   I. Title.

QA76.76.S46W43 2004
005.3—dc22   2003056916

Contents

Preface

Several years ago when I began thinking about open source software, I had to convince just about everyone I talked to, outside of a narrow technology community, that this was a real phenomenon and something worth studying in a serious way. I no longer have to make that case. Open source has become a subject of real interest to a wide-ranging swath of people and organizations. I hope this book will explain to many of those people how the open source process works and why the success of open source is broadly significant.

I'm a political scientist and I worry more about how communities are governed than I do about technology per se. I became interested in open source as an emerging technological community that seemed to solve what I see as very tricky but basically familiar governance problems, in a very unfamiliar and intriguing way. In the end I've decided, and I argue in this book, that the open source community has done something even more important. By experimenting with fundamental notions of what constitutes property, this community has reframed and recast some of the most basic problems of governance. At the same time, it is remaking the politics and economics of the software world. If you believe (as I do) that software constitutes at once some of the core tools and core rules for the future of how human beings work together to create wealth, beauty, new ideas, and solutions to problems, then understanding how open source can change those processes is very important.

I had a huge amount of help and support in writing this book. The

University of California at Berkeley, the Ford Foundation, the Markle Foundation, the Social Science Research Council, the Institute on Global Conflict and Cooperation, and University of California's Industry-University Cooperative Research Program made bets that I would produce something valuable. My close friends and colleagues at the Berkeley Roundtable on the International Economy, Global Business Network, and the Monitor Group made their bets as well but more importantly gave me the gift of great ideas and probing questions. More people than I can possibly remember from many different walks of life read versions of chapters, talked me through sticky problems, and put up with my sometimes naïve questions. I owe particularly large thanks to Jonathan Aronson, Michael Barnett, David Bollier, Denise Caruso, Peter Cowhey, Jerome Feldman, Brad DeLong, Rana Nanjappa, Elliot Posner, AnnaLee Saxenian, Janice Stein, Mark Stone, Nick Ziegler, John Zysman, and a group of the best graduate students in the world. And a special thanks to Michael Aronson and Elizabeth Collins from Harvard University Press.

And of course I owe the greatest thanks to the open source communities I have studied and to the people who contribute their time and energy to that work. I know you weren't trying to build a huge data set for some researcher to come in and understand how you were doing what you were doing. You are just trying to build the best software you can in the way that makes sense to you. I hope I've done some justice to that effort in my attempts to understand what makes open source succeed and why that success matters as much as I think it does.

I want to dedicate this book to my three life partners, who helped me through every day I worked on it. Even though only one of them walks on two legs.

CHAPTER 1

Property and the Problem of Software

This is a book about property and how it underpins the social organization of cooperation and production in a digital era. I mean "property" in a broad sense—not only who owns what, but what it means to own something, what rights and responsibilities property confers, and where those ideas come from and how they spread. It is a story of how social organization can change the meaning of property, and conversely, how shifting notions of property can alter the possibilities of social organization.

I explain the creation of a particular kind of software—open source software—as an experiment in social organization around a distinctive notion of property. The conventional notion of property is, of course, the right to exclude you from using something that belongs to me. Property in open source is configured fundamentally around the right to distribute, not the right to exclude. If that sentence feels awkward on first reading, that is a testimony to just how deeply embedded in our intuitions and institutions the exclusion view of property really is.

Open source is an experiment in building a political economy—that is, a system of sustainable value creation and a set of governance mechanisms. In this case it is a governance system that holds together a community of producers around this counterintuitive notion of property rights as distribution. It is also a political economy that taps into a broad range of human motivations and relies on a creative and evolving set of organizational structures to coordinate behavior. What would a broader version of this political economy really look like? This book uses the open source story as a vehicle for proposing a set of pre-liminary answers to that very large question.

The way in is to answer two more immediate questions about open source. How is it that groups of computer programmers (sometimes very large groups) made up of individuals separated by geography, corporate boundaries, culture, language, and other characteristics, and connected mainly via telecommunications bandwidth, manage to work together over time and build complex, sophisticated software systems outside the boundaries of a corporate structure and for no direct monetary compensation? And why does the answer to that question matter to anyone who is not a computer programmer?

Let me restate these questions as an observation and two general propositions that together provoked me to write this book. The observation is that collaborative open source software projects such as Linux and Apache have demonstrated that a large and complex system of software code can be built, maintained, developed, and extended in a nonproprietary setting in which many developers work in a highly parallel, relatively unstructured way. The first proposition is that this is an important puzzle for social scientists worrying about problems of both small- and large-scale cooperation (which is just about every social scientist, in one way or another). It is also an important puzzle for anyone who struggles, in theory or in practice, with the limits to very complex divisions of labor and the management of knowledge in that setting.

The second proposition is that the open source software process is a real-world, researchable example of a community and a knowledge production process that has been fundamentally changed, or created in significant ways, by Internet technology. Understanding the open source process can generate new perspectives on very old and essential problems of social cooperation. And it can provide an early perspective on some of the institutional, political, and economic consequences for human societies of the telecommunications and Internet revolutions.

This book explains how the open source software process works. It is broadly a book about technology and society, in the sense that changes in technology uncover hidden assumptions of inevitability in production systems and the social arrangements that accompany them. It is also about computers and software, because the success of open source rests ultimately on computer code, code that people often find more functional, reliable, and faster to evolve than most proprietary software built inside a conventional corporate organization. It is a business and legal story as well. Open source code does not obliterate profit, capitalism, or intellectual property rights. Companies and individuals are creating intellectual products and making money from open source software code, while inventing new business models and notions about property along the way.

Ultimately the success of open source is a political story. The open source software process is not a chaotic free-for-all in which everyone has equal power and influence. And it is certainly not an idyllic community of like-minded friends in which consensus reigns and agreement is easy. In fact, conflict is not unusual in this community; it's endemic and inherent to the open source process. The management of conflict is politics and indeed there is a political organization at work here, with the standard accoutrements of power, interests, rules, behavioral norms, decision-making procedures, and sanctioning mechanisms. But it is not a political organization that looks familiar to the logic of an industrial-era political economy.

The Analytic Problem of Open Source

Think of a body of software code as a set of instructions for a computer—an artifact, a "thing" in and of itself. In that context, what is open source software and how is it different from the proprietary software products that companies like Microsoft and Oracle build and sell?

Consider a simple analogy to Coca-Cola.[1] Coca-Cola sells bottles of soda to consumers. Consumers use (that is, drink) the soda. Some consumers read the list of ingredients on the bottle, but that list of ingredients is surprisingly generic. Coca-Cola has a proprietary formula that it will not divulge, on the bottle or anywhere else. This formula is the knowledge that makes it possible for Coke to combine sugar, water, and a few other readily available ingredients in particular proportions with a secret flavoring mix and produce something of great value. The point is that the bubbly liquid in your glass cannot be reverse-engineered into its constituent parts. You can buy Coke and you can drink it, but you can't *understand* it in a way that would let you reproduce the drink, or improve upon it and distribute your cola drink to the rest of the world.

Standard economics of intellectual property rights provides a straightforward account of why the Coca-Cola production regime is organized this way. The core problem of intellectual property is supposed to be about creating incentives for innovators. Patents, copyrights, licensing schemes, and other means of "protecting" knowledge ensure that economic rents are created and that some proportion of those rents can be appropriated by the innovator. If that were not the case, a new and improved formula would be immediately available in full and for free to anyone who chose to look at it. The person who invented the formula would have no special and defensible economic claim on a share of the profits that might be made by selling drinks engineered from the innovation. And so the system unravels, because that person no longer has any rational incentive to innovate in the first place.

The production of computer software is typically organized under a similar regime, with a parallel argument behind it. You can buy Microsoft Windows and you can use it on your computer, but you cannot reproduce it, modify it, improve it, and redistribute your own version of Windows to others. Copyright, licenses, patents, and other legal structures provide a layer of legal protection to this regime, but there is an even more fundamental mechanism that stops you from doing any of these things. Just as Coca-Cola does not release its formula, Microsoft and other proprietary software makers do not release their source code.

Source code is a list of instructions that make up the "recipe" for a software package. Software engineers write source code in a programming language (like C++ or FORTRAN) that a human can read and understand, as well as fix and modify. Most commercial software is released in machine language or what are called "binaries"—a long string of ones and zeros that a computer can read and execute, but a human cannot read.[2] The source code is basically the recipe for the binaries; and if you have the source code, you can understand what the author was trying to accomplish when she wrote the program—which means you can modify it. If you have just the binaries, you typically cannot either understand or modify them. Therefore, shipping binary code is a very effective way for proprietary software companies to control what you can do with the software you buy.

Proprietary source code is the touchstone of the conventional intellectual property regime for computer software. Proprietary source code is supposed to be the fundamental reason why Microsoft can sell Windows for around $100 (or why Oracle can sell its sophisticated data management software for many thousands of dollars) and distribute some of that money to programmers who write the code—and thus provide incentives for them to innovate.

Open source software simply inverts this logic. The essence of open source software is that source code is free. That is, the source code for open source software is released along with the software to anyone and everyone who chooses to use it. "Free" in this context means freedom (not necessarily zero price). Free source code is open, public, and nonproprietary. As Richard Stallman puts it, freedom includes the right to run the program for any purpose, to study how it works and adapt it to your own needs, to redistribute copies to others, and to improve the program and share your improvements with the community so that all benefit.[3] Programmers often explain it with simple shorthand: when you hear the term free software, think "free speech" not "free beer." Or, in pseudo-French, software libre not software gratis.

The core of this new model is captured in three essential features of the semiofficial "Open Source Definition":

- Source code must be distributed with the software or otherwise made available for no more than the cost of distribution.
- Anyone may redistribute the software for free, without royalties or licensing fees to the author.
- Anyone may modify the software or derive other software from it, and then distribute the modified software under the same terms.[4]

If you array these terms against the conventional intellectual property story for software, open source software really should not exist. Or at best it should be confined to small niches outside the mainstream information technology economy, perhaps among a tightly bound group of enthusiastic hobbyists who create and share source code for the love of the challenge.

Here's the empirical problem: Open source software is a real, not marginal, phenomenon. It is already a major part of the mainstream information technology economy, and it increasingly dominates aspects of that economy that will probably be the leading edge (in technological and market terms) over the next decade. There exist thousands of open source projects, ranging from small utilities and device drivers to office suites like OpenOffice, database systems like MySQL, and operating systems like Linux and BSD derivatives.[5] Linux and Apache attract the most public attention. Apache simply dominates the web server market—over 65 percent of all active web sites use Apache.[6] Nearly 40 percent of large American companies use Linux in some form; Linux is the operating system for more than a third of active web servers and holds almost 14 percent of the large server market overall.[7]

Sendmail is an open source email transfer and management program that powers about 80 percent of the world's mail servers. BIND is an open source program that acts as the major addressing system for the Internet. If you use Google to search the web, you use a cluster of 10,000 computers running Linux. Yahoo! runs its directory services on FreeBSD, another open source operating system. If you saw the movies *Titanic* or *Lord of the Rings,* you were watching special effects rendered on Linux machines that are running at companies like Disney, DreamWorks, and Pixar. Increasingly, open source software is running major enterprise applications for large and small corporations alike. Amazon, E*Trade, Reuters, and Merrill Lynch are examples of companies that have recently switched backend computer systems to Linux. Large parts of the U.S. government, including the Defense Department, the Department of Energy, and the National Security Agency, work with open source software. National, state, and municipal governments from Germany to Peru to China are considering and in some cases mandating the use of open source software for e-government applications. IBM is now a major champion of open source after publicly declaring in 2001 a $1 billion commitment to developing technology and recasting central parts of its business models around Linux and other open source programs. Hewlett-Packard, Motorola, Dell, Oracle, Intel, and Sun Microsystems have all made serious (if less radical) commitments to open source software.

The fact that Linux is probably not running your desktop computer today does not diminish the significance of what is happening with open source. That is partly because more PCs and computing appliances will run Linux and open source programs in the next few years.[8] But Windows on your desktop is not important for a more fundamental reason, and that is because your PC desktop is becoming much less important. Even Microsoft knows and acknowledges this—that recognition is at the heart of the company's move toward web services and the "dot-net" architecture. Sun Microsystems claimed a long time ago that "the network is the computer" and the technology is upholding that claim. Your desktop is like the steering wheel to your car—important, but not nearly as important as the engine. The engine is the Internet, and it is increasingly built on open source software.

Computer scientists and software engineers value Linux and other open source software packages primarily for their technical characteristics. But as open source has begun over the last several years to attract more public attention, it has taken on a peculiar mantle and become a kind of Internet era Rorschach test. People often see in the open source software movement the politics that they would like to see—a libertarian reverie, a perfect meritocracy, a utopian gift culture that celebrates an economics of abundance instead of scarcity, a virtual or electronic existence proof of communitarian ideals, a political movement aimed at replacing obsolete nineteenth-century capitalist structures with new "relations of production" more suited to the Information Age.

It is almost too easy to criticize some of the more lavish claims. Like many things about the Internet era, open source software is an odd mix of overblown hype and profound innovation. The hype should be at least partly forgiven. The open source phenomenon is in some ways the first and certainly one of the most prominent indigenous political statements of the digital world. Unlike the shooting star that was Napster, the roots of open source go back to the beginning of modern computing; it is a productive movement intimately linked to the mainstream economy; and it is developing and growing an increasingly self-conscious identification as a community that specifies its own norms and values.

Some of those values sound extraordinarily compelling, particularly when compared to darkly dystopic visions of the Internet-enabled society as one in which computer code leads to a radically privatized, perfectly regulated, tightly controlled world in which technology enforces upon the many the shape of a market that is preferred by and benefits the few. In the widely read book *Code and Other Laws of Cyberspace*, Lawrence Lessig repeatedly invokes the idea of open source as a major challenge and counterpoint to the possibilities for government and corporate control of the architecture that will help shape the e-society. He implies that this is part of an almost epochal battle over who will control what in the midst of a technological revolution, and that open source is on the right side of that battle.[9] Lessig is hardly alone in this view.[10] And it is an important point to make, although I will show that the situation is considerably more complicated than "open= good, closed=bad."[11] To get to a more nuanced understanding of what is at stake, we first should confront in detail the problem of how open source comes to be, what its boundaries and constraints are, what makes it work as a social and economic system, and what that system in turn makes possible elsewhere. That is the purpose of this book.

The Political Economy of Open Source

My starting point for explaining the open source process is the lens of political economy. I will situate the puzzle to start in modern concepts from political economy and then say more precisely why open source challenges some conventional theories about the organization of production, and how it affects and is affected by society. This lens represents a choice: There are other starting points you could choose; and the choice does matter in terms of where you come out as well as where you start. One of the strengths of the political economy perspective in fact is that it can naturally open up to a much broader set of discussions, and I will do so particularly in the conclusion to the book. The point is to take the political economy perspective as a useful focusing device for a discussion of a very complex set of human and social behaviors.

One of the foundational problems of political economy is collective action. People do not easily work together in large groups toward a joint goal. There are many reasons for this: People have different preferences around the goal, they have different tolerances for costs and effort, they find it difficult to evaluate the importance of others' and their own contributions, and in many cases they would come out better if they were able to sit back and allow somebody else to contribute in their place. The classic modern statement of the problem is Mancur Olson's book *The Logic of Collective Action*. Olson's arguments have been refined over time, but the core logic has become almost the equivalent of an instinct for people who think about politics and organization. And thus the natural attraction of the open source process to this conceptual frame: Intuition tells us that thousands of volunteers are unlikely to come together to collaborate on a complex economic project, sustain that collaboration over time, and build something that they give away freely, particularly something that can beat some of the largest and richest business enterprises in the world at their own game.

Marc Smith and Peter Kollock took that intuition a step further when they wrote about Linux as "the impossible public good."[12] Linux is nonrival and nonexcludable. Anyone can download a copy of Linux along with its source code for free, which means it is truly nonexcludable. And because it is a digital product that can be replicated infinitely at zero cost, it is truly nonrival. For well-known reasons that track with the intellectual property rationale, public goods tend to be underprovided in social settings. In other words, it is hard for a community of human beings to organize and sustain organization for the production and maintenance of public goods. The situation with Linux ought to be at the worse end of the spectrum of public goods because it is subject additionally to "collective provision." In other words, the production of this particular good depends on contributions from a large number of developers. Stark economic logic seems to undermine the foundations for Linux and thus make it impossible.

The elementary political economy question about open source software is simple. Why would any person choose to contribute—voluntarily—to a public good that she can partake of, unchecked, as a free rider on the effort of others? Because every individual can see that not only her own incentives but the incentives of other individuals are thus aligned, the system ought to unravel backward so no one makes substantial contributions, and the good never comes to be in the first place.

But Linux is also an impossibly complex good. An operating system is a huge, complicated, intricate piece of code that controls the basic, critical functions of a computer. Everything depends on it. It is the platform on which applications—be they word processors, spreadsheets, databases, or anything else—sit and run. To design a robust operating system and to implement that design in software code is a gargantuan task. Testing, debugging, maintaining, and evolving the system over time are even harder. Computer users will run an operating system in a nearly infinite number of settings, with functionally infinite permutations of behavior, leading to infinite possible paths through the lines of code. Complex software is not like a book, even the longest and most complex book ever written. It is more like a living organism that must continually adapt and adjust to the different environments and tasks that the world puts in front of it.

There was a time when a single determined individual could write the core of a simple operating system for a primitive computer. But given the demands of computer applications and the capabilities of hardware technology at present, that is no longer conceivable. The task needs to be divided somehow. This immediately raises a second core political economy question, about coordination of a division of labor. The standard answer to this question has been to organize labor within a centralized, hierarchical structure—that is, a firm. Within the firm an authority can make decisions about the division of labor and set up systems that transfer needed information back and forth between the individuals or teams that are working on particular chunks of the project. The boundaries of the firm are determined by make-or-buy decisions that follow from the logic of transaction cost economics. The system manages complexity through formal organization and explicit authority to make decisions within the firm as well as price coordination within markets between firms.[13]

Even this caricatured model of industrial-era organization for production is hardly perfect. It is expensive and sometimes awkward to move information and knowledge around, to monitor the actions of labor, and to enforce decisions on individuals. No one says that hierarchical coordination in a complex production task like software development is efficient, only that it is less inefficient than the alternatives. And it does seem to work at some level. Within companies, the job gets done and complex software—imperfect, buggy, and expensive, but functional—does get produced. And thus a third core political economy question arises: Is this an inevitable way of organizing the production process for software (and, perhaps by implication, other complex knowledge goods)? Is it the best way?

Eric Raymond, computer hacker turned unofficial ethnographer of the open source movement, draws a contrast between cathedrals and bazaars as icons of organizational structure. Cathedrals are designed from the top down, then built by coordinated teams who are tasked by and answer to a central authority that implements a master plan. The open source process seems to confound this hierarchical model. Raymond sees instead a "great babbling bazaar of different agendas and approaches."[14] Yet this bazaar has produced software packages that develop "from strength to strength at a speed barely imaginable to cathedral builders."[15]

There is some hyperbole here, and the imagery of chaos and invisible hands in the bazaar misleads by distracting attention from what are the real organizational structures within open source. But focus for the moment on Raymond's core observation. Many computer programmers believe that Linux and other open source software packages have evolved into code that is superior to what hierarchical organizations can produce. The quality of software is to some degree a subjective judgment; and like "good art," a lot depends on what you want to do with the software and in what setting. But the technical opinions are serious ones. Ultimately, so are the opinions expressed in market share, and particularly in the success of open source software in taking away market share from proprietary alternatives.

To summarize and set the problem, open source poses three interesting questions for political economy:

- *Motivation of individuals:* The microfoundations of the open source process depend on individual behavior that is at first glance surprising, even startling. Public goods theory predicts that nonrival and nonexcludable goods ought to encourage free riding. Particularly if the good is subject to collective provision, and many people must contribute together to get something of value, the system should unravel backward toward underprovision. Why, then, do highly talented programmers choose voluntarily to allocate some or a substantial portion of their time and mind space to a joint project for which they will not be compensated?
- *Coordination:* How and why do these individuals coordinate their contributions on a single focal point? The political economy of any production process depends on pulling together individual efforts in a way that they add up to a functioning product. Authority within a firm and the price mechanism across firms are standard means of coordinating specialized knowledge in a

highly differentiated division of labor, but neither is operative in open source. Instead, individuals choose for themselves what they want to work on. Money is not a central part of the equation. And any individual can freely modify source code and then redistribute modified versions to others. A simple analogy to ecology suggests what might happen over time as modifications accumulate along different branching chains. Speciation—what computer scientists call code-forking—seems likely. In effect the system evolves into incompatible versions. Synergies in development are lost. And any particular developer has to choose one or another version as the basis for his future work. This is essentially what happened to another major operating system, Unix, in the 1980s. How does the open source process sustain coordinated cooperation among a large number of contributors, outside the bounds of hierarchical or market mechanisms?

- *Complexity:* Software is an extraordinarily complex technical artifact. In *The Mythical Man-Month,* a classic study of the social organization of computer programming, Frederick Brooks noted that when large organizations add manpower to a software project that is behind schedule, the project typically falls even further behind schedule.[16] He explained this with an argument that is now known as Brooks's Law. As you raise the number of programmers on a project, the work that gets done scales linearly, while complexity and vulnerability to mistakes scales geometrically. This is supposed to be inherent in the logic of the division of labor—the geometric progression represents the scaling of the number of possible communication paths and interfaces between pieces of code written by individual developers. Chapter 3 considers in detail the deeper line of reasoning behind this argument, which is an incredibly interesting statement about the relationship between complex systems of meaning and the imperfections of human communication. Recognize for the moment the challenge it poses to organization. What is the nature of governance within the open source process that enables this community to manage the implications of Brooks's Law and perform successfully with such complex systems?

The book answers these questions by developing a multilayered explanatory model of the open source process. Throughout the book, including the analytic history and descriptions in Chapters 2, 3, and 4, I portray open source as a social phenomenon, like any difficult collaborative project. It is also a political phenomenon because collaboration is governed by formal and informal institutions, norms, and conflict-management procedures. And it is self-evidently an economic phenomenon as well, in both the micro and the macro sense. At the center of the process are individuals who engage in some kind of cost-benefit analyses according to some kind of utility function. And open source has real implications for the organization of production, for corporate structures, and possibly for the economy as a whole.

All models simplify reality, and all analytic perspectives have baselines, be they implicit or explicit. My goal here is to take the political economy perspective seriously, but not too seriously, as a baseline. It would be taking it too seriously to posit that the lack of money is the big puzzle to be explained (although it is certainly part of the puzzle). It would be taking it too seriously to doubt or ignore what are obvious truths about people: Human beings often have a passionate relationship to their creative endeavors and their work; they wish to share their creativity with others; and value inheres in things other than monetizable rewards. Each of these attitudes exists within the open source community. But none of them is unique to that community or distinctive to the Information Age.[17] Human motivation and behavior is always and everywhere an elaborate mix of factors. An analytic perspective grounded in economic assumptions is a useful heuristic that helps to start structuring a story that explains that behavior. But a starting point is all it is.

The Bigger Picture

The other purpose of a heuristic is to open up discussion toward much broader questions that surround and embed the open source process. I will do that throughout this book in at least four general areas.

The first is simply the context of the Internet revolution. The collapse of the dot-com stock market extravaganza can lead to unadulterated pessimism that is just as intellectually diverting as was the irrational exuberance of the 1990s boom. Open source too has ridden some of the waves of public interest and hype over the last few years, with particular attention focused on Linux. Recognize right now that the future of the open source process is a bigger question than the future of Linux. Linux will not last forever. Someone will break Linux up and use pieces of it as a tool kit to build another major operating system or something else. Remember what is potentially durable and possibly deserving of the term "revolutionary"—not a particular manifestation of a process but the process itself. After all, the logistics revolution was not any single container ship or a company building tractor-trailer trucks; it was a new way of moving goods around the world.

The rapid introduction into human affairs of extensive telecommunications bandwidth, configured as a neutral network, does not change everything.[18] But it does change some very important things about the constraints and opportunities that face individuals and organizations in the new economy. The open source story opens up a significant set of questions about the economics and sociology of network organization, not just network economics. And it demonstrates the viability of a massively distributed innovation system that stretches the boundaries of conventional notions about limits to the division of labor.[19]

There is a subtle but important point that will emerge here, overlapping with Lessig's case that in a computational environment, software code plays a structuring role much like law does in conventional social space. The open source process is a bet on the idea that just as important as the code itself and probably more fundamental is the *process* by which the code is built. Consider a slightly different analogy, to physical architecture, not law (after all, if Lessig had been an architect and not a lawyer, he would have probably emphasized physical structures and his book might have been titled "Code and Other *Buildings* in Cyberspace"). Stewart Brand wrote that "all buildings are predictions. And all predictions are wrong." His point is that some buildings are designed to "learn" from their users over time and others are not, and that matters much more in the long run than what the building looks like on the day it opens.[20] Human-computer interface designers are deeply aware of the fact that what they build embodies decisions about policy, and underlying that rights, values, and even basic philosophical views on human action in the world.[21] But they have paid less attention to the process by which those decisions about design are made. Open source is one sign that the information politics discussion is growing up and taking itself seriously enough to confront those tricky questions. Some of these questions and their evolving answers will have significant and long-lasting consequences beyond the lifespan of Linux or any other open source software program.

The second broad area is the evolving relationship between communities, culture, and commerce. The open source "community" (as it calls itself) is indeed marking out a set of organizing principles. These include criteria for entering (and leaving), leadership roles, power relations, distributional issues, education and socialization paths, and all the other characteristics that describe a nascent culture and community structure. At the same time the community is figuring out how it relates to commerce and the capitalist economy that embeds it. These characteristics are evolving and are not always transparent. And the technology that lies at the heart of the community sometimes distracts attention from what may become really important changes in the way people relate to each other around creativity and economic production.

Peter Drucker argues consistently that technology may change the costs of doing things but that is ultimately a marginal adjustment in political-economic behavior. What make a significant difference in human life are the ideas, theories, and institutions that are themselves a product of experimentation and imagination, of a different sort. The steam engine was the metal behind the first industrial revolution; but the revolution was a set of ideas about organizing factories, limited liability corporations, trade unions, and daily newspapers. The second industrial revolution was a story about the publicly traded corporation, the commercial bank, business schools, the professionalization of women, and so on. None of these is a technology, and neither is the open source process. They are ideas—ideas that create institutions and ways of organizing that were nearly unimaginable beforehand and nearly unrecognizable when they first emerged.

My point is that during the early stages of economic and social change, analysts often pay more attention to what is going away than what is struggling to be born. To use Schumpeter's phrasing, it is easier to see precisely the destructive side of creative destruction, than it is to see the creative side.[22] We know how the old and familiar institutions function and we know when they are being challenged. The significance and meaning of a new way of doing things is unfamiliar. That new way may not be a functional replacement for institutions that are being destroyed.[23] And there is always a great deal of noise that accompanies any signal. That counsels caution, but it also recommends an open attitude toward unfamiliar possibilities that demonstrate themselves even within relatively specific economic and social conditions.

The third general area is the nature of collaboration and production in knowledge-intensive economic processes. The software world is almost a limiting case for the study of knowledge economies, in the sense that it is made up of digitally encoded knowledge all the way through from top to bottom.[24] Production processes that evolve in this space are not a hard test of limits but rather a leading indicator of change and a place where experiments can be seen at a relatively early stage.

Open source is an experiment in social organization for production around a distinctive notion of property. The narrow problem in thinking about property is simply who owns what. Broader theories of property differentiate among bundles of rights—rights to access, rights to extract, rights to sell or lease other rights, and so on—that can be combined in different ways. While these differentiating arguments remain important, the open source process is experimenting with some of the most fundamental aspects of property. That is, what does it mean to "own" something? What rights does ownership confer upon whom and for what purpose?

The intuition around "real" property is that to own something is to be able to exclude nonowners from it. In practical implementations, of course, property often carries with it expectations and obligations as well as rights. But the right of exclusion is essential because it brings with it opportunities to sell access or transfer the right of exclusion to someone else, under terms that the owner can set. Free riding is an unfortunate imperfection that governance systems try to minimize. For intellectual property, copyright and particularly the fair use provision is a pragmatic compromise between the interest of the owner-creator in having exclusive rights and the aggregate interests of society in gaining access to ideas. This argument sounds intuitive, but it is not encoded in the facts of nature.

Open source radically inverts the idea of exclusion as a basis of thinking about property. *Property in open source is configured fundamentally around the right to distribute, not the right to exclude.* This places the open source process a step beyond standard norms of sharing in a conventional scientific research community. The entire research product and the process of generating the product is made open; copying is allowed and encouraged; and under the most commonly used open source licenses, modifications and improvements of any sort must be given back to the community fully and without any restriction. It is almost as if the concept of fair use were extended without boundaries, along with a guarantee that no individual's fair use will be permitted to constrain subsequent fair use by any other individual, and for any purpose. What does "ownership" then mean, and what is the significance of free riding in this context? Ultimately the open source process poses a simple but provocative challenge: Is it possible to build a working economic system around the core notion of property rights as distribution? What kinds of characteristics would that system take on?

The fourth broad area is probably the most obvious. How big a phenomenon is this, and how broad is its scope? I argue in this book for the demonstrated importance of the minimum case. Even if open source were just a story about software, it would still be an interesting problem for social scientists thinking about large-scale cooperation. And it would still have significant implications for economic growth and development.

At the same time I build the contours of a more ambitious case: The open source process has generalizable characteristics, it is a generic production process, and it can and will spread to other kinds of production. The question becomes, are there knowledge domains that are structured similarly to the software problem? If we take the structure of the knowledge domain and the nature of demand that people have to solve particular kinds of problems in that domain as independent variables, then allow organization in the broadest sense (how people organize themselves to solve the problem) to be the dependent variable, can we sketch out some of the boundaries within which an open source–type process might work? In addition to the practical implications, this is a reasonably good test of how well we understand what makes the open source process succeed.

The Plan of the Book

This chapter sets the overall problem of open source in a political context and suggests some of the directions in which the arguments of the book proceed.

Chapter 2 traces the early history of the open source process. It focuses on the interaction between technology, culture, and politics. It explains how open source grew out of early programming needs, how it established a technical aesthetic and a nascent political culture, and how both were affected by Justice Department antitrust actions, corporate strategies, and changes in the way mainstream technology users behaved.

Chapter 3 gives a more precise description of the phenomenon. How does the open source process function? I present data that capture an important part of what we know about the open source process and the people who contribute to it. I use this to build an ideal-type description of open source as a production process for complex knowledge goods.

Chapter 4 continues the history of open source to the present. It was in the 1990s that open source acquired a self-conscious identity as a community. By the end of the 1990s, open source had become a phenomenon, in product markets, capital markets, mainstream corporate settings, and in the imagination of many people inside and outside the software engineering world. This history demonstrates the viability of (at least) two discrete ways of organizing the production of software, each of which is embedded in distinctive notions of property, policy, business models, and ideas in the popular imagination.

Chapters 5 and 6 are the core explanation of the open source process. I break the explanation into two separate buckets along the lines I outline in this introductory chapter. The first is about microfoundations. Why do individuals choose voluntarily to allocate a portion of their time, effort, and mind space to the open source process? What is the economic logic of the collective good that is being built that frames these decisions? This is the focus of Chapter 5. The second bucket is macro-organizational. How do individuals work with each other and govern that process, in a way that makes their contributions add up to a joint product? This is the focus of Chapter 6.

Chapter 7 explores some business and legal issues. The open source process does not exist on its own; it enters an ecology of business and law that is densely populated by institutions that do things according to a different set of principles and rules. Yet open source needs to interact, deeply and effectively, with existing structures of capitalist economies and legal structures like copyright, patent law, and licensing.

The most interesting set of propositions begins to emerge where the two interface.

Chapter 8 summarizes the book and draws out implications. I explore some nascent answers to the broader questions that open source raises about political economy in the Internet-enabled environment. And I spell out implications for thinking about the problem of cooperation in a general sense, and specifically in an international setting. The general topics include the importance of shifting property rights, the function(s) of a technological commons, the logic of distributed innovation, technology transfer and economic growth, new forms of power within networked communities, and the very interesting and timely problem of understanding interactions between differently structured organizations, specifically networks and hierarchies.

CHAPTER 2

The Early History of
Open Source

The history of modern computing is a complicated story about interactions between human beings, organizations, and technology. Here I
focus on the social organization of software production, how individuals come together to write complex instructions that tell computers
what to do. As is true of many stories about industrial organization, the
history of software includes alternative approaches to organizing production. The differences between these approaches are as much about
embedded worldviews as about "efficient" means of transforming inputs into outputs. Proponents of a particular way of building software
may claim that their worldview is self-evident and that the form of organization that goes along with it is technological destiny, a necessary
outcome of the material forces and constraints in computing. But a
careful reading of the history argues against this position. Neither proprietary nor free software, as a general paradigm of industrial organization for software, is a technologically determined endpoint. This
chapter recounts the ways in which the first several decades of modern
computing shaped the terms of the competitive dance between these
two paradigms.

Software Is a Tool

"In the beginning . . . was the command line."[1] The catchy title of Neal
Stephenson's popular tale of computer operating systems assumes too
much. In the beginning there was only an on-off switch. Put enough of

these together and you have a binary computer, a bunch of electric circuits that transform inputs into outputs through on-off (or 0–1) calculations. To get all the way to a command line—at which a person can enter a string of letters or numbers as a command and direct the computer to respond—requires a great deal of additional work.

"In the beginning" there was no meaningful distinction between what we call today hardware and software, or between user and programmer. There was only the computer and the people who worked with it. And, as with many emerging technologies, there was not a great deal that these user-programmers could do with their machines. The early generation of modern computers was awkward, expensive, tricky to maintain, and not very powerful. The capabilities we take for granted today—huge memories, fast processors, reliable and vast storage media, and, most importantly, connectivity—were hardly imaginable in 1952 when IBM put on the market the 701, its first commercial electronic computer.

To lease this machine cost $15,000 a month. Most of the organizations that did so were either within the U.S. Department of Defense (DoD) or contractors who worked for DoD (hence the 701's nickname, "Defense Calculator"). In 1953 some businesses started buying the IBM 705, a commercial derivative model, for an average price of $1.6 million.

Price aside, the hard part of owning this machine was writing the instructions, or software, that told the machine what to do. For example, the software that was needed to render dynamic radar images on an IBM 704 contained nearly 80,000 lines of code.[2] The user-programmers writing software for these machines started largely from scratch, without many tools. Their task would have been much easier if they had had a compiler, which is software that translates higher-level programming languages (the words and symbols that programmers use) into machine language (the instructions that the computer can understand and execute).

To write a compiler from scratch is difficult. The engineers facing this challenge recognized the obvious next step: get everyone together who was using the machine, regardless of what company they worked for, and build a compiler that everyone could use. In today's business jargon, this would be called precompetitive collaboration: Competitors share early stages of research that benefit all. In 1952 there was no such label or accompanying ideology. Everyone needed a set of basic tools, nobody could afford to build them alone (at least not quickly enough), and efficiency dictated collaboration across corporate boundaries. It was ultimately this argument about efficiency that helped programmers convince their skeptical managers that this approach made sense. PACT (the Project for the Advancement of Coding Techniques) brought together software engineers from Lockheed, Douglas, RAND, and other large defense contractors mainly on the West Coast to build a set of shared tools.

All technological systems sit within particular cultural frames. The early framing of software as a tool had a pragmatic foundation. In 1956 it would acquire a legal foundation as well. On January 24 1956, the Eisenhower Administration Justice Department entered a consent decree with Western Electric and AT&T to settle a Sherman antitrust act complaint that the Truman administration had filed almost precisely seven years earlier. The common interpretation of this decree is that it banned the companies from entering markets having to do with anything other than telephones.

In fact the terms were more subtle. The consent decree specified that AT&T and Western Electric could not engage in manufacturing or sales outside of telephone, telegraph, and "common carrier communications" services. The AT&T lawyers had a conservative view of what fell within the boundaries (particularly the last, which was open to interpretation). It was the AT&T lawyers who read the agreement essentially to mean "no business other than phones and telegrams," so as not to aggravate an already strained relationship with the Department of Justice. That understanding filtered up through AT&T management to become part of the company's self-understanding. The lawyers also took a conservative view of an additional consent decree provision that required AT&T, Western Electric, and Bell Telephone Laboratories (BTL) to license patents at nominal fees. They understood this as signaling the Justice Department's intention to accelerate the dissemination of communications technology but also other, related innovations that were happening at Bell Labs.

The cultural and legal interpretations of software as a precompetitive tool would play a critical role in the future of Unix, a computer operating system that a group of BTL researchers developed in the late 1960s.

From CTSS to Unix

The information revolution depended on a massive decline in the costs of computing power. Digital Equipment Corporation (DEC) played a major role in this process early on, in part because its founder Ken Olsen rejected what he interpreted as the elitist attitude at IBM that characterized computers as expensive machines that would be owned by only the privileged few. DEC undermined that position when it delivered its first PDP-1 computer in 1960 for $120,000. In 1965 DEC introduced the PDP-8 minicomputer for about $18,000; over 50,000 of these machines were eventually sold.

But the key DEC innovation for disseminating computing power to "the masses" of the time was the PDP-11, released in 1970. The PDP-11 was the first minicomputer with a low enough starting price ($11,000) and good enough performance to entice university departments and corporate research units. By the end of the 1970s, IBM's prediction that the entire market for computers would be fewer than 300,000 machines was swept away by a wave of minicomputers. Even so, the computing environment remained centralized in a way that sounds bizarre today, when we are used to having laptop supercomputers on our desks. This was a culture of scarcity, not abundance.

In the 1960s mainframe era (and similarly with the dissemination of minicomputers), computing time was far too expensive to waste. To run the steps of a computing process linearly—that is, load the compiler into memory, assemble it, load a program, do things with it, and then print out the results—would waste precious computing time. The solution was to overlap jobs in time. A programmer could handle this task with several machines, but the real innovation was figuring out how to overlap jobs on a single machine. Buffers (memory spaces that temporarily store data) and spooling (a procedure for decoupling relatively slow devices from the main process) were necessary for this approach to work.

To allocate computing time to different tasks and then bring the pieces of the process back together requires a programming trick called job scheduling, which in turn requires multiprogramming. It's like instructing the computer to make the filling for a pie while the pie crust is baking. The next step in multiprogramming is true multitasking. Just like a person who is checking email, answering calls, and opening letters at the same time by mobilizing all available resources, multitasking maximizes the speed of a complex computing process when time really matters.

If a computer could multitask for one user, there is no reason why it could not multitask for many users. This realization was the genesis of time-sharing. The concept was simple, though writing the software to implement it was not. The MIT Computation Center developed one of the first systems, CTSS (Compatible Time-Sharing System) in the early 1960s. CTSS could host about thirty users at one time, each connected to the computer by a modem.

In 1964 researchers at MIT began a joint project with colleagues at Bell Labs and General Electric to build a second-generation time-sharing system called Multics (Multiplexed Information and Computing Service). The Multics project was too ambitious for the state of technology at the time.[3] It did not help that three project collaborators had different goals for the system, and that they were hamstrung by an awkward structure for decision-making. The project quickly ran into severe problems. The programming language (PL/I) turned out to be hard to implement. The group hired an outside contractor to write a compiler for the system, which never was delivered. The *Multics Systems Programmers Manual* was over 3,000 pages long. A system designed to handle 1,000 users at once could barely handle 3. By 1968 many of the project staff realized that Multics was a failure. The Advanced Research Projects Agency (ARPA) of DoD reviewed the project in 1968 and gave a lukewarm endorsement to its continuation.

In the spring of 1969, BTL announced that it was withdrawing from Multics. BTL had spent substantial resources on the project and its failure left behind a strong management bias against research on operating systems. Ken Thompson and Dennis Ritchie, two ambitious Bell researchers on the Multics project, were left with little direction and even less enthusiasm in the organization for their work.

But Ritchie and Thompson (along with several colleagues) felt they had learned important lessons from the Multics experiment, lessons that could be used in architecting a new and simpler operating system. The energy behind this initiative was not solely technical. The mid-1960s had brought a sea change in the culture and organization of computer programming work, a change that was not welcomed by many programmers. As computers moved into the mainstream of business operations (at least for large companies) over the course of the

1960s, the demand for programmers grew rapidly. Many managers were uncomfortable with the power programmers held as a result. The stereotype of programmers at the time was not that different from the hacker stereotype of today: free-wheeling, independent, research oriented to the point of playfulness, and not particularly concerned with narrow business concerns.

In fact many programmers perceived themselves as craftspeople. They saw their culture as one of artisanship as much as engineering.[4] Like traditional craftspeople, they wanted to be responsible for a project from start to finish—from specifying the problem with the client, to writing the code, to operating the machine. This approach ran up against management prerogatives and also, of course, against contemporary "Fordist" production theory, which emphasized the division of tasks to increase efficiency. For computing, Fordist thinking prescribed a separation of the conceptual work of programming from the physical work of operating a machine. The aerospace industry began to reorganize computer work along these lines in the late 1950s. The practice spread through much of the business world in the mid-1960s. Under the new "rules," operators were located in the machine room with the computer while programmers sat in a different room to write the instructions. Programmers experienced this change as a serious loss of autonomy: "those of us in the field remember feeling that a firm division of labor had been introduced almost overnight."[5] The narrative of the programmer is not that of the worker who is gradually given control; it is that of the craftsperson from whom control and autonomy were taken away.

Some years later, systems analysts would see more clearly what programmers knew almost viscerally: the high costs of separating out sets of tasks that were much more integrated, often in a tacit way, than they appeared. Ken Thompson understood this principle intuitively and saw the Multics failure as evidence of a skewed development and organizational paradigm, not of faulty or inadequate technology. The solution was to start over.

The Early Days of Unix

In the summer of 1969 Ken Thompson stayed at home while his wife took their new baby to California to visit the grandparents. With four quiet weeks and access to a PDP-7 (an older and not very powerful computer), he allocated one week each to writing an operating system kernel, a shell, an editor, and an assembler. By the end of the month, Thompson had something he called UNICS (uniplexed information and computing services), an intentional pun on Multics. Unics would later be renamed Unix.

The programming philosophy behind Unix and its derivatives still reflects these modest beginnings—and it is central to the intellectual culture of open source. With just one man-month and very basic hardware, Thompson had to leave behind big-system mentality and do something simple—as Dennis Ritchie put it, "build small neat things instead of grandiose ones."[6] The Unix philosophy would become more elaborate over the years, but this doctrine of smallness and simplicity would remain at the core.

Certainly none of the early Unix programmers could have foreseen that more than thirty years later (an eternity in the computer industry), Unix would remain a mainstay operating system for researchers, custom applications, major business software packages, and perhaps most importantly the Internet. Eric Raymond writes:

> Unix has found use on a wider variety of machines than any other operating system can claim. From supercomputers to personal micros, on everything from Crays down to handheld computers and embedded networking hardware, Unix has probably seen more architectures and more odd hardware than any three other operating systems combined. . . . Other technologies have come and gone like mayflies. Machines have increased a thousandfold in power, languages have mutated, industry practice has gone through multiple revolutions—and Unix hangs in there . . . still commanding loyalty from many of the best and brightest software technologists on the planet.[7]

These are central pillars for both the economic and cultural foundations of open source.

Scarcity of computing power characterized the Unix development process during its early days. In fact, Ritchie and Thompson could not convince BTL to buy a computer for their research group until the summer of 1970. Even then, the PDP-11/20 came to them only because another group at BTL was interested in experimenting with a primitive word processing system. This new PDP-11 came with a standard DEC OS (operating system), but Ritchie and Thompson never installed it. Instead, they ported their latest version of Unix onto the machine and had it up and running even before a storage disk had arrived. They then needed a line editor to write programs on top of the OS. But because the machine had been acquired to build a word processor, they needed a program that could also edit text and "masquerade" as a primitive word processor. The easiest way to do this, it turned out, was to hack together pieces of existing editors, one of which Thompson had worked on for CTSS at MIT.[8] The text processor worked well enough that BTL's patent department took over the machine and transferred money to the Computing Research group for a new and more powerful machine, the PDP-11/45.

Naturally, Unix began to grow with new sets of instructions and subroutines and so on. But until November 1971, there was no official documentation or manual for Unix. You learned the program by playing with it and then sitting down with one of the authors to ask questions. The pressure to document grew as it became increasingly clear that Unix might turn out to be more than just an experimental toy. Ritchie and Thompson turned the necessity of writing a programmer's manual into a virtue. Clean and well-designed programs are easy to document; conversely, documenting an ugly piece of code makes it painfully clear just how ugly the code really is. As Doug McIlroy (a colleague of Ritchie's and Thompson's) said, "Cleaning something up so you can talk about it is really quite typical of Unix."[9] This first edition of the programmer's manual established another important Unix cultural tradition: listing each subprogram with an "owner," the person principally responsible for writing and maintaining that particular block of code. Unix spread, although relatively slowly, within certain parts of BTL. By the summer of 1972, there were about ten installations; by the beginning of 1973, there were about sixteen, all within AT&T.

The next major conceptual innovation in Unix was the pipe. A pipe is a uniform mechanism for connecting the output of one program to the input of another. It is a key element for programming modularization, which is the division of a complex task into a series of simple tasks that can be carried out by essentially autonomous modules that communicate through standard interfaces. Modularization led to the idea of software not as a tool *per se* but as a "toolbox." Programmers could then think of Unix not as a single integrated operating system but as a toolbox of small and simple modules that could be combined and recombined to create complex functions. The idea was McIlroy's; Thompson did the original code implementation of the major Unix components *in one night.*

Although it seems obvious in retrospect, the toolbox concept and its implementation was at the time a novel way of thinking about software. Pipes made it possible to practice what was becoming known as a Unix philosophy, with three major tenets:

- Write programs that do one thing and do it well.
- Write programs that work together.
- Write programs that handle text streams because that is a universal interface.

The Spread of Unix

By this time, Unix had its own nascent philosophy and a dedicated group of users within AT&T, but no larger audience. This situation changed dramatically after Thompson and Ritchie presented a paper on Unix to several hundred programmers gathered at the ACM Symposium on Operating Systems in October 1973. Even before the paper was published in July 1974, BTL received requests for copies of the operating system; after July, the requests flooded in.

This response might have looked like a business opportunity for AT&T, were it not for the consent decree and the strict interpretation of it favored by AT&T lawyers. Unix was software, not a common carrier activity, which meant that AT&T could not sell it. In fact the AT&T lawyers wanted a clear statement that the company had no intention of pursuing software as a business. They went yet a step further, arguing that the provision of the consent decree requiring AT&T to license patents meant that the company had to license Unix as well. The sensible thing was to license Unix to university departments and research units and later to the military and commercial users. The terms of the early Unix licenses were minimal: The software came "as is" with no royalties to AT&T, but also no support and no bug fixes. These terms were meant to separate AT&T from any business interest in Unix, but they also had an immediate and critical effect on users, who then had a clear incentive to share support and bug fixes with one another because no one at AT&T was going to help them.

Unix was a unique windfall for university computer science departments. For a few hundred dollars license fee, AT&T supplied the Unix source code, which the BTL research group had rewritten in the high-level programming language C. Unix could run on any machine that had a C compiler, not just on the DEC machines on which it had been developed. With the source code at hand, users could and did treat Unix as a research and learning tool, as much as they used it for a functional operating system. Graduate and undergraduate students tinkered with and enhanced the code, tailoring it for specific monitors, printers, storage systems, and the like.

By 1975 Unix had spread to at least forty institutions in the United States. Australia after 1974 had an active set of users, as did England. The University of Tokyo introduced Unix to Japan in 1976. In each country users organized meetings and newsletters to share ideas, support, and bug fixes. Much of this work had to be done via tapes, disks, and other awkwardly physical means of transmission. The ARPANET was up and running (as of 1969); and by the early 1970s, computer mail was in common use—but not for computers running Unix. The first de facto email standard protocol, written in 1973, was for the TENEX operating system running on DEC-10 machines. Before an AT&T research fellow wrote a Unix-to-Unix copy program (UUCP) in late 1976, it was almost impossible to send files over the Internet from one Unix machine to another. So Unix spread in the most traditional of ways—scholars on sabbatical and research fellows going back and forth between BTL, Xerox PARC, and university departments. There was a physical community of Unix users long before anything like a virtual community could have been imagined.

Unix at Berkeley

UC Berkeley computer science professor Robert Fabry was an early member of that community. Fabry heard Thompson and Ritchie deliver their first Unix paper in November 1973 and wanted to get the system installed at Berkeley. First, though, he had to buy a computer (Berkeley at the time had only large mainframes). Fabry put together a group from the Computer Sciences, Statistics, and Math departments to buy a PDP-11/45. He got a Unix tape from Thompson. In January 1974 one of Fabry's graduate students installed the software. Notably, this was the first Unix installation with which Ken Thompson was not directly involved, although Thompson did help with remote debugging over the phone. This first installation set the tone for an extraordinary cooperation between Berkeley and Bell Labs that would be instrumental in the evolution of Unix.

Unix spread through the computer science research group at Berkeley from the bottom up. At the start, the sharing arrangement for the PDP-11/45 was a problem. The Math and Statistics departments wanted to run a DEC operating system for their particular applications. The compromise reached was that each department would get an eight-hour shift on the machine—thus, Unix would run for eight hours, followed by sixteen hours of DEC RSTS.[10] To make matters worse, the time slots rotated each day so the machine ran Unix from 8 am to 4 pm on one day, 4 pm to midnight the next day, and midnight to 8 am the third day. And yet the students taking Fabry's operating systems course followed the bizarre schedule because they preferred to work on Unix than on the batch processing mainframe machines that they could have used at more convenient hours of the day.

The demand for Unix spread among the faculty as well. Two professors (Eugene Wong and Michael Stonebraker) working on a database project (called INGRES) in the spring of 1974 bought another machine, a PDP-11/40 running the newly available Unix version 5. A few months later they were distributing a working version of the INGRES software to other Unix installations. In early 1975 Stonebraker and Fabry got money to buy two additional 11/45 machines but decided instead to buy just one of DEC's new and much improved machines, the PDP-11/70.

The autumn of 1975 was a key watershed for Unix at Berkeley. Just as the new 11/70 arrived on campus, so did Ken Thompson, who had decided to take a sabbatical from BTL to spend a year at Berkeley as a visiting professor. Thompson brought with him Unix version 6, which he promptly installed on the 11/70. That same fall semester, Chuck Haley and Bill Joy arrived at Berkeley as graduate students. They began work on a Pascal system that Thompson had brought with him, expanding and improving the Pascal interpreter to the point at which it became the programming system of choice for the Berkeley students.

That summer Joy and Haley took a screen editor named "em" and developed it into an early screen editor for Unix, called "ex" (which Joy subsequently would develop into the better known screen editor "vi"). When Thompson left at the end of the summer of 1976, Joy and Haley started working on the guts of Unix, the kernel. By the end of the summer they were installing kernel fixes from Bell Labs and suggesting additional small changes to the code that would improve the performance of Unix.

News spread around the Unix community about Bill Joy's Pascal system. As requests for the software arrived at Berkeley, Joy put together a package of tools and utilities he called the Berkeley Software Distribution, which later came to be known as BSD. Joy sent out in 1978 about thirty free copies of the software, which included the Pascal system and the ex text editor. As Peter Salus says, the essential elements of a collaborative culture as well as a primitive mechanism for software sharing and creation were now in place:

> Something was created at BTL. It was distributed in source form. A user in the UK created something from it. Another user in California improved on both the original and the UK version. It was distributed to the community at cost. The improved version was incorporated into the next BTL release.

BSD, of course, improved on its own, through Joy's own efforts and through feedback he received from users. In the middle of 1978 Joy released an update with an enhanced Pascal system, the vi editor, and other improvements. The second Berkeley Software Distribution, which became known as 2BSD, went to at least seventy-five different sites over the next year.

2BSD was a package of tools and utilities, not a standalone operating system. The next step in BSD evolution to that end came out of a de facto and largely unintentional collaboration with AT&T that developed around Unix version 7. When Bell Labs released Unix version 7 in June 1979, it impressed many users with its new enhancements and reliability. The bad news was that its performance overall was notably slower than most version 6 systems, particularly those that had been customized by sophisticated users.

Those users went to work immediately on the source code of version 7. Bill Joy and others at Berkeley as well as researchers at RAND and at the University of New South Wales made major modifications to the system. But by this time, it was not just high-powered computer scientists who were contributing: Students in a high school outside Boston wrote a set of programs that allowed version 7 to run on a PDP-11 with particular disk drives for which it was not originally compatible.[11] All of these improvements were shared back with the community of Unix users and were incorporated into future releases of both BSD and AT&T Unix.

Probably the most important event that happened with version 7 was that it was ported to a variety of different machines and architectures. To port a piece of software is to rewrite it so it can run on a processor or machine architecture different from the original. (Porting requires access to the source code.) Many people wanted to use version 7 on their machines, which led to a port for the Intel 8086 chip, which was at the heart of most PCs; a port for the Motorola 68000 chip, which Apple, among others, was using; and, most significantly, the 32V port, which ran on DEC's new machine, the VAX-11/780, at the computer science department at Berkeley.

But it was not DEC itself that wrote the 32V port for its machines. In fact, DEC had a very ambivalent relationship with Unix. Although a significant number of DEC's customers bought DEC machines to run Unix, DEC had several proprietary operating systems (most importantly, VMS). At least through the 1970s, DEC did not officially support Unix. Ken Olsen, DEC's chairman, saw Unix as a competitor to VMS and was never fully behind the DEC engineers who wanted to write a native Unix for the VAX machine. In return, Ken Thompson and Dennis Ritchie resented DEC management: They felt that their work on Unix had helped DEC to sell machines and that the business logic for supporting Unix was clear.

In early 1978 DEC engineers went to another group at Bell Labs, in Holmdel, for help. Six months later a small group of engineers at Holmdel finished the 32V port of Unix version 7, which ran nicely on the new VAX. Several universities badly wanted this software. Unfortunately, the intensity of the demand began to illustrate for AT&T management the potential commercial value of the Bell Labs software. Although the company still regarded itself as tightly constrained by the antitrust consent decree, the mood was shifting. It took a great deal of negotiation between the engineers and the Patents and Licensing Department of AT&T to release the 32V port. And it was given to only one university—Berkeley—for "research purposes" under the terms of a "special research agreement" in the autumn of 1978.

The 32V port did not live up to expectations, particularly when it came to the use of memory. So the Berkeley group went to work on the system, rewriting parts of the kernel (particularly to enable the use of virtual memory) and porting over additional utilities, Bill Joy's Pascal interpreter, and the like. By the end of 1979, 32V had been transformed into something fundamentally new, which Bill Joy called 3BSD.

3BSD was a complete UNIX operating system distribution for the VAX. This was significant because, while AT&T was moving toward stable commercially oriented releases of its Unix products, Berkeley had de facto stepped into the role of managing the cutting edge of ongoing Unix research. That in turn would be a critical consideration for the Pentagon's Defense Advanced Research Projects Agency (DARPA) when, in the late 1970s, it had to make some difficult decisions about the practical future of a protocol for packet-switched communication between networks of computers, something called ARPANET.

Unix and the Internet

ARPANET began in 1968 as a small-scale research experiment. Over the course of the 1970s, the net grew to link most of DARPA's major research centers, configured as a network of many local networks. This growth demonstrated the need for a common communications protocol within the meta-network, thereby catalyzing the development of the TCP/IP protocols (the rules for communication that currently underlie the Internet).[12] By the late 1970s, the embryonic Internet was in trouble from another source. Many of the computers at DARPA-funded research institutions were nearly obsolete. DARPA worried about the huge costs of porting software onto new machines, particularly as its contractors were using many different kinds of hardware and a diversity of incompatible operating systems.

DARPA needed some kind of a common base for the sake of efficiency. But to get people to choose a single hardware vendor was not a serious proposition. Even though the VAX was the sure favorite, research groups needed different computers and no one liked the idea of becoming dependent on a single large hardware manufacturer at what was obviously a very early stage in the evolution of modern computing.

The solution was to try to achieve greater compatibility at the level of software, particularly operating systems. And in that discussion UNIX had several advantages over DEC's own VMS and other alternatives. According to at least one DARPA official, the availability of the source code for Unix was a decisive consideration. The researchers who were going to use the network disliked VMS because, as a closed source proprietary operating system, it was simply not very interesting for researchers.[13] In addition, Bill Joy played a central role in convincing DARPA that Unix's proven ability to move relatively easily to other systems would ensure that the network would not be too tightly tied to the VAX.

Berkeley professor Bob Fabry in the fall of 1979 made a formal proposal to DARPA to develop an enhanced version of 3BSD for the network. After difficult negotiations, DARPA granted to Fabry an eighteen-month contract in April 1980. This allowed Fabry to set up a more elaborate organization at Berkeley that he called the Computer Systems Research Group, or CSRG—in part so graduate students like Joy could spend their time writing code. And the researchers went quickly to work.

CSRG released 4BSD late in 1980. It was not a high-performance piece of software—in fact, on some benchmark measures, 4BSD did not do as well as VMS. Bill Joy led a systematic initiative to improve the performance of 4BSD so it would run well on the newest DEC computer (the VAX-11/750). In June 1981 Berkeley released 4.1BSD, which was "tuned to a fine hone especially for the 750."[14]

Conventions for naming software releases may seem arcane. But in this case, the decision to call the new release 4.1BSD signaled a further change in AT&T's attitude toward Unix and toward the de facto collaboration with Berkeley. CSRG had intended to call the new release 5BSD. AT&T objected, fearing possible confusion with AT&T's commercial release of Unix system V. The Berkeley group resolved the issue by promising that future releases of BSD would use 4.1, 4.2, 4.3, and so on. The easy-going collaboration between AT&T and Berkeley was clearly coming under strain as the products of that collaboration became increasingly valuable to both parties, for different reasons.

DARPA, on the other hand, was focused on taking 4.1BSD to the next stage of networking efficiency. Bolt, Beranek, and Newman (BBN, a Boston-based computer company under DARPA contract) released an early version of the TCP/IP stack for Unix.[15] Bill Joy integrated this software into 4.1BSD and tuned it up to increase its performance, particularly for use in local area networks. The Berkeley group also redesigned the network software interfaces so, in the future, Unix would be able to use other networking protocols as well, besides the DARPA standard.

In September 1983 Berkeley released 4.2BSD, a major system revision that (among other changes) fully integrated TCP/IP networking into Unix. Within eighteen months Berkeley shipped more than a thousand site licenses for 4.2BSD, which was more than all of the previous BSD distributions combined. In fact, most Unix vendors decided to ship 4.2BSD rather than AT&T system V (at least until many of the improvements in 4.2BSD were incorporated into system V, as they were over the next couple of years). In a real sense 4.2BSD lies at the foundation of the Internet as we know it today. Peter Salus put it this way: "TCP/IP, which enabled greater connectivity, was integrated into Berkeley Unix; Unix became increasingly popular, increasing connectivity."[16] This was a simple, but powerful, manifestation of positive feedback effects in a network economy.

Alternative Tracks: The Mid-1970s

In fact, the industry structure associated with BSD Unix (positive network externalities, at cost distribution, nonproprietary source code) was only a part of the picture. In other, sometimes overlapping segments of the computing community, a different industry structure was evolving concurrently. As noted earlier, managers in large business settings began in the mid-1960s to separate the conceptual work of programming from the physical work of operating a computer. In the mid-1970s this embryonic division of labor moved forward with the emergence of a formal separation between systems analysts and programmers. Systems analysts designed what they called "solutions" on the basis of their understanding of the customers' needs and problems. And then they specified the tasks, which they gave to programmers to be rendered into code.

Like most routinization, this structure was supposed to increase efficiency while cutting costs. And predictably there was disagreement over whether the new division of labor did either. Specifications were often not quite right, because much of what users end up doing with software is different from what they think they will do and certainly different from what they can communicate in anticipation of a product. By insulating the end user yet another step from the guts of the software development process, this division of labor probably made it harder still for software to meet the needs of people rather than machines. Just as important, it reinforced a cultural image at least in large corporate settings of programmers as technicians, not as artisans, and as implementers of other peoples' guidelines, not as creative designers.

The early manifestations of the personal computer might have reversed this trend. Clubs like the Homebrew Computer Club, which started around 1975, brought together scrappy enthusiasts and hobbyists who were a lot more interested in experimenting and having fun with computers than being efficient.[17] For the personal computer (PC) experimenters, there was no distinction between programmer and user, and certainly no meaningful distinction between hardware and software. As in the early days of computing, the code was the machine in a real sense. And code was something you naturally collaborated on and shared. This was natural because everyone was just trying to get their boxes to do new and interesting things, reasonably quickly, and without reinventing the wheel. And so it came as a shock when in February 1976, Bill Gates released an "open letter to hobbyists" about copying software. Gates and his partner Paul Allen had written a version of the BASIC computer language that could run on the Altair, one of the first mass-produced PCs. The Altair actually couldn't do very much at all without the BASIC program installed, so Microsoft's BASIC was a very popular program. The problem was that users were simply copying the program from and for each other rather than paying Microsoft for copies. At Homebrew, the rule was that you could take a tape of the software only under the condition that you returned to the next meeting with two copies to give away.

Gates's letter was simple, direct, and accusatory: "As the majority of hobbyists must be aware, most of you steal your software." Gates went on to make a familiar argument about intellectual property rights and innovation. This practice of "thieving" software, in his view, would stifle innovation. "Who can afford to do professional work for nothing? What hobbyist can put three man-years into programming, finding all the bugs, documenting his product, and distributing for free?"

The Homebrew hackers had their own answers to these questions, but they were not answers that Gates would have accepted or really even understood. This was not a marginal disagreement or a quarrel over how to interpret rules about intellectual property. Rather it was a clash between two distinct and incompatible cultural frames. Part of the difference was broad and philosophical, a perspective about human motivation—do people write software to make money, or to create and experiment as true artists do? Part of the difference was more mundane—a disagreement about the evolving structure of the computing industry. Where, in the chain of products that made up computing, was value being added?

In either case (or in both), the differences arose from starting assumptions and thus the worldviews could not really be reconciled. Lines of conflict were drawn here, lines that would shift and reposition over the next twenty-five years but would never go away. Making it harder still was the fact that the lines of conflict blurred ethical claims about what was right or fair or basic to human motivation, with instrumental economic claims about what was adding value in an industry and what should therefore be protected (and how).

Both sides claimed (and continue to claim) that their worldview was self-evident, obvious, and an inevitable consequence of the material forces and constraints that exist in computing. But neither proprietary nor free software is "blind destiny." Both continue to coexist, in a kind of software industry "dualism" reminiscent of what Charles Sabel calls technological dualism in industrial economies.[18] Different ways of organizing work, "based on different markets, rooted in correspondingly different patterns of property rights," simultaneously prosper. Neither is a technological necessity, and neither can claim to have "won out" in any meaningful sense.

Into the 1980s

The 1980s contain a submerged story about the continued vigor of the open software paradigm. Unix did not prosper in many markets during this decade, but it evolved technically and remained strong within important niches of computing. The long shadow of Microsoft and the growth of proprietary software models obscured the underlying vitality of Unix. Unix suffered, to be sure, from a loss of important people and other resources that were drawn away by the economics of proprietary alternatives, as well as from unintended consequences of legal maneuvering around the AT&T antitrust suit. But the core energy behind the open paradigm was still in place at the end of the decade. And the very success of the proprietary paradigm increased the demand for alternatives. Mass Internet connectivity would provide the necessary catalyst in the early 1990s to spark a huge revival in the Unix "way of doing things" and lead to the birth of the modern open source software phenomenon.

AT&T released version 7 of Unix in June 1979. Ten years into its development, AT&T management now understood Unix to be a valuable commercial product and so for the first time seriously restricted the distribution of the source code. This did not immediately affect the Berkeley group because of its special arrangement with AT&T, but it did affect many other universities and particularly their teaching programs. Many dropped the use of Unix as a teaching tool.[19]

Meanwhile the legal background for AT&T's Unix mindset was shifting. Five years earlier (in November 1974) the U.S. government had filed perhaps its most celebrated antitrust suit, alleging that AT&T, Western Electric, and Bell Telephone Labs had acted as monopolists in a broad variety of telecommunications services (this despite the Consent Decree of 1956). The famous trial of this suit, which took place before Judge Harold Greene, did not begin until January of 1981, just a few days before the new President Ronald Reagan took office.

The Reagan Justice Department certainly had a different view of the AT&T problem than had its predecessors, and tried to settle the case with a "modification" of the 1956 Consent Decree rather than the dissolution of AT&T that had been sought in the 1974 action. Judge Greene rejected this deal and in the early summer of 1982 brought forward a proposed decree that would, among other things, lead to the divestiture of the operating companies from AT&T, essentially breaking up the company. It took two more years of legal wrangling to settle the details. In 1984 Bell Labs was made autonomous, Western

Electric was dissolved, and the Baby Bells were split off as operating companies.[20]

The "new," post–Greene decision AT&T was no longer bound by the strictures that had stopped it from entering the computer business. And it entered with a vengeance, changing dramatically the licensing terms for Unix in 1983. AT&T created a separate division called Unix Systems Laboratory. Licensing fees for Unix skyrocketed, to around $100,000 in 1988 and as high as $250,000 a few years later. IBM and DEC could afford these prices, but very few university researchers or smaller companies could. This was a major impetus behind the growth of BSD, which increasingly came to look like an alternative and a competitor to AT&T Unix rather than a cotraveler.

Evolution of BSD

Berkeley released 4.2BSD in the summer of 1983. 4.2BSD suffered from some performance problems (as had 4BSD) that needed tuning. After two years of work, the CSRG group announced in June 1985 that it would release an optimized 4.3BSD later that summer. In fact the release was held up for almost another year by arguments over whose implementation (Berkeley's or BBN's) of the crucial TCP/IP networking protocols would be included.[21] CSRG finally released 4.3BSD in June 1986, with an updated version of the Berkeley code base for TCP/IP.

CSRG's next big project was to split the BSD kernel into machine-dependent and machine-independent parts so it would be easier to port the software to different kinds of hardware. Bill Joy had started this work a couple years earlier, anticipating that the VAX architecture was nearing the end of its lifespan. In June 1988 CSRG released the result of this work under the name 4.3BSD-Tahoe, which made it increasingly easy to port BSD to machines other than DEC's VAX.

4.3BSD and particularly the Tahoe version came face to face with the shift in AT&T's licensing provisions. Remember that BSD Unix, since it had evolved out of an early relationship with software from Bell Labs, was based on and still contained a good deal of code that "belonged to," or at least had been written by, AT&T. And because each BSD release was truly "open source—that is, it came with the complete source code for every part of the system—recipients of BSD had to have an AT&T source license to receive the software. Before 1983 this was not a problem, because AT&T had been happy to share its Unix source code relatively freely in return for contributions and bug fixes by users.

But the shift toward commercialization of AT&T Unix made the open source nature of BSD increasingly problematic. An AT&T source license in 1988 could cost as much as $100,000, making it prohibitive for many would-be users of BSD. But the increasing popularity of TCP/IP networking in particular meant that the demand for BSD was huge. One possible solution was for Berkeley to break out the networking code and related utilities from the rest of the system and distribute just those pieces. This could be done without an AT&T license, because the TCP/IP networking code had been developed at Berkeley without any direct AT&T contribution. In June 1989 the Berkeley group took just this approach, releasing the TCP/IP code and a set of supporting utilities that had been written without any AT&T code, as Networking Release 1.

Networking Release 1 came with generous licensing terms. This was the first example of what would later be called a BSD-style license. It was liberal in the extreme. In fact, a licensee could do just about anything with the code. You could release or distribute it, modified or unmodified, with source code or without source code (in other words, in binary-only form), in all cases without paying any royalties to Berkeley. You could build a proprietary software product out of it and sell it for whatever price the market would bear. You could also give it away for free, which many licensees did. The only firm requirement was that credit be given to Berkeley in the documentation and that copyright notices in the source file be left intact. Berkeley charged $1,000 for an original tape; but of course under the terms of the license, anyone who bought a tape could immediately copy it and give it to others.[22]

The immense popularity of Networking Release 1 made a huge impression on the Berkeley group. One of the key CSRG people, Keith Bostic, soon brought up the idea of expanding the release and trying to incorporate as much of the BSD code as possible. To do this under the BSD-style license terms, the group would have to replace any code that "belonged" to AT&T in what was called a "clean room" operation. The idea of a clean room is that individuals reverse-engineer code based only on the published documentation of what the software is supposed to do, without ever looking at the original source code (that still belonged, in principle, to AT&T).

To do this for the entire BSD system would be an elaborate, almost audacious, undertaking. Kirk McKusick and Michael Karels went along in principle with Bostic, in part because they thought it would never really happen. They agreed that if Bostic would figure out how to re-implement the utilities (hundreds of them, in fact) and the huge C library that BSD needed, McKusick and Karels would work on the kernel of the operating system.[23]

It was Keith Bostic who led the way in putting together a consciously designed, public, decentralized, voluntary mass involvement, Internet-based development effort to write software. (It didn't always feel so voluntary to Bostic's friends: Bostic was known for pressuring them in all sorts of ways to take on one or another task.) Beyond this circle of friends, Bostic solicited contributors at Unix user group meetings, in public speeches, and over the net. He promised in return one thing only: Each contributor would have his name listed in the credits, specifying the utility that he wrote.

This was the de facto formalization of a distributed development process, which grew naturally out of the research orientation of the Berkeley group that led it. At the core of the process was a small group, usually about four people, who coordinated the contributions of a larger network of volunteer programmers who sent in contributions. It wasn't a perfect arrangement. Bill Joy feels that most of what came in to Berkeley through the network was not very good code and thus most of the valuable work was done internally at CSRG. McKusick acknowledges that they received a lot of junk but feels that some very important ideas and code did in fact come from the network.[24] Both agree that the process was constrained in the 1980s by poor network communications and insufficient bandwidth to collaborate efficiently. The growth of the Internet and particularly increased bandwidth would later make the role of outside contributions more important.

Bostic's effort started slowly but picked up momentum over time. After about eighteen months, and with the contributions of almost 400 developers, the rewrites of nearly all the key utilities and libraries were ready. McKusick and Karels had had their bluff called. Together with Bostic, they went to work re-engineering the kernel and systematically removing from the entire software package any remaining code that they could identify as having come from AT&T. It was a huge and complicated job, which was more or less finished by the spring of 1991.

In fact at this point the rewritten code was *almost* a complete operating system. There were only six remaining files still "contaminated" with AT&T code, but these were deemed too hard for the CSRG folks to rewrite at that time. So the group decided instead to release the slightly incomplete system and hope that someone else would finish the work.

In June 1991 Berkeley began distributing the system, which was called Networking Release 2. This was really a misnomer, because the software was much more than simply a set of tools for networking. The point of calling it Networking Release 2 was to save time by avoiding the process of having to get University of California lawyers to come up with a whole new licensing scheme. Instead, Berkeley released the software under the same terms as Networking Release 1: $1,000 per tape, source code provided, freely redistributable as long as proper credit was given.

Bill Jolitz picked up Networking Release 2. Jolitz's key insight (really a bet at the time) was that the newly emerging Intel x86 chip architecture (the heart of the IBM PC, and the precursor to today's Pentium chips) was set to evolve much more quickly than DEC's Alpha or other competing processors. It was Jolitz (not Linus Torvalds) who launched the first Unix-based operating system for personal computers to be distributed over the Internet. Less than six months after Networking Release 2 was distributed, Jolitz had written replacements for the six omitted files. He released onto the net a full operating system for the Intel 386 chip (then state-of-the art in PCs).

The system, 386/BSD, was licensed for free redistribution and modification as long as attribution remained intact. Within a short period of time, thousands of users downloaded it. Many started sending back to Jolitz bug fixes, enhancements to the code, and other ideas about next steps in its evolution.

This was exactly the time at which a graduate student in Finland named Linus Torvalds was trying to find a Unix-style operating system to play with on his PC. Torvalds was not aware of what Jolitz was doing with 386/BSD. This may sound bizarre; but in 1991 there effectively was no World Wide Web, and the Internet itself was in its infancy. USENET newsgroups flourished, but information found its way unevenly around these groups. Torvalds would later say that if he had known about the availability of 386/BSD, he probably would have worked with it, rather than setting out to write his own software (which would eventually become Linux).

In any case 386/BSD was a major development. In a complicated series of spin-offs, it gave birth first to NetBSD and then variants FreeBSD and OpenBSD. Each project had a slightly different objective. The idea behind NetBSD was to support as many different hardware architectures as possible, in a research mindset. FreeBSD was optimized for ease of use and performance on the Intel x86 architecture. OpenBSD focused on security. The detailed story of how and why BSD split in these different directions is important and complicated; I consider it in greater detail in Chapter 4 as an example of the politics of "forking."

Networking Release 2 had one other major offspring. Remember that under BSD license terms, it was legal to build a proprietary product out of BSD code. This is exactly what a new company, Berkeley Software Design Incorporated (BSDI), did. BSDI took Jolitz's code, wrote the six missing files, and began selling its own operating system in early 1992 for just under $1,000. BSDI took out a series of advertisements that specifically compared its operating system to AT&T Unix (which was orders of magnitude more expensive). Adding insult to injury, the phone number for BSDI was 800-ITS-UNIX. AT&T may not have liked the fact that 386/BSD and its free derivatives were posted on the net for anyone to use. But the clear commercialization and competitive stance of BSDI seemed a more potent threat to AT&T's Unix business. This would be the source of the 1992 legal battle between AT&T and the University of California.

Proliferating Standards

BSD and its offspring were not the only important Unix derivatives. In fact Unix began to suffer a familiar dilemma of success: proliferating implementations and standards. Sun Microsystems, a startup in Mountain View that hired Bill Joy away from CSRG, intended to build hardware optimized for Unix. The Sun Workstation, announced in summer 1982, was to be a graphics-oriented, personal desktop machine based on the Motorola 6800 chip, running Unix (at first version 7 and later derivatives of 4.2BSD). In late 1982 Hewlett-Packard announced its own series of desktop workstations running an operating system called HP-UX, derived from AT&T Unix system III. In 1983 IBM made available its own Unix version for the Intel 8088 processor. Within a few years the proliferation of partly compatible or incompatible hardware and software was daunting. Apollo, DEC, Integrated Solutions, NSC, and other companies built further versions of BSD. AT&T, Altos, Apollo, Compaq, HP, IBM, Intel, Microsoft, Silicon Graphics, and others had AT&T Unix system V derivatives. Cray, DEC, Data General, Motorola, and Unisys offered proprietary Unix systems, most of which were based on 4.2BSD. The Unix "market" was a mess.

These differences led predictably to pressures for standardization of some kind. Unix user groups were some of the earliest de facto standards bodies for operating systems. But they were fighting an uphill battle. The user groups had no official authority and inadequate market power in a traditional sense. It was clear to everyone that particular standards would probably advantage different people and companies, so the distributional stakes were large. Even more important were the simple economics of rapid innovation taking place across different Unix implementations. Accepted standards were difficult to sustain. The deeper disagreements came over deciding when, in fact, a particular area should be standardized—that is, when innovation was locking in to a desirable pathway and the overall Unix market should try to standardize on it. And it wasn't just economics or even the politics of competition that made standardization difficult. Ultimately Unix programmers carried with them the cultural legacy of researchers. And as researcher-innovators, many Unix programmers were almost instinctively nervous about locking anything in to standards that might constrain fundamental technologies.

The commercial market had a different logic, which AT&T in its new competitive mindset around Unix understood perfectly well. In late 1987 AT&T bought about 20 percent of Sun Microsystems. Suddenly the Unix community faced an alliance between the original source of the system software and the most aggressive competitor making workstations optimized for that software. Worse still, AT&T acknowledged that Sun would now get preferential treatment as AT&T developed new software. As Peter Salus puts it, "a frisson of horror ran through a good part of the Unix world" when Sun announced that its next operating system release would be derived from AT&T's proprietary Unix system V, rather than from BSD Unix.[25]

The fear that Sun was moving along with AT&T in a strongly proprietary direction and turning its back on the scientific community prompted an extraordinary meeting among many of the other major

Unix players in January 1988. Apollo, DEC, Hewlett-Packard, Honeywell, MIPS, NCR Silicon Graphics, and others met at DEC's offices (on Hamilton Avenue) in Palo Alto and released a telegram to the CEO of AT&T expressing their concern about the importance of open Unix standards. Over the next few months there were several meetings between representatives of this so-called Hamilton Group and senior AT&T officials. But AT&T gave no ground. IBM was invited to join the Hamilton Group in March. In May, the major Hamilton players (Apollo, DEC, HP, IBM, Bull, Nixdorf, and Siemens) created a new organization, the Open Software Foundation, with the goal of building their own Unix offshoot free of AT&T licenses. Almost immediately, AT&T and Sun fired back, creating Unix International for the purpose of promoting the proprietary System V.

The intense rivalry soon waned, but not because the two sides found any real accommodation. Rather, the entire computing industry suffered from an exogenous shock, the recession in 1991 at the end of the Cold War. Many of the major antagonists started losing money, including IBM. AT&T sold off its portion of Sun to raise cash. Sun adopted a user interface (called Motif) that had been developed by the Open Software Foundation. Unix International was dissolved. The Open Software Foundation ran out of money and gave up the idea of creating an AT&T license–free operating system.

These events might have ended up as small footnotes in history. The reason they were much more important was because of the timing. The late 1980s and early 1990s were a major watershed for computing and for the Internet. As the U.S. economy emerged from the 1991–1992 recession, computing and Internet communications would come front and center to corporate investment, economic growth, and an intellectual trajectory of arguments about a "new economy."[26] The proliferating standards and the looming controversy between AT&T and its "open" competitors undermined people's confidence in the future of Unix, just at the moment that major investments in future systems were being determined.

The AT&T–University of California lawsuit over Unix was simply the icing on an already very troubled cake. The late 1980s and early 1990s created a disquieting image in people's minds about the dangers of multiple incompatible versions of Unix software and legal uncertainty. This image would dog public understanding of the Open Source movement in the late 1990s and is still a part of the public cultural legacy of Unix.

The Free Software Foundation

The history of the 1980s as I have told it so far has a utilitarian and business-competitive tone to it. It is a story about people trying to advance the science of computing and positioning their companies in markets. At MIT the history unfolded with an additional, very strong element of moral and ethical fervor. The MIT Artificial Intelligence Lab had in the 1960s and 1970s been a major center for the development of software and particularly computer communications and time-sharing systems. It was also a place where the intellectual culture was founded on openness, sharing, and collaboration. Richard Stallman describes it this way: "We did not call our software 'free software' because that term did not yet exist, but that is what it was. Whenever people from another university or a company wanted to port and use a program, we gladly let them. If you saw someone using an unfamiliar and interesting program, you could always ask to see the source code, so that you could read it, change it, or cannibalize parts of it to make a new program."[27]

Steven Levy's book *Hackers* gives a compelling account of the impact of the growth of proprietary software in the late 1970s and early 1980s on the MIT community. Many of the best programmers were hired away into lucrative positions in spin-off software firms. MIT began to demand that its employees sign nondisclosure agreements. The newest mainframes came with operating systems that did not distribute source code—in fact, researchers had to sign nondisclosure agreements simply to get an executable copy.

Richard Stallman led the backlash. As he tells it, the problem crystallized in a very practical way as early as 1979 when the MIT lab got a new laser printer from Xerox. The printer suffered from paper jams. Stallman and his colleagues wanted to deal with this little problem in the same way they had always dealt with problems—experiment with and modify the software so it would work better. But Xerox would not give them the source code for the software that drove the printer. Stallman was annoyed and frustrated. At this point it was just a practical reaction—the inability to fix the printer on his own was a nuisance, not a moral issue.[28]

The tone of Stallman's thinking would soon change. Software for him was not just a tool to run computers. It ultimately was a manifestation of human creativity and expression. Even more importantly, software represented a key artifact of a community that existed to solve problems together for the common good. It was as much about the kind of society you lived in as the technology you used. Proprietary software ran directly against the moral sentiments of a decent society. Stallman did not (and does not) accept the prior assumptions behind standard intellectual property rights arguments, about human motivations to create. Traditional, exclusionary property rights do not incentivize people to write good software, as mainstream intellectual property rights law would have it. Rather, imposing traditional property rights on software makes "pirates" out of neighbors who want to help each other. In this guise law effectively forbids the realization of a cooperating community.[29] Proprietary software was something to be opposed because it was a moral bad, regardless of whether it might in some cases be a practical good.

In 1984 Stallman resigned his position at MIT to devote himself to what he called "free software." He founded the Free Software Foundation as a nonprofit organization to support the work. The goal was to produce an entirely free operating system that anyone could download, use, modify, and distribute freely. Naturally, given the technical setting at MIT, Stallman's training, and the preferences of the people he would work with, the general model for the operating system would be Unix. But to separate himself clearly from AT&T's increasingly proprietary attitude, Stallman named his project the recursive acronym GNU—(GNU's Not Unix). Stallman's 1984 "GNU Manifesto" lays out the logic of the project and, crucially, the meaning of the word "free" in "free software."

Free does not and never did imply zero price. Free means *freedom*—libre, not gratis. This is a language problem that often causes confusion in popular discourse. The Free Software Foundation is crystal clear about the distinction. Stallman writes: "Since free refers to freedom, not to price, there is no contradiction between selling copies and free software. In fact, the freedom to sell copies is crucial . . . selling them is an important way to raise funds for free software development."[30]

Stallman specified four freedoms essential to his vision:

- Freedom to run the program for any purpose
- Freedom to study how the program works and to modify it to suit your needs
- Freedom to redistribute copies, either gratis or for a monetary fee
- Freedom to change and improve the program and to redistribute modified versions of the program to the public so others can benefit from your improvements

To make these freedoms effective in practice, users would need to have full access to source code. And they would need to be able to make changes to source code without constraint.

Stallman realized early on that these freedoms did not add up to a self-reinforcing equilibrium. Put differently, a social system or intellectual property regime that began with these four freedoms needed additional constraints and structure to ensure that it would stay free. If Stallman simply put software into the public domain and let anyone do anything they wanted with it, someone could take the code and use it to build another piece of software that they could then release as a proprietary product, without showing the source code. In that event, the next generation of users would not have the freedoms that Stallman wanted them to have.

This requirement was the genesis of the General Public License (GPL). Stallman cleverly inverted copyright to something he called "copyleft," which in effect reverses the logic of keeping software source code secret. Instead, the GPL uses copyright law to ensure that free software *and derivative works from free software* remain free. The central idea of the GPL is that it uses copyright law to extend the four freedoms, by preventing any users from adding restrictions that could deny these rights to others.

Software that is licensed under the GPL cannot be made proprietary. Derivative works from free software must also be free. The GPL goes further. It does not allow the use of GPL'ed code in any proprietary implementation at all. It is not permitted under the GPL to combine a free program with a nonfree program *unless* the entire combination is then released as free software under the GPL.[31]

This last point is sometimes referred to as the "viral clause" of the GPL. The reference to a virus is not pejorative. It is meant to emphasize that free software "infects" other software with its licensing terms, if a programmer chooses to use GPL'ed code. (For the legal and practical implications of the GPL, as well as its underlying philosophy and the complex relationship to the open source movement, see Chap. 6.) These complications aside, the GPL was a major innovation. Regardless of its status as formal rule or law, the GPL established a clear social regime with specific principles and norms that defined free software.

The Free Software Foundation has created some of the most elegant and widely used pieces of Unix-compatible software. The GNU Emacs text editor is legendary among programmers. The GCC compiler and GDB debugger programs are almost as celebrated. As these and other popular GNU programs were ported to run on almost every version of Unix, they helped to cement Unix as the operating environment of choice for free software advocates.

The popularity of these programs had a downside. GNU developers put their time and energy into maintaining the ports of these existing programs and adding new features to them, rather than building the additional components necessary to create a full operating system under the GPL. That had been Stallman's original goal in starting the Free Software Foundation; but in a peculiar sense, it fell victim to the interim success of the smaller programs. Some of the energy that might have gone into finishing the Free Software Foundation's operating system kernel was also siphoned off into a related (but distinct) project that built heavily on the GNU utilities. That project was called Linux.

BSD Versus AT&T

The BSDI version of Networking Release 2 was a complete operating system and a viable competitor to AT&T Unix. The problem (from AT&T's perspective) was that for $1,000 BSDI was an order of magnitude less expensive. AT&T's Unix System Laboratories decided that its best option was to take the battle into the courts. In late 1991 AT&T threatened BSDI with a lawsuit charging that BSDI was infringing

AT&T's rights to Unix as a trademark. BSDI tried to calm matters by changing its provocative advertisements and telephone number. This wasn't enough to satisfy AT&T. Unix System Laboratories went ahead and filed suit against BSDI, seeking a preliminary injunction to bar the distribution of its software, on the grounds that BSDI had infringed copyright and "misappropriated USL trade secrets."[32]

The second proposition in the lawsuit was the critical one. USL claimed that BSDI stole proprietary source code from AT&T. BSDI argued that they were simply using source code that was freely distributed by the University of California and that they were using it under the terms of the UC license, plus the six additional files that BSDI had written. The implication was clear. If AT&T had a problem with the source code being distributed by Berkeley, they needed to take that up with Berkeley, not BSDI. The judge accepted this argument and instructed USL that he would dismiss the case unless USL chose to restate its complaint against BSDI to focus only on the six additional files.

This put AT&T into a tough spot. There was no sensible case to be made against the six files that BSDI had written autonomously. USL had either to drop the lawsuit altogether, or go back and file suit as well against its long-time collaborator, the University of California.

This was an important decision for AT&T, but it was critical for the future of the open source software movement. A legal cloud of uncertainty over who really owned the BSD code and who could do what with it, particularly one that cast gloom for months or years, would surely sap the energy of developers to contribute to BSD and its derivatives. Why write code for a set of programs that might be locked up under court injunction indefinitely, or locked up as a proprietary product afterward? In the fast-moving software economy of the early 1990s, having to operate under this kind of fundamental uncertainty even for a few months would have undermined confidence. That is exactly what happened: It took nearly two years—an eternity—to resolve the legal dispute.

In the fall of 1992 Unix Systems Laboratories refiled its suit, this time against both BSDI and the University of California, and asked a federal court near AT&T headquarters in New Jersey for an injunction on shipping of Networking Release 2 as well as BSDI software. A legal chill fell over the Berkeley CSRG as faculty, graduate students, and researchers were deposed for the suit. On a Friday afternoon in early 1993 a U.S. district court judge in New Jersey denied the injunction and narrowed the complaint to cover recent copyrights and the loss of trade secrets. Just as important, he suggested that the dispute belonged in a state court system rather than in the federal courts.

On the Monday morning following, the University of California filed a countersuit against USL in California State Court.[33] The UC suit argued that it was AT&T that had broken the law. UC claimed that AT&T had willfully violated the extraordinarily permissive terms of the BSD license by stripping copyright notices from Berkeley code that AT&T had imported into Unix system V. If so, AT&T would have failed to provide proper credit to Berkeley, and thus violated the only substantial requirement of the BSD license.

The case did not go to trial. Not long after UC filed its suit, AT&T sold Unix Systems Laboratories to the software company Novell. The CEO of Novell took advantage of this opportunity to open the door to negotiations. Settlement talks began in the summer of 1993. In part because of the complexity of the ownership issues, but also because there were intense feelings of betrayal on both sides, it took until January of 1994 to reach an agreement.

The precise details of the settlement are sealed. McKusick has written that UC agreed to remove a few files from Networking Release 2, make changes to some other files, and add USL copyrights to some (although those could still be freely redistributed). In June 1994 Berkeley released the new, unencumbered package that it called 4.4BSD-Lite. Unix Systems Laboratories agreed that BSD license terms covered this new release and thus that they would not have a legal claim against anyone using 4.4BSD-Lite code as a basis for their software.[34]

The various groups building versions of BSD software (including BSDI, NetBSD, and FreeBSD) had to go back and rebuild their code bases around the 4.4BSD-Lite source code, to cement this legal protection. This forced the groups to synchronize and update their work, but the process caused further delays and sapped more momentum from BSD development. Bug reports and other code contributions coming back to Berkeley slowed down.

In June 1995 CSRG released an updated code base as 4.4BSD-Lite Release 2. Then the CSRG was disbanded, cutting off the BSD derivatives from their birthplace and accelerating a maturation process for

BSD that, like most maturations, would be fractious and demanding. I pick up this strand of the history in Chapter 4.

Into the 1990s

There are two competing narratives that try to capture the feel of free or open source software development in the 1980s. The first is a narrative of decline. In this story, the good old days of Unix, the ARPANET, sharing, and collaborative development were beaten down by deregulation, privatization, and the enclosure of source code by profit-hungry proprietary players. The Free Software Foundation was fighting a battle with this narrative on philosophical grounds. To reverse the decline, Stallman sought to recapture what he thought was essential about software—the ideology of cooperative social relations embedded within the knowledge product. The philosophy implanted in the software was as important as the code.

The Free Software Foundation's success was in some sense self-limiting. In part, this was due to the moral fervor underlying Stallman's approach. Not all programmers found his strident attitudes to be practical or helpful. In part it was a marketing problem. Free software turned out to be an unfortunate label, despite Stallman's vigorous attempts to convey the message that it was about freedom, not price. In part, the problem lay in the nature of the General Public License, which was the practical manifestation of the philosophy. The "viral" clause of the GPL clashed with the pragmatic views of many programmers. Programmers trying to solve a particular coding problem wanted to use what worked. And many programmers who were sympathetic to the FSF's goals nonetheless wanted to use pieces of proprietary code along with the free code when the proprietary code was technically good. The GPL did not permit this kind of flexibility. And Stallman's vehement rhetoric raised the stakes.

BSD and its derivatives grew up around a subtly different narrative. The success of Berkeley's CSRG was wound up in its intimate relationship to AT&T. BSD was built out of early Unix code that came from AT&T. As Peter Wayner put it, "The AT&T code was good, it was available, and many of the folks at Berkeley had either directly or indirectly helped influence it."[35] They saw no reason to give it up or reject it then, as long as the code was technically useful.

The change in AT&T's views about the proprietary value of Unix and the resulting problems for the BSD collaboration model posed less of a moral dilemma than a practical problem that needed a solution. The BSD license was less restrictive than the GPL, in the fundamental sense that it did not require derivatives to remain free but instead allowed the creation of proprietary products from open code.

In a deep sense, the tension between the BSD-style license and the GPL reflects different views about human motivation and its relationship to creativity and productivity (see Chapter 6 for a discussion of the social structure imposed on the software production process by licensing schemes). The important point here is that the tension deeply affected the development of free software in the 1980s. By the end of the decade, the FSF was running into its self-imposed limits and the operating system kernel project was bogged down. BSD was mired in a legal quagmire that made its future uncertain, for several critical years. This created a de facto opportunity for the development of a third major strand in the open source movement, called Linux.

CHAPTER 3

What Is Open Source and How Does It Work?

In January 1991 a computer science graduate student at the University of Helsinki named Linus Torvalds bought himself a personal computer with an Intel 80386 processor, 4 megabytes of memory, and a 40-megabyte hard drive—quaint in today's computing environment, but quite a powerful personal setup for 1991. Like most PCs at the time, the machine came with Microsoft DOS (disk operating system) as its standard software. Torvalds had no love for DOS. He strongly preferred the technical approach of the UNIX-style operating systems that he was learning about in school. But he did not like waiting on long lines for access to a limited number of university machines that ran Unix for student use. And it simply wasn't practical to run a commercial version of Unix on his PC—the available software was too expensive and also too complicated for the hardware.

In late 1990 Torvalds had heard about Minix, a simplified Unix clone that Professor Andrew Tanenbaum at Vrije University in Amsterdam had written as a teaching tool. Minix ran on PCs, and the source code was available on floppy disks for less than $100. Torvalds installed this system on his PC. He soon went to work building the kernel of his own Unix-like operating system, using Minix as the scaffolding. In autumn 1991, Torvalds let go of the Minix scaffold and released the source code for the kernel of his new operating system, which he called Linux, onto an Internet newsgroup, along with the following note:

I'm working on a free version of a Minix look-alike for AT-386 computers. It has finally reached the stage where it's even usable (though it may not be, depending on what you want), and I am willing to put out the sources for wider distribution. . . . This is a program for hackers by a hacker. I've enjoyed doing it, and somebody might enjoy looking at it and even modifying it for their own needs. It is still small enough to understand, use and modify, and I'm looking forward to any comments you might have. I'm also interested in hearing from anybody who has written any of the utilities/library functions for Minix. If your efforts are freely distributable (under copyright or even public domain) I'd like to hear from you so I can add them to the system.[1]

The response was extraordinary (and according to Torvalds, mostly unexpected). By the end of the year, nearly 100 people worldwide had joined the newsgroup. Many of these contributed bug fixes, code improvements, and new features to Torvalds's project. Through 1992 and 1993, the community of developers grew at a gradual pace—even as it became generally accepted wisdom within the broader software community that the era of Unix-based operating systems was coming to an end in the wake of Microsoft's increasingly dominant position.[2] In 1994, Torvalds released the first official Linux, version 1.0. The pace of development accelerated through the 1990s.

By the end of the decade, Linux was a major technological and market phenomenon. A hugely complex and sophisticated operating system had been built out of the voluntary contributions of thousands of developers spread around the world. By the middle of 2000 Linux ran more than a third of the servers that make up the web. It was making substantial inroads into other segments of computing, all the way from major enterprise-level systems (in banks, insurance companies, and major database operations) to embedded software in smart chips and appliances. And in 1999 Linux became a public relations phenomenon. VA Linux and Red Hat Software—two companies that package and service versions of Linux as well as other open source programs—startled Wall Street when they emerged among the most successful initial public offerings on NASDAQ. Suddenly the arcane subjects of operating systems and source code had moved from the technical journals to the front page of *The New York Times*. And open source became a kind of modern day Rorschach test for the Internet-enabled society.

Chapter 4 contains a detailed history of how open source evolved from about 1990 to the present. This chapter describes the phenomenon: What is open source and how does it function? To make sense of the data that captures what we know about the open source movement and the people who contribute to it requires an understanding of what we are measuring and why. That sounds obvious, but putting this principle into practice is not so simple. Linux is just one example of an extremely diverse phenomenon. To approach this analytic problem, I use a two-pronged strategy. First, I present a simple and sparse ideal-typical description of an open source project. As an ideal type it captures the major shared characteristics of open source, although it is not itself "true" for any single project.[3]

Second, I situate this ideal type within the framework of a *production process,* a conceptual move central to the logic of this book. The essence of open source is not the software. It is the *process* by which software is created. Think of the software itself as an artifact of the production process. And artifacts often are not the appropriate focus of a broader explanation. If I were writing this book in 1925 and the title was *The Secret of Ford,* I would focus on the factory assembly line and the organization of production around it, not about the cars Ford produced. Production processes, or ways of making things, are of far more importance than the artifacts produced because they spread more broadly. Toyota, for example, pioneered lean production in a factory that made cars. Twenty years later, this way of making things had spread throughout the industrial economy. Similarly, open source has proved itself as a way of making software. The question becomes, what are the conditions or boundaries for extending open source to new kinds of production, of knowledge and perhaps of physical (industrial) goods as well? Intriguing questions—but not answerable until we have a more sophisticated understanding of what the open source production process is, how it works, and why.

This chapter describes the open source process by situating it within the "problem" that it is trying to "solve" and then focusing on the people who contribute to open source software and how they relate one to another. I pose and answer, as far as possible given the limitations of the data and the variation among different open source projects, four ideal-type questions.

- Who are the people who write open source code?
- What do these people do, exactly?
- How do they collaborate with each other?
- How do they resolve disagreements and deal with conflict?

This sets the stage for explaining the deeper puzzles of the open source process in Chapter 5.

The Software "Problem"

To build complex software is a difficult and exacting task. The classic description of what this feels like comes from Frederick Brooks, who likened large-scale software engineering to a prehistoric tar pit:

> One sees dinosaurs, mammoths, and sabertoothed tigers struggling against the grip of the tar. The fiercer the struggle, the more entangling the tar, and no beast is so strong or so skillful but that he ultimately sinks. Large-system programming has over the past decade been such a tar pit, and many great and powerful beasts have thrashed violently in it . . . Large and small, massive or wiry, team after team has become entangled in the tar. No one thing seems to cause the difficulty—any particular paw can be pulled away. But the accumulation of simultaneous and interacting factors brings slower and slower motion.[4]

In 1986 Brooks chaired a Defense Science Study Board project on military software. Afterward he wrote a paper entitled "No Silver Bullet: Essence and Accidents of Software Engineering."[5] This paper, while controversial, still stands as the most eloquent statement of the underlying structure of the software engineering problem—and why it is so hard to improve. Brooks uses Aristotelian language to separate two kinds of problems in software engineering. *Essence* is the difficulty inherent in the structure of the problem. *Accident* includes difficulties that in any particular setting go along with the production of software, or mistakes that happen but are not inherent to the nature of the task.

Brooks's key argument is that the fundamental challenge of software lies in the essence, not in the accidents. The essence is the conceptual work of building the interlocking concepts that lie behind any particular implementation—data sets, relationships among data, the algorithms, the invocations of functions. To implement this essence by writing working code is hard, to be sure. But those kinds of practical coding difficulties, for Brooks, fall into the realm of accident. Accidents can be fixed or at least made less common by evolving the process. But software will remain hard to write because "the complexity of software is an essential property not an accidental one."[6]

If this is correct, simple models fail because the complexities at the core of the task cannot be abstracted away. A physicist dealing with complexity has the advantage of being able to assume that models can be built around unifying physical principles. The software engineer cannot make that assumption. Einstein said that there must be simplifiable explanations of nature because God is not arbitrary. But there is no such stricture for software engineering because the complexity at play is "arbitrary complexity, forced without rhyme or reason by the many human institutions and systems to which [the programmer's] interfaces must conform."[7]

To make matters worse, humans use software in an extraordinarily diverse technological and cultural matrix that changes almost continuously. If an auto engineer has to envision the range of conditions under which people will drive a car, the software engineer is faced with a harder task, if for no other reason than that much of the technological environment in which a piece of software will be used has not even been invented at the moment that the software is being written. Highways and bridges, in contrast, don't change that fast, and they are not configurable by users in the way that software is.

Another aspect of this complexity is that software is invisible and, more importantly, "unvisualizable." Brooks means that software is hard or perhaps even impossible to represent in a spatial or geographical model. Silicon chips have wiring diagrams that are incredibly intricate but at least they exist on one plane. Software structure exists on multiple logical planes, superimposed on one another. Software is conceptually more like a complex poem or great novel in which different kinds of flows coexist across different dimensions. To represent any one of these flows is possible. You can diagram the syntax of a poem or write an essay about an underlying theme. To represent all at once— and to do so in a way that communicates effectively to an outside observer—is a problem of a different order of magnitude, perhaps insoluble.

That is why great poetry is almost always the product of a single creative mind. It can be helped along, of course. Design practices and general rules can be and are taught to aspiring poets, and to aspiring software designers. Technology provides both with tools to assist their work, from word processors to elegant test programs for software modules. But technology cannot now, and will not in the foreseeable future, solve the problem of creativity and innovation in nondecomposable complex systems. The essence of software design, like the writing of poetry, is a creative process. The role of technology and organization is to liberate that creativity to the greatest extent possible and to facilitate its translation into working code. Neither new technology nor a "better" division of labor can replace the creative essence that drives the project.

Hierarchical and Open Source "Solutions" as Ideal Types

There is more than one way to skin this cat.[8] The fairy tale solution would be to place a brilliant young eccentric in an isolated basement room with a computer and lots of coffee and let her write software until the point of exhaustion. In fact a great deal of software does get written in exactly this way. But most of this software is used only by the author or perhaps a few friends. And there are inherent limits to software that can be built by one or two people. One person can write a utility, a device driver, or some other small program in a matter of days or weeks. A modern operating system, however, consists of millions of lines of code. And scale is not the only issue. Like a modern car, with its engine, brakes, electronics, hydraulics, and so on, software is made up of components that call on very different kinds of expertise. Yet the result must be conceptually coherent to the single mind of the user.

One way or another, the software problem leads inexorably to some kind of division of labor. Putting large numbers of people into the correct slots in a division of labor is important. But getting the numbers of people right and putting them in the right places is really a secondary problem. The primary question is, *What kind of division of labor, organized how?*

In 1971 Harlan Mills put forward an evocative image in response to this question. It was obvious to him that a large software project must be broken up so separate teams can manage discrete pieces. The key to Mills's argument was that each team should be organized as a surgical team, not a hog-butchering team. In other words, "instead of each team member cutting away on the problem, one does the cutting and the others give him every support that will enhance his effectiveness and productivity."[9]

Frederick Brooks took this argument a step further with an analogy to the building of medieval cathedrals. But Brooks meant a particular kind of medieval cathedral. He was talking about Reims, not Chartres. In fact most European cathedrals are a mishmash of architectural designs and styles, built at different times according to the aesthetic of their designers. Norman transepts may abut a Gothic nave. These contradictions produce a certain kind of splendor in a cathedral, because the human eye can move with ease across boundaries and find beauty in the dissonance. Data cannot do this, which is why similar design contradictions are a nightmare in software.

The key to software design, for Brooks, is conceptual integrity, the equivalent of architectural unity that comes from a master plan. His argument about the appropriate division of labor follows directly from this commitment. Conceptual integrity "dictates that the design must proceed from one mind, or from a very small number of agreeing resonant minds."[10] Only a single great mind can produce the design for a great cathedral. The division of labor for coding (in other words, building the cathedral) then proceeds along two clear lines.

First, draw a separation as cleanly as possible between architecture and implementation. The architect designs the system, creates the master plan, and owns the mental model of the intended outcome. The architect is also responsible for dividing the system into subsystems, each of which can be implemented as independently as possible. Second, structure implementation teams like surgical teams, as Mills argued. Each surgical team has its own subarchitect who is responsible for organizing the implementation team that works under him (just as a chief surgeon assigns tasks in the operating room). The process, in principle, can advance recursively into a multilayered division of labor, depending on the complexity of the project that the master architect is trying to construct.

Stripped to its core, the Brooks approach is really a slightly modified Fordist style of industrial organization. That is no criticism: Fordist divisions of labor are incredibly successful at building certain kinds of products. A clear division between architecture and implementation, segmentation of tasks into subsystems that are then supposed to "snap" together, reporting hierarchies with command and control from above, are all familiar techniques of industrial organization. And they all fit well within a traditional sketch of an ideal-typical corporate hierarchy. An authority assigns tasks, monitors for performance, and compensates according to measurable indicators of execution.

This is not nearly a perfect solution, even in theory. The dilemmas are familiar. Monitoring and evaluating the performance of a complex task like writing code is expensive and imperfect. Proxy measures of achievement are hard to come by. Quality is as important (often more important) than quantity, and simple measures are as likely to be misleading as informative (someone who produces a large number of lines of code may be demonstrating poor implementation skills, not productivity). Shirking within teams and free riding on the efforts of others is hard to isolate. One person's good efforts can be rendered ineffective by another person's failure to produce.

Much of the software engineering and organization literature focuses on ways to ameliorate at least some of these problems in practice. The underlying notion is just like Winston Churchill's views about democracy: Building software this way is the worst possible system except for all the others. Improve the implementation (by removing what Brooks called "accident") over time and you move gradually toward a better industrial organization for software. Substantial progress has in fact been made in exactly this way.

But the essence of the problem according to Brooks—the conceptual complexity of design—will remain. This argument is now commonly called Brooks's Law and it is foundational in programming lore. The simple version of Brooks's Law is this: Adding more manpower to a software project that is late (behind schedule) will make the project even later. Hence the phrase "the mythical man-month."

What lies behind the mythical man-month is a subtle line of reasoning about the relationship between complex systems of meaning and the imperfections of human communication. Brooks says that, as the number of programmers working on a project rises (to n), the work that gets done scales at best by n—but vulnerability to bugs scales as the square of n. In other words, the production system tends to create problems at a faster rate than it creates solutions.

Too many cooks spoil the broth is an old argument. What Brooks's Law adds is a statement about *the rate at which that happens*. Why does vulnerability to bugs scale as the square of n? Brooks argues that the square of n represents a decent estimate of the number of potential communications paths and code interfaces between developers, and between developers' code bases. Human communication about complex, often tacit goals and objectives is imperfect and gets more imperfect, *and at an increasing rate,* as it must travel among larger numbers of people. The complexity of technological interfaces between code modules increases in similar geometric fashion. This is the essential problem of software engineering. Removing Aristotelian accidents only reduces the rate at which the underlying problem gets worse. Indeed, as software systems evolve toward greater complexity, organizations will be challenged to keep up, running faster to stay in the same place.

The open source process takes on this challenge from a different direction. The popular image of open source as a bazaar does capture the feeling of an ideal type. It is an evocative image. But it is analytically misleading and it is best to drop it. *The key element of the open source process, as an ideal type, is voluntary participation and voluntary selection of tasks.* Anyone can join an open source project, and anyone can leave at any time. That is not just a free market in labor. What makes it different from the theoretical option of exit from a corporate organization is this: Each person is free to choose what he wishes to work on or to contribute. There is no consciously organized or enforced division of labor. In fact the underlying notion of a division of labor doesn't fit the open source process at all. Labor is *distributed,* certainly—it could hardly be otherwise in projects that involve large numbers of contributors. But it is not really divided in the industrial sense of that term.

The ideal-type open source process revolves around a core code base. The source code for that core is available freely. Anyone can obtain it, usually over the Internet. And anyone can modify the code, freely, for his or her own use. From this point the process differs among projects, depending largely on how they are licensed. BSD-style licenses are minimally constraining. Anyone can do almost anything with this code, including creating from it a proprietary product that ships without source code. The GPL is much more constraining. In essence, anyone is free to do anything with GPL code *except things that restrict the freedom of others to enjoy the same freedoms.* In practice this means that a program derived from GPL code must also be released under the GPL with its source code.

The key to the open source process is only partly what individuals do for themselves with the source code. It is also in what and how individuals contribute back to the collective project. Again there are differences. BSD-style projects typically rest with a small team of developers who together write almost all the code for a project. Outside users may modify the source code for their own purposes. They often report bugs to the core team and sometimes suggest new features or approaches to problems that might be helpful. But the core development team does not generally rely heavily on code that is written by users. There is nothing to stop an outside user from submitting code to the core team; but in most BSD-style projects, there is no regularized process for doing that. The BSD model is open source because the source code is free. But as an ideal type, it is not vitally collaborative on a very large scale, in the sense that Linux is.

The vital element of the Linux-style process is that the general user base can and does propose what are called "check-ins" to the code. These are not just bug reports or suggestions, but real code modifications, bug fixes, new features, and so on. The process actively encourages extensions and improvements to Linux by a potentially huge number of developers (any and all users). If there is a general principle of organization here, it is to lower the barriers to entry for individuals to join the debugging and development process. As an ideal type, the Linux process makes no meaningful distinction between users and developers. This takes shape in part through a common debugging methodology that is derived from the Free Software Foundation's GNU tools. It takes shape in part through impulsive debugging by someone trying to fix a little problem that she comes across while using the software. And it takes shape in part through individuals who decide to make debugging and developing Linux a hobby or even a vocation.

But the process of developing and extending Linux is not an anarchic bazaar. The email discussion lists through which users share ideas and talk about what they like and don't like, what works and what doesn't, what should be done next and shouldn't (as well as just about everything else) do have a raucous, chaotic feel to them. Conflict is common, even customary in these settings. Language gets heated. There are indeed norms for the conduct of these discussions that bound what kinds of behaviors are considered legitimate. The principal norm is to say what you think and not be shy about disagreeing with what others, including Linus Torvalds, might think. Yet the procedure for reviewing submissions of code and deciding whether a submission gets incorporated into the core code base of Linux is ordered and methodical. A user-programmer who submits a patch for inclusion in Linux is expected to follow a procedure of testing and evaluation on his own, and with a small number of colleagues, before submitting the patch for review. The submission then travels up through a hierarchy of gatekeepers or maintainers who are responsible for a particular part of the code base, lieutenants who oversee larger sections of code, and eventually Linus Torvalds, who de facto makes the final decision for all official code modifications.

This hierarchy has evolved and grown more elaborate over time as Linux itself has grown. Smaller open source projects have simpler and often more informal decision-making systems. Apache, on the other hand, has a formal de facto constitution that is built around a committee with explicit voting rules for approval of new code. The big question is, Why are these systems stable? Why do people obey the rules and accept decisions that go against their own work?

In fact, sometimes they don't. And in an open source setting there is no reason why they must. An individual whose code patch gets rejected always has a clear alternative path. He can take the core code, incorporate the patch, set the package up as a "new" open source project, and invite others to leave the main project and join his. This is called "forking the code base" or simply "forking." Open source guarantees this right—in fact, some developers believe that the essential freedom of free software is precisely the right to fork the code at any time.

In practice, major forks are rare. In practice, most participants in open source projects follow the rules most of the time. There is a lot to explain here. The point of this discussion is simply to set the context for that explanatory challenge.

Decentralized voluntary cooperation is always an interesting phenomenon in human affairs. For some social scientists, it is almost foundational. For studies of how the Internet may change political economy and society by enabling new kinds of communities and other cooperative institutions, it is crucial. The problem certainly gets more interesting when it involves highly motivated and strongly driven individuals who clearly have attractive options to exit any particular cooperative arrangement.

Brooks's Law adds a particularly challenging dimension to the problem as it manifests in software development. To explain the open source process, we need a compelling story about why individuals contribute time and effort to write code that they do not copyright and for which they will not be directly compensated for a collective project whose benefits are nonexcludable. In other words, any individual can take from the project without contributing in return.

But explaining individual motivations does not explain the success of open source. In a peculiar way, it makes the problem of explanation harder. *If Brooks is even partially right about the nature of complexity, then the success of open source cannot simply depend on getting more people or even the "right" people to contribute to the project. It depends also, and crucially, on how those people are organized.*

The reason a great poem is written by a single person and not by thousands of contributors from all over the world is not that it would be hard to get those thousands of people to contribute words to the collective poem, but that those words would not add up to anything meaningful. They would simply be a mess of uncoordinated words that no one would see as a poem (certainly not a great poem). Eric Raymond famously said about the open source development process, "with enough eyeballs all bugs are shallow."[11] Whether he is right depends on how those eyeballs are organized.

What do we know, descriptively, about the important parameters to help answer these questions?

Who Participates in the Open Source Process?

I would like to start with a clean number that decently estimates how many people participate in open source development. It's not possible to do that, and the problem is not just about measurement. It's about conceptualization: Should we define as an open source developer a high school student who modifies some source code for her unusual configuration at home, or reports a bug to one of thousands of small open source projects listed on the website SourceForge.net? Should we limit the definition to people who contribute a certain threshold number of lines of code to a major project like Linux or Apache? Rather than try to define *a priori* the conceptual boundaries, I think it is better for now to remain agnostic and look broadly at what kinds of data are available, to give a more textured view of the size and characteristics of an (evolving and dynamic) open source community.

SourceForge is a major website for open source development projects that provides a set of tools to developers. It is also a virtual hangout, a place that open source developers visit regularly to see what kinds of projects are evolving and who is doing what in specific areas.[12] In July 2001 SourceForge reported 23,300 discrete projects and 208,141 registered users; in September 2003 there were 67,400 projects and over 600,000 registered users. Most of these projects are very small, both in technical scope and in the number of people working on them. Some are essentially dead in the water or abandoned. With these caveats, the numbers are suggestive of the scope of activity in at least one very active part of the open source community.

Counter.li.org is an effort to count the number of active Linux users over time. It relies on voluntary registration for one bottom line measure, but also tries to estimate the size of the community by a variety of techniques that vary in sophistication and plausibility. The range of estimates is huge, with a consensus guesstimate of about 18 million as of May 2003.[13] This roughly tracks estimates made by Red Hat Linux, the major commercial supplier of packaged versions of the Linux operating system (and thus the company most highly motivated to generate a serious assessment of market size). Even if this number is right in some very broad sense, it says nothing about the scope of contributions. Only a subset of users contributes in significant ways to the development of Linux.

There are several large research efforts, both completed and ongoing, aimed at collecting more precise statistics about active contributions and contributors to open source software development.[14] Probably the most ambitious effort is the Orbiten Free Software Survey, carried out over eighteen months in 1999 and 2000 by Rishab Ghosh and Vipul Ved Prakash.[15] Prakash wrote a software tool called CODD that tries to automate the process of identifying credits in source code.[16] He and Ghosh ran this tool across an important but still quite limited subset of open source projects.[17] Within this subset, making up about 25 million lines of code, they found 3,149 discrete open source software projects and 12,706 identifiable developers. Another 790 developers were unidentifiable within the data.

Many other efforts to collect raw data on developers focus specifically on Linux. These studies show that the community of developers contributing to Linux is geographically far flung, extremely large, and notably international. It has been so nearly from the start of the project. The first official "credits file" (which lists the major contributors to the project) was released with Linux version 1.0 in March 1994. This file included seventy-eight individual developers from twelve countries and two developers whose home countries were not disclosed. Ilka Tuomi adjusted these numbers to take account of the different sizes of home countries to show the disproportionate influence of Europeans and the relatively small contribution of developers living in the United States (Figure 1).[18]

Of the major developers listed in the credits file for the 2.3.51 release (March 2000), the United States had the largest absolute number, but Finland was still by far the most active on a per capita basis. Thirty-one countries were represented. Clearly, the international aspect of Linux development has not decreased over time or with the increasing notoriety of the software (Figure 2).

Gwendolyn Lee and Robert Cole looked at the institutional affiliation of contributors to the Linux kernel from the 2.2.14 credits file.[19] The top-level domain of a contributor's email address (such as .org,

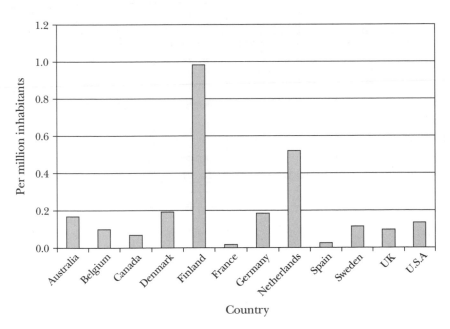

Figure 1 Linux code authors listed in first credits file (1994), concentration by country.

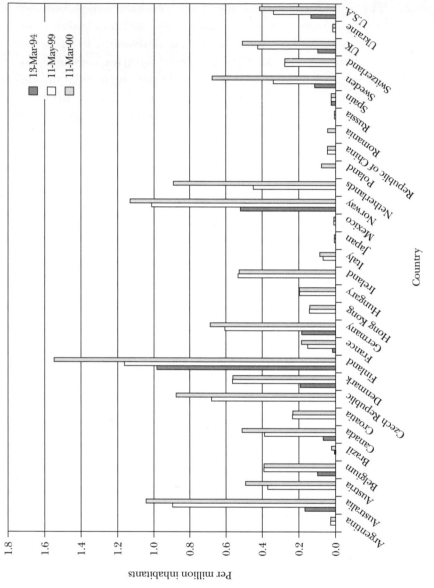

Figure 2 Linux code authors listed in credits files, concentration over time.

.com, or .edu) is an imperfect measure of institutional affiliation, but it is a reasonable proxy.[20] Their observation that more developers have .com than .edu addresses at least calls into question another common perception. Academics and computer science students (who presumably write code for research and teaching) may not dominate the open source process (see Figure 3).

But these numbers count only the major contributors to the Linux kernel. Other active developers report and patch bugs, write small utilities and other applications, and contribute in less elaborate but still important ways to the project. The credit for these kinds of contributions is given in change logs and source code comments, far too many to read and count in a serious way. It is a reasonable guess that there are at least several thousand, and probably in the tens of thousands, of developers who make these smaller contributions to Linux.[21]

A 1999 assessment of these so-called application contributors used Linux software maps (LSMs) located at University of North Carolina's Metalab, one of the oldest and most comprehensive repository sites for Linux software.[22] LSMs are small descriptive metadata files that

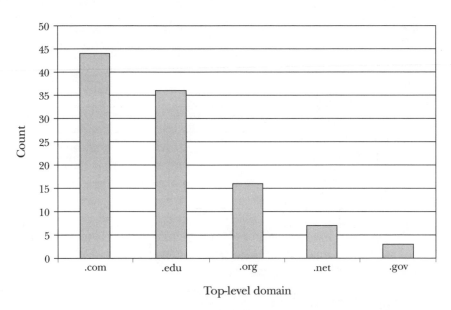

Figure 3 Linux code authors in 2.2.14 credits file, by top-level domain of email address.

many (but not all) developers use to announce their new software and describe its functions.[23] In September 1999 the Metalab archives contained 4,633 LSMs. The distribution among top-level domains reinforces the results of the kernel surveys about geographic distribution of contributors, but shows an even more pronounced European influence (see Figure 4).

In fact 37 percent of the LSMs have email suffixes representing European countries (.de for Germany, .fr for France, and so on) compared to the 23 percent that have .com suffixes. And this method undercounts European participation because at least some authors with .com and other addresses would be located in Europe.

Each of these studies attempts to measure the relative concentration of contributions. In any collective project, not all contributors work equally hard or make contributions that are equally important, and those two variables are not necessarily correlated. Anyone who has worked or played on a team knows the apocryphal 80–20 rule: 80 percent of the work seems to be done by 20 percent of the people.

Although the studies use measures like lines of code or gross numbers of submissions as (deficient) proxies for the value of an individ-

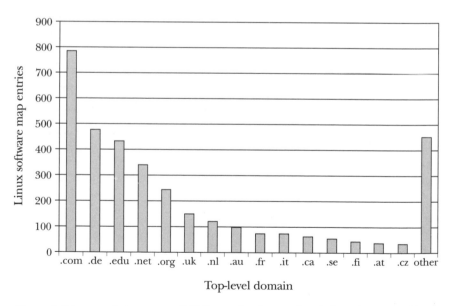

Figure 4 Linux software map (LSM) entries, by top-level domain of email address.

ual's contributions, the open source process is not seemingly much different in this respect from other team efforts. The Orbiten Free Software Survey found that the most prolific 10 percent of developers are credited with about 72 percent of the code; the second decile contributes another 9 percent. In fact the top ten individual authors are responsible for almost 20 percent of the total code. Authors tend to focus their attention tightly: About 90 percent of software developers participate in only one or two discrete projects; a small fraction (about 1.8 percent) contributes to six or more projects. The UNC Metalab data shows a similar distribution of effort: Large numbers of LSM authors (about 91 percent) have contributed only one or two items to the archive, with only a few developers (about 1 percent) contributing more than six.[24] A more recent study on the code repository for the GNOME project (a desktop environment that runs on top of an operating system) finds similar patterns—a relatively small inner circle of developers who contribute a majority of the code and are the most active participants in the email list discussions of the project, surrounded by a larger group of less active coders and discussion group participants.[25]

This data certainly tempers the image of a babbling anarchic bazaar. Open source is a distributed production process, but clearly the distribution is lumpy and somewhat top heavy. The data on Linux is consistent with an image of several *hundreds* of central members who do most of the coding, and several *thousands* of comparatively peripheral participants who contribute in more indirect and sporadic fashion. For the most part contributors work on one or a very small number of programs, rather than spread their efforts more widely over a broad range of projects. It is important to remember the caveats. Each survey relies on a limited sample. More important, none of this data speaks directly to the relative importance of any particular contribution or even the level of effort that any individual puts in. One could in a few days write many lines of relatively simple code to solve a shallow bug, or spend weeks working on a small piece of code that solves a very difficult problem and removes a major roadblock from a project. Still, the data does say something about the demography of the open source community, including its profoundly international nature and its superficial (at least) resemblance to many other communities in which the 80–20 rule seems to apply.

The data also suggests tentative hypotheses about *why* particular individuals write open source software. For example, the prevalence of developers with .com addresses may indicate that many people write open source code in the course of their everyday work. This possibility is consistent with the narrative that many open source developers tell about themselves: People within commercial organizations like to use open source software because they can customize it for their needs and configurations. These in-house developers write bug fixes and other patches for their own work and then contribute that code back to the community for others to use in similar settings.

Several surveys have tested this story as well as other claims about what motivates individuals to contribute to the open source process. Again there are serious data problems, not the least of which follow from the uncertain boundaries around the overall population (and subpopulations) of open source developers from whom these surveys sample. The more important caveat is the manner in which surveys about individual motivations are embedded, deeply, in the explanatory problem that the researcher believes should guide the study of open source. Put simply, if you accept the simple collective action story as capturing the problem to be solved, you then frame the question of motivation in terms of what drives individuals to make contributions. You design a survey instrument to ask questions aimed at eliciting motivations that would counter the behavioral driving forces (in other words, egoistic rationality) that are assumed to set up the collective action problem in the first place. The survey findings about motivations (however inexact they may be as data) thus are linked to assumptions about explanation in a profound, conceptual way. As I have said, the collective action problematic is too narrow to capture the most interesting puzzles about open source and thus I do not present that data in this chapter. For this reason I do not want to present survey data about individual motivations in this chapter, which is dedicated to describing the open source process. That survey data is best understood in the context of contending explanatory claims, and I present both in Chapter 5.

What Do They Do?

The conventional language of industrial-era economics identifies producers and consumers, supply and demand. The open source process scrambles these categories. Open source software users are not consumers in the conventional sense. By that I mean more than the simple fact that no one consumes software in the sense that one consumes a loaf of bread because software can be copied an infinite number of times at no cost. I mean, more fundamentally, that users integrate into the production process itself in a profound way.

Not all users do this, of course. You can choose to consume open source software in the same way as you consume a copy of Windows. But with open source, that is a voluntary decision, not one that is made for you in the technology and legal protections around the product. On the contrary, the technology and the licensing provisions around open source positively encourage users to be active participants in the process. Many do so, and at many different levels.

The logic of what open source user-programmers do did not emerge from abstract theory. No one deduced a set of necessary tasks or procedures from a formal argument about how to sustain large-scale, decentralized collaboration. It was a game of trial and error—but a game that was played out by people who had a deep and fine-grained, if implicit, understanding of the texture of the community they were going to mobilize. Over time, observers studied the behavior as it played out in practice and tried to characterize its key features. Drawing heavily on Eric Raymond's keen analysis supplemented by a set of interviews and my own observations, I offer eight general principles that capture the essence of what people do in the open source process.

1. MAKE IT INTERESTING AND MAKE SURE IT HAPPENS. Open source developers choose to participate and they choose which tasks to take on. There is naturally, then, a bias toward tasks that people find interesting, significant and "cool," in the community vernacular. Anyone who has done programming knows that much of the work involved in writing (and particularly in maintaining) code is boring, grunt work.

Open source developers clearly look for cool opportunities to create new and exciting functions or do hard things in an elegant way. They also look for opportunities to learn and to improve skills. These are two different kinds of benefits to the volunteer, and either one (or some combination of both) is balanced against the costs. Given a large base of volunteers with diverse interests and expertise, a project leader can hope that someone "out there" will find a particular task either cool or valuable as a learning experience relative to the time and energy costs, and choose to take it on. Project leaders often engage in friendly marketing, explaining to the "audience" why it would be a great thing for someone to do x, y, or z. A charismatic leader like Torvalds can go a step further, acknowledging (as he often does) that a particular task is not very interesting but someone really should step up to the plate and do it. There are implied benefits within the community for taking on these kinds of tasks.

Volunteers, regardless of why they choose to volunteer, don't like to see their efforts dissipated. A cool program is really only as cool as others say it is; and for the developer to get that kind of feedback, the program needs to be used. Even if someone takes on a task primarily for the sake of her individual learning, she gains additional satisfaction if the task contributes to something more than her own human capital. These may be side benefits of a sort; but if they were not important, individuals would go to problem sets in textbooks rather than to SourceForge.net.

This sets up an interesting problem for a project leader, who needs to search out a workable balance between exciting challenges and a credible assurance that the challenges will indeed be met. User-programmers look for signals that projects will generate significant products rather than turn into evolutionary dead ends. They want interesting puzzles to solve along the way.

2. SCRATCH AN ITCH. Public radio fund-raisers know intuitively what economists have formally argued: One way to get voluntary contributions is to link the contribution to a private good. Hence KQED offers you a T-shirt in "exchange" for your membership dollars. The open source process knows this as well. Most computer programmers love T-shirts. But what they love even more is a solution to a tangible problem that they face in their immediate environment. This is the "itch" that the developer feels, and scratching it is a reliable source of voluntary behavior.

To understand just how important this is, you need to understand something that outsiders generally do not know about the structure of the software industry. Software code written for sale outside the enterprise that writes it is just the tip of a huge programming iceberg, the rest of which is invisible to most people. Mainstream estimates are that 75 percent of all code is written in-house, for in-house use, and not sold by software vendors.[26] For example, NASA engineers spend a great deal of time writing software to orient the solar panels on the space shuttle. Most software is like this—beneath the surface, in-house code built for financial and database system customizations, technical utilities specific to a particular setting, embedded code for microchip-driven toasters, and so on. And most of what programmers get paid to do is debugging and maintaining this code as the environment in which it is being used evolves.

Scratching an itch is usually about solving one of these immediate and tangible problems in an enterprise setting. Or it might be about a computer hobbyist at home trying to get a particular application to talk to a particular device on that person's uniquely configured hardware. Open source developers scratch these itches, just like all programmers do. What is different about the open source process is that the community has developed a system for tapping into this vast reservoir of work and organizing it in a useful way so at least some of it can be brought back in to benefit collaborative projects. This system blurs the distinction between a private good and a public good and leads directly to the third principle.

3. MINIMIZE HOW MANY TIMES YOU HAVE TO REINVENT THE WHEEL.   A good programmer is "lazy like a fox." Because it is so hard and time consuming to write good code, the lazy fox is always searching for efficiencies. Open source developers have a particularly strong incentive to take this approach because they are not compensated directly for their time. The last thing a programmer, particularly a volunteer programmer, wants to do is build from scratch a solution to a problem that someone else has already solved or come close to solving.

Open source developers have two major advantages here. First, the code moves freely across corporate boundaries. A huge repository of code gets bigger as more developers use it and contribute to it. The second advantage is at least as important. Developers know that source code released under an open source license like the GPL will always be available to them. They don't have to worry about creating dependencies on a code supplier that might go bankrupt, disappear down the road, or change the terms of access. They don't have to worry about a single supplier trying to exploit a lock-in by later enclosing code or raising price barriers.

Developers working in proprietary corporate settings often complain about the inefficiencies associated with what they call the NIH (not invented here) syndrome. They perceive corporate hierarchies as irrational in their desire to own or at least build for themselves code that they know exists in other corporate hierarchies. But in the context of proprietary software, the NIH syndrome is not necessarily irrational, because dependence on source code that someone else owns can create exploitable dependencies over a very long term.[27] Open source developers are free of this constraint, what Oliver Williamson calls the "hold-up" problem. As a result, they do not have to reinvent the wheel quite so many times.

4. SOLVE PROBLEMS THROUGH PARALLEL WORK PROCESSES WHENEVER POSSIBLE. Computer scientist Danny Hillis has said, "There are only two ways we know of to make extremely complicated things. One is by engineering, and the other is evolution."[28] A software bug fix or a desired feature in a complex program is often an extremely complicated thing. What do open source developers do to "make" it?

Frederick Brooks's description of the traditional software development process relies on the engineering archetype. The architect sets the definition of the problem that the hierarchy below her is going to solve. She plots out a conceptual course (or perhaps more than one potential course) to a solution and then divides the implementation work among a certain number of carefully selected people. Three decisions are critical. What route (or routes) is most promising to take toward a solution? How many people need to be tasked with that job? And which people?

Open source developers rely on the evolution archetype. In some cases, but not all, a project leader does set the effective definition of the problem that needs to be solved. Regardless, if it is an important problem, it will probably attract many different people or perhaps teams of people to work on it. They will work in many different places at the same time, and hence in parallel. They will experiment with different routes to a resolution. And they will produce a number of potential solutions. At some point a selection mechanism (which is messy and anything but "natural selection") weeds out some paths and concentrates on others. This evolutionary archetype works through voluntary parallel processing. No central authority decides how many paths ought to be tested, how many people ought to be placed on each path, or which people have the most appropriate skills for which tasks.

Remember that these are archetypes and real-world development processes are not so starkly differentiated. It's also important to remember that both archetypes contain their own inefficiencies. Engineering is great if the chief engineer makes all the right decisions. Parallel problem solving at best is messy, like evolution. It is not possible to say *a priori* which is more efficient and less wasteful for a given setting. The point here is that the open source process enables voluntary parallel processing by as many (or as few) developers as the problem can attract, developers who make their own choices about where and how to allocate their resources.

5. LEVERAGE THE LAW OF LARGE NUMBERS. The key to field testing products such as washing machines or cars is to try out the product in as many different settings as possible. Field testers try to predict all the ways in which people will use the product and then test whether the product works for those applications.

The field-testing problem is orders of magnitude more complicated for software and different in kind than it is for a car—but not only because the hardware on which the code must run changes so much faster than roads and bridges. The issue is that even a moderately complex program has a functionally infinite number of paths through the code. Only some tiny proportion of these paths will be generated by any particular user or field-testing program. Prediction is actually the enemy in software testing. The key is to generate patterns of use that are inherently *unpredictable* by the developers. As Paul Vixie puts it, "The essence of field testing is *lack* of rigor."[29]

The more bugs you generate and the sooner you generate them, the better your chances are that you will fix a decent proportion of what will go wrong once the software is in general use. Hence the benefit of large numbers. Proprietary software companies are constrained in this game. Of course they engage in beta testing, or prerelease of an early version to testers and users who are asked to report back on bugs. But companies face a very tricky calculation: How buggy a piece of software are they willing to put out for public assessment? From a developer's perspective, the earlier the beta is, the better. From a marketer's perspective, buggy software is a nightmare. The cost to a company's reputation as a builder of reliable software can be prohibitive. Customers expect a finished or almost finished product. (Academics understand this calculation all too well. If I were to distribute early drafts of scholarly articles to a broad community of readers to get a diverse set of critical comments, I would quickly destroy my reputation. Instead I give them to a few close friends; but their base of knowledge and expertise tends to be parallel to mine, so what I get in feedback (my beta test result) is narrow and ultimately less useful.)[30]

The open source process has a distinctly different culture that leverages the law of large numbers and exploits the strength of weak ties. The expectations are different: In a real sense open source software is always in beta. The difference in part is the availability of the source code, which empowers continual modification. There is also a collective perception of the open source software process as ongoing research. Open source developers think of themselves as engaging in a continuing research project in which bugs are challenges (not problems) and puzzles (not weaknesses).

As with other evolutionary processes, large numbers and diversity should accelerate adaptation to the environment—in this case, the identification and the fixing of bugs. Again, "with enough eyeballs all bugs are shallow." What this really means is four things. First, different people doing different things with the software will surface more bugs, and that is good. Second, the bugs will be characterized and that characterization communicated effectively to a large group of possible "fixers." Third, the fix will be relatively obvious to someone. And fourth, that fix can be communicated back and integrated efficiently into the core of the project.

Large numbers require organization to work effectively. This principle becomes more apparent when you take into account the observation, common among software developers, that the person who finds a bug and the person who fixes it are usually not the same person. There are probably interesting psychological reasons why that tends to be true, but the observation is an *a priori* argument for the desirability and relative efficacy of parallel debugging. Of course this approach also vastly increases organizational demands on the software development process.

6. DOCUMENT WHAT YOU DO.   Source code is readable, but that does not mean it is easy to read. In a sufficiently complex program,

even excellent code may not always be transparent, in terms of what the writer was trying to achieve and why. Like a complex set of blueprints, good documentation explains what the designer was thinking and how the pieces of the design are supposed to fit together. Good documentation takes time and energy. It is often boring and has almost no immediate rewards. The incentives for a programmer to carefully document code are mainly to help others and to ensure that future developers understand what functions a particular piece of code plays in the larger scheme. In corporate settings detailed documentation tends to carry a low priority relative to more immediate tasks. Much of the communication about code happens in less formal settings in which exchange of tacit knowledge substitutes, at least in the short term, for strict documentation.

Open source developers, in contrast, have to rely more heavily on good documentation. A voluntary decentralized distribution of labor could not work without it. Potential user-programmers, connected in most cases only by bandwidth, need to be able to understand in depth the nature of a task they might choose to take on. Members of this community understand that documentation is a key means of lowering the barriers to entry for user-programmers, particularly those whom they will never meet. An additional incentive comes from the knowledge that open source code will be available for people to use and work with "forever." Because code is nearly certain to outlive the developer (or at least to outlive the developer's interest in that specific project), documentation is a means of transferring what the author knows across time as well as space.

But reality is not so generous. In fact open source developers are not always good at documentation, and some of the reasons (in particular, time pressure) are the same as what developers face in a proprietary setting. The culture of open source programming historically has had an intimate relationship to documentation—and like most intimate relationships, it is complicated. In the early days of Unix, programmers learned about the system by playing with it and then talking to Dennis Ritchie or Ken Thompson. Obviously, this approach didn't scale; and as Unix grew in popularity, documentation became increasingly important. Developers' documentation of bugs as well as features and processes eventually became a fundamental principle of Unix and one that was quite novel at the time. Documentation forces programmers to think clearly about what it is they are trying to do. Rewriting code so it is easier to document, as Ritchie said, is quite characteristic of the Unix culture. Of course, documentation is also a vital part of the scientific, research-oriented tradition in which replicability of methods, as well as results, is considered essential.

7. RELEASE EARLY AND RELEASE OFTEN. User-programmers need to see and work with frequent iterations of software code to leverage fully the potential of the open source process. The evolutionary archetype is not just about voluntary parallel processing among geographically distributed developers; it is also about accelerating the turnover of generations so the rate of error correction can multiply. (Evolutionary biologists know this kind of argument well. Bacteria evolve as quickly as they do for two reasons: their large number *and* the speed with which they reproduce. The first creates a diversity of variation and is the substrate for natural selection; the second is the mechanism for "locking in" to the genetic code that works well and getting rid of what does not.) The open source process in principle mimics this evolutionary strategy, with a feedback and update cycle (at least for larger projects) that is an order of magnitude faster than most commercial software projects. In the early days of Linux, for example, there were often new releases of the kernel on a weekly basis, and sometimes even daily.

But while rapid turnover of generations is tolerable for populations of bacteria (because bacteria can't complain about it), a similar kind of evolutionary process would not be acceptable in software. Rapid evolution is an extremely dynamic process. The vast majority of changes that occur in an evolutionary system are highly *dysfunctional* and they cause the organism to die. That is tolerable for an ecology of bacteria, but not for the ecology of a human-oriented technological system. Of course because changes in software are the result of design, not random variation, a smaller percentage of them are likely to be lethal. But it is still true that one great software feature in an evolutionary "package" of 100 crashing programs would not be an acceptable outcome of a human-oriented development process. More fundamental is that rapid evolution poses the risk of overwhelming the system that selects among variations—and thus introducing errors more quickly than the system can fix them. If this dynamic is set in motion, a system can undergo very rapid deterioration toward the equivalent of extinction through a downward evolutionary spiral.

What open source developers do as individuals, does not guarantee that this will not happen. Put differently, the evolutionary stability of open source software is something that needs to be explained at the macro level because it does not follow directly from the behavior of individual developers.

8. TALK A LOT. Peter Wayner captures something essential about the open source process in this aphorism: How many open source developers does it take to change a light bulb? His answer is, "17. 17 to argue about the license; 17 to argue about the brain-deadedness of the light bulb architecture; 17 to argue about a new model that encompasses all models of illumination and makes it simple to replace candles, campfires, pilot lights, and skylights with the same easy-to-extend mechanism; 17 to speculate about the secretive industrial conspiracy that ensures that light bulbs will burn out frequently; 1 to finally change the light bulb, and 16 who decide that this solution is good enough for the time being."[31]

Open source developers love to talk about what it is they are doing and why. These discussions range from specific technical problems in a project to general issues associated with the politics or business of software development. The email lists for the Linux kernel are enormous and bubble with activity. Beyond Linux, there are huge lists on Slashdot, Kuro5hin, Freshmeat, and other popular websites.[32] People talk about projects in progress, about new ideas, about old bugs, about new hardware, about the politics of antitrust suits against Microsoft; almost nothing seems off limits. Some of these discussions are tightly organized around a specific technical problem and are clearly aimed at gaining consensus or defending an argument about how to proceed with a project. Others are general opinion-venting or discussions about the merits and demerits of the open source development process.

"Talking" among open source developers does not mean calm, polite discussion. One of the common and most misleading fallacies about the open source process is that it involves like-minded geeks who cooperate with each other in an unproblematic way because they agree with each other on technical grounds. Even a cursory glance at the mailing lists shows just how wrong this concept is. Discussion is indeed generally grounded in a common belief that there exist technical solutions to technical problems, and that the community can see good code for what it is. But this foundation of technical rationality is insufficient to manage some of the most important disagreements. It works fairly well to screen out arguments that are naïve or have little technical support. And it tends to downplay abstract "good" ideas unless and until there is some actual code to talk about. But it does not cleanly define problems, identify solutions, or (most importantly) discriminate up front among contending strategies for solving problems.

And technical rationality hardly restricts the tone of the conversation. When open source developers disagree with each other, they do not hold back. They express differences of opinion vehemently and vent their frustrations with each other openly. Even by the relatively pugnacious standards of contemporary academic discourse, the tone of exchange is direct and the level of conflict, at least in language, is quite high. Torvalds set the standard for this kind of behavior in Linux mail lists when in 1992 he wrote to Andrew Tanenbaum (the author of Minix): "Linux still beats the pants off Minix in almost all areas . . . your job is being a professor and a researcher, that's one hell of a good excuse for some of the brain-damages of Minix."[33]

How Do Open Source Developers Collaborate?

All complex production processes face a problem of collaboration. Individuals make efforts, but they need to work together, or at least their contributions need to work together. The open source process is no different. To get past the boundary where the complexity of software would be limited by the work one individual programmer can do on his own, the development process has to implement its own principles of collaboration. To explain the collaboration principles and mechanisms of the open source process is to explain the guts of that process. But first the problem needs to be described more accurately.

It is common to see open source collaboration explained away with a slogan like "the invisible hand" or "self-organizing system." But these are not very useful descriptions and, for the most part, they obfuscate the explanatory issue more than they illuminate it. What do they really mean? The term "invisible hand" is a placeholder for an argument about coordination by price signals, which is supposed to happen in markets. The term "self-organizing system" is a placeholder for an argument about how local forces, those that act between nearby agents, sum to global or at least greater-scale organization. When used carelessly, both often really mean, "I don't understand the principles of organization that facilitate collaboration."

It is better to drop both these notions for now. I am not assuming they are wrong. I am simply taking the position that any argument about principles of collaboration in open source should be built from the ground up, relying on a careful description of actual behavior rather than assumed from abstract principles. Given that, there are three important aspects of behavior to describe in this chapter: the use of technology, the development of licensing schemes, and the emergent similarities between the configuration of technology, and the social structures that create it.

TECHNOLOGY IS AN ENABLER. Networking has long been an essential part of the open source development process. Before computer-to-computer communications became common, prototypical open source communities grew up in spaces bounded by geography. The main centers in the United States were Bell Labs, the MIT AI Lab, and UC Berkeley. The density of networks really did fall off with something approximating the square of the distance from these geographic points. Extensive sharing across physical distances was difficult, expensive, and slow. It was possible for programmers to carry tapes and hard drives full of code on buses and airplanes, which is exactly what happened, but it was not very efficient.

The Internet was the key facilitating innovation. It wiped away networking incompatibilities and the significance of geography, at least for sharing code. As a result, the Internet made it possible to scale the numbers of participants in a project. There are downsides to working together virtually: The transferring of tacit knowledge at a water cooler is a reminder that face-to-face communication carries information that no broadband Internet connection can.[34] But the upside of TCP/IP as a standard protocol for communication was huge because it could scale the utility of electronic bandwidth in a way that physical space could not. Put 25 people in a room and communication slows down, whereas an email list can communicate with 25 people just as quickly and cheaply as it communicates with 10 or 250. As the numbers scale and the network grows, the likelihood of proliferating weak ties—that is, pulling into the process people with very different sets of expertise and knowledge—goes up as well.

To simply share code over the Internet became a seamless process.

As bandwidth increased over time, the Internet also enabled easy access to shared technical tools, such as bug databases and code-versioning systems, that further reduced the barriers to entry for user-programmers.

The more complicated issues, such as communication about the goals of a project or working out disagreements over directions to take, are not seamless over the Internet. In principle the Internet ought to reduce the costs (in a broad sense) of coordinating by discussion and argumentation rather than by price or corporate authority. In practice there is really no way to measure the overall impact because the costs are paid in such different currencies. What practice does reveal is that open source developers make enormous use of Internet-enabled communications to coordinate their behavior.

LICENSING SCHEMES AS SOCIAL STRUCTURE. Another pernicious myth about open source developers is that they are hostile to the concept of intellectual property rights. Actually, open source developers are some of the most vehement defenders of intellectual property rights. Rarely do these developers simply put their software in the public domain, which means renouncing copyright and allowing anyone to do anything with their work.[35] Open source collaboration depends on an explicit intellectual property regime, codified in a series of licenses. It is, however, a regime built around a set of assumptions and goals that are different from those of mainstream intellectual property rights thinking. The principal goal of the open source intellectual property regime is to maximize the ongoing use, growth, development, and distribution of free software. To achieve that goal, this regime shifts the fundamental optic of intellectual property rights away from protecting the prerogatives of an author toward protecting the prerogatives of generations of users.

The basic assumptions behind open source is that people want to be creative and original and they don't need much additional incentive to engage in this manner. The only times when innovation will be "undersupplied" is when creative people are prevented from accessing the raw materials and tools that they need for work. Distribution of raw materials and tools, then, is the fundamental problem that an intellectual property rights regime needs to solve. Solving that problem allows the system to release fully the creative energies of individuals. Even better, it promises to ratchet up the process over time as a "commons" of raw materials grows. Open source intellectual property aims at creating a social structure that expands, not restricts, the commons.

The regime takes shape in a set of "licenses" written for the most part in the language of standard legal documents. For now, think of these licenses as making up a social structure for the open source process. In the absence of a corporate organization to act as an ordering device, licensing schemes are, in fact, the major formal social structure surrounding open source.

Open source licensing schemes generally try to create a social structure that:

- Empowers users by ensuring access to source code.
- Passes a large proportion of the rights regarding use of the code to the user rather than reserving them for the author. In fact, the major right the author as copyright holder keeps is enforcement of the license terms. The user gains the rights to copy and redistribute, use, modify for personal use, and redistribute modified versions of the software.
- Constrains users from putting restrictions on other users (present and future) in ways that would defeat the original goals.

Precisely how these points are put into practice differs among open source licenses. The differences are core explanatory elements of the open source process. They depend in large part on underlying assumptions about individuals' motivations, and the robustness of the commons, as well as some fundamental quarrels about the moral versus pragmatic values connected to software. BSD-style licenses are much less constraining than is the GPL. Arguments over the "appropriate" way to conceive of and implement licenses are an important part of the story of open source in the 1990s (see Chap. 4). In a very real sense, the open source community figures out its self-definition by arguing about licenses and the associated notions of property, what is worth protecting, that they embody. Remember that licenses act as the practical manifestation of a social structure that underlies the open source process.

The Debian Project, which Ian Murdock started in 1993 to produce an entirely free operating system around a GNU/Linux distribution, is most explicit but characteristic on this point. In 1997 Bruce Perens (who followed Murdock as the leader of Debian) wrote a document he called the Debian social contract to articulate the underlying ideals.[36] The Debian social contract clearly prioritizes the rights of users, to the point at which it recognizes that many Debian users will choose to work with commercial software in addition to free software. Debian promises not to object to or to place legal or other roadblocks in the way of this practice. The basic principle is nondiscrimination against any person, group of people, or field of endeavor, including commercial use. (There are sharp ethical differences here with at least some free software advocates. These differences became a major point of contention in the late 1990s when Perens and others recast the Debian Free Software Guidelines as "The Open Source Definition," in sharp contrast to the Free Software Foundation's stance against commercial software on principle.) The principle of collaboration at work here is clear: Do nothing to complicate or slow down the widespread distribution and use of open source software. On the contrary, do everything you can to accelerate it by making open source software maximally attractive to users. This is intellectual property to be sure, but it is a concept of property configured around the right and responsibility to distribute, not to exclude.

ARCHITECTURE TRACKS ORGANIZATION.   More than thirty years ago, Melvin Conway wrote that the relationship between architecture and organization in software development is driven by the communication needs of the people who are trying to collaborate.[37] Conway's Law argues that the structure of a system—in this case, a technological system of software code—mimics the structure of the organization that designed it. Because the point of organization ultimately is to facilitate successful coordination of the technology development process, Conway's Law has been interpreted to mean that the technology architecture should drive thinking about the organization, not vice versa.[38]

The problem is that early formulations of software architecture are best guesses and are likely to be unstable, while a formal organization set up to support those guesses locks in quickly and is hard to change. As the architecture evolves, new communication paths are necessary for collaborative work to succeed, but those communication paths are not hardwired into the organization. This is one reason (not the only one, of course) why informal, unplanned communication is so critical within organizations. It is not just tacit knowledge that gets passed around at the water cooler; it is also communicable knowledge that would travel through standard pathways quite easily, if those pathways did exist.

Herbsleb and Grinter documented some of the ways in which these informal knowledge transfers become more difficult with distance and physical isolation, regardless of Internet connections.[39] The existence of a formally structured organization can, ironically, exacerbate the problem. The formal organization puts a stake in the ground and marks out particular communication paths, which makes it more awkward to step outside those paths. Developers sometimes say they feel like they are working in silos. When they need to talk to someone in another silo, the initial difficulty comes in knowing exactly whom to contact. The next is the difficulty of initiating contact and then following up. This is a familiar feeling for anyone who has wondered how to interpret an unreturned phone call or email when the other party is a stranger (did the person not receive my message? Is she on vacation? Does she just not care?)

In commercial software development, this silo problem causes more than just social awkwardness. Developers communicate outside their silos less frequently than they should; they are inclined to take a risk that problems will not arise. Furthermore, developers in other silos say they are not consulted frequently enough on decisions that affect what they do. When communication does traverse silos, it takes longer to find the right contact and then even longer to solve problems (what developers call "cycle time"). Disagreements that cross silos frequently have to be escalated to higher management for resolution.[40] The really interesting observation is the way these communication problems reflect themselves back into the code—how the organization comes to influence the architecture. At least some of Herbsleb and Grinter's developers reported that they "strove to make absolutely minimal changes, regardless of what the best way to make the change would be, because they were so worried about how hard it would be to repair the problem if they 'broke the system.'"[41] Whatever their technical predilections, developers are clearly going to be influenced to write code that compensates for the imperfections of the organizational structure that sets the parameters for collaboration.

Open source developers know this problem well. Because their organization is voluntary and most often informal, Conway's Law makes extraordinary demands on the technological architecture. This is one of the major reasons why technical rationality is not deterministic in the open source process. Technical rationality always is embedded in a cultural frame, which for open source generally means Unix culture. Technical rationality also is embedded in the organizational character- istics of the development model. When people talk about "clean" code and so on, they are making statements not only about some distinct characteristic of source code but also about the way in which the tech- nical artifact can interface with and be managed by a particular orga- nized community.

Open source developers often say, "Let the code decide." This sounds on the face of it like an unproblematic technical rationality, but it is not so in practice. The most important technical decisions about the direction of software development are those that have long- term consequences for the process of development. Many imply a set of procedures that will need to be carried out in the development path going forward. Implicitly then, and often explicitly, technical decisions are influenced by beliefs about effective ways to organize develop- ment. Technical discussions on how things should work and should be done are intimately related to beliefs about and reflections on social practices. Modularization of source code is an intimate reflection of the complex collaboration problem invoked by voluntary large-scale parallel processing in open source development. Technical rationality may be a necessary part of the foundation for the open source process, but it is not sufficient.

How Do Open Source Developers Resolve Disagreements?

Anyone who has dabbled in software engineering recognizes that dis- agreement is the rule. A large number of very smart, highly motivated, strongly opinionated, often brazenly self-confident, and deeply cre- ative minds trying to work together creates an explosive mix.

Successful collaboration among these highly talented people is not simple. Conflict is customary. It will not do to tell a story about the avoidance of conflict among like-minded friends who are bound to- gether by an unproblematic technical rationality, or by altruism, or ex- changes of gifts.[42] The same bandwidth that enables collaboration on the Internet just as readily enables conflict. People could use the Internet to break off and create their own projects, to skewer the efforts of others, and to distribute bad code just as quickly and widely as good code. They do use the Internet on a regular basis to argue with each other, sometimes quite bitterly. What needs to be explained is not the absence of conflict but the management of conflict—conflict that is sometimes deeply personal and emotional as well as intellectual and organizational.

Major conflicts within the open source process seem to center on three kinds of issues.[43] The first is who makes the final decision if there are deep and seemingly irreconcilable disagreements over the goodness of a specific solution, or a general direction for dealing with a problem. The second is who receives credit for specific contributions to a project. (Ironically, this second source of conflict can become worse in more successful collaborations, because much of what is good in these collaborations is created in the context of relationships as much as by any particular individual.) The third major source of conflict is the possibility of forking. The right to fork *per se* is not at issue. What causes contention is the issue of legitimacy. It is a question of who can credibly and defensibly choose to fork the code, and under what conditions.

Similar issues arise when software development is organized in a corporate or commercial setting. Standard theories of the firm explain various ways in which these kinds of conflicts are settled, or at least managed, by formal authoritative organizations. Most of these mechanisms are just not available to the open source community. There is no boss who can implement a decision about how to proceed with a project; there is no manager with the power to hire and fire; and there is no formal process for appealing a decision.

In open source much of the important conflict management takes place through behavioral patterns and norms. There are two descriptive elements of these norms that I consider here: the visible nature of leadership and the structures of decision-making.

Leadership is a peculiar issue for the open source community. The popular media as well as most extended treatments of open source focus on one project—Linux—and its remarkable leader, Linus Torvalds. There certainly is something unique about the man as an individual. His style of leadership is alternatively charismatic and self-deprecating. Torvalds (surprisingly to some) is a shy person whose self-effacing manner seems authentic, not manufactured for effect. Developers respect Torvalds for having started Linux, but much more so for his extraordinary intellectual and emotional commitment to the Linux project through graduate school and later through a Silicon Valley programming job. Although he does not claim to be the very best programmer, he has maintained a clear vision about the evolving nature of Linux, as well as the structure and style of the code that he incorporates into the kernel; and that vision has turned out over time to look "right" more often than not. His vision has never been enforced in an aggressively authoritative way. When challenged about his power over Linux early on, Torvalds posted to the Linux mail list (on February 6, 1992) this revealing comment: "Here's my standing on 'keeping control,' in 2 words (three?): I won't. The only control I've effectively been keeping on Linux is that I know it better than anybody else."

In fact, one of the most noteworthy characteristics of Torvalds's leadership style is how he goes to great lengths to document, explain, and justify his decisions about controversial matters, as well as to admit when he believes he has made a mistake or has changed his mind. Torvalds seems intuitively to understand that, given his presumptive claim on leadership as founder of the Linux project, he could fail his followers in only one way—by being unresponsive to them. That does not in any way rule out disagreement. In fact it prescribes it, albeit within a controlled context. In the end, Torvalds is a benevolent dictator, but a peculiar kind of dictator—one whose power is accepted voluntarily and on a continuing basis by the developers he leads. Most of the people who recognize his authority have never met him and probably never will.

But Torvalds's charismatic leadership style is clearly not the only way to lead an open source project. Richard Stallman has a very different leadership style that has developed from his extraordinary prowess as a code writer. He is self-consciously ideological and (in sharp contrast to Torvalds's fervent pragmatism) sees his leadership role at the Free Software Foundation as piously defending an argument about ethics and morality. Brian Behlendorf, one of the central figures behind the Apache web server, has yet another leadership style and is known for engaging deeply in the development of business models around open source software. This kind of variance does not demonstrate that leadership is irrelevant; instead, it suggests that there are different ways to lead and that a satisfying explanation of the open source process needs to go beyond the question of leadership.

There is just as much variance in decision-making structures for open source projects. In the early days of Linux, Linus Torvalds made all the key decisions about what did or did not get incorporated into the kernel. Many small-scale open source projects are run this way, with one or a few decision makers choosing on the basis of their own evaluations of code.

Chapter 4 describes how the decision-making system for Linux was restructured in the mid-1990s, as both the program itself and the community of developers who contributed to it grew enormously. Linux today is organized into a rather elaborate decision-making structure. Torvalds depends heavily on a group of lieutenants who constitute what many programmers call "the inner circle." These are core developers who essentially own delegated responsibility for subsystems and components. Some of the lieutenants onward-delegate to area-owners (sometimes called "maintainers") who have smaller regions of responsibility. The organic result looks and functions like a decision hierarchy, in which responsibility and communication paths are structured in something very much like a pyramid. Torvalds sits atop the pyramid as a benevolent dictator with final responsibility for managing disagreements that cannot be resolved at lower levels. The decision hierarchy for Linux is still informal in an important sense. While programmers generally recognize the importance of the inner circle, no document or organization chart specifies who is actually in it at any given time. Everyone knew for years that the British programmer Alan Cox was responsible for maintaining the stable version of the Linux kernel (while Torvalds spends more of his time working on the next experimental version) and that Torvalds pro forma accepted what Cox decided. This made Cox close to something like a vice-president for Linux. But Torvalds did not handpick or formally appoint Cox to this role; he simply took it on as he established his expert status among the community over time.[44]

The BSD derivatives on the whole follow a different decision-making template, organized around concentric circles. A small core group controls final access to the code base. This group grants (or revokes) the rights to the next concentric circle, who can modify code or commit new code to the core base. These are the "committers." In the third concentric circle are the developers, who submit code to committers for evaluation. The boundaries of the circles are generally more definite: FreeBSD, for example, has a core of 16 and about 180 committers in the second circle.

Larry Wall, the originator of the programming language Perl, in the mid-1990s developed a different version of a delegated decision-making structure.[45] There is an inner circle of Perl developers, most of whom took an informal leadership role for a piece of the code during the transition from Perl version 4 to Perl version 5. Wall would pass to another developer the leadership baton, that person would work on a particular problem and then release a new version of the code, and then pass the baton back to Wall. This process developed into what Wall called "the pumpkin-holder system."[46] The pumpkin holder acts as chief integrator, controlling how code is added to the main Perl source. In a kind of rotating dictatorship pattern, the pumpkin gets passed from one developer to another within the inner circle.

Apache has evolved a more highly formal decision-making system. The Apache Group is an elite set of developers that together make decisions about the Apache code base. The Group began in 1995 with eight core developers who worked together to build Apache out of a public domain http daemon, which is a piece of server software that returns a web page in response to a query. There was no single project leader *per se*, and the group was geographically diverse from the start, with core developers in the United States, Britain, Canada, Germany, and Italy. The Apache Group devised a system of email voting based on minimal quorum consensus rule. Any developer who contributes to Apache can vote on any issue by sending email to the mailing list. Only votes cast by members of the Apache Group are binding; others are simply expressing an opinion. Within the Apache Group, code changes require three positive votes and no negative votes. Other decisions need a minimum of three positive votes and an overall positive majority. The Apache Group itself expands over time to include developers who have made excellent and sustained contributions to the project. To join the Apache Group, you must be nominated by a member and approved unanimously by all other members.[47]

Each of these decision-making systems has strengths and weaknesses as coordination mechanisms. As Conway's Law suggests, they make different demands on the technology architecture. What they share is the fundamental characteristic of the open source process—there is no authority to enforce the roles and there is nothing to stop an individual programmer or a group of programmers from stepping outside the system. On a whim, because of a fundamental technical disagreement, or because of a personality conflict, anyone could take the Linux code base or the Apache code base and create their own project around it, with different decision rules and structures. Open source code and the license schemes positively empower this option. To explain the open source process is, in large part, to explain why that does not happen very often and why it does when it does, as well as what that means for cooperation.

This chapter painted a picture of the open source process, the problem(s) it is trying to solve, and what we can recognize about how it seems to do that. These functional characterizations together describe a set of important interactions among the developers who create open source software—what they do, how they work together, and how they resolve disagreements. Clearly these do not constitute by themselves a robust explanation, and I have pointed out at various junctures why not. To answer the broader question with which I began this chapter— what are the conditions or boundaries for the open source process in software engineering, or for extending a version of that process to different kinds of production?—we need a more general and deeper explanation. That explanation needs to elucidate more precisely the basis of the equilibrium "solution" that open source has found, and to illustrate either why it is not challenged or why challenges do not disrupt it. The next chapter returns to a historical account of open source software in the 1990s. Chapters 5 and 6 build the explanation.

CHAPTER 4

A Maturing Model
of Production

At the start of the 1990s open source software could claim an implicit development model, some formal organizations, a nascent culture, the beginnings of business models, and—most importantly—a good deal of code. Ironically, it did not yet have the name "open source" or the distinctive community self-identification that often goes with an agreed name.[1] By the end of the 1990s open source had become a phenomenon—in product markets, capital markets, mainstream corporate settings, and in the imagination of many people outside the software engineering community. It also had a discrete identity (contested, like all identities) and an image of itself as a technological and political community that was building at once the very best software code and a new model of collaboration.

The road to this particular stage of maturation was a rocky one (as these journeys tend to be) because the stakes were high.[2] Developers devoted their lives and companies bet their futures on the product of a community that was struggling to build its own narrative about what it was doing and why. These struggles continue. Of course, it is in seeing how a community navigates its hard times and its struggles, including the struggles that are the dilemmas of success, that demanding tests of a model emerge.

In 1990 it would have been easy to predict the demise of the Unix world, the full marginalization of the Free Software Foundation, and the decisive triumph of the proprietary software development model exemplified by Microsoft. The prediction would have rested on an argument about basic forces of industrial organization. It would claim that source code, the key knowledge asset for a software company, is created most effectively in a market setting when innovators capture directly the rents associated with their innovation. The proprietary software development model maximizes the incentives to innovate because it can generate those rents by keeping source code secret. Proprietary software, then, is the equilibrium result of fundamental economic forces, not historical accident, policy choices, or something else.[3] Alternative models of software production might survive at most in some small niches on the periphery of the "real" market. Free software would be the vestige of a peculiarly inefficient set of arrangements, fated to play a marginal role in the shadow of a superior logic of production. Certainly evidence from the software market in 1990 would not have been able to prove this argument wrong. But the evidence today suggests a very different perspective.

The history of the 1990s demonstrates the viability of (at least) two discrete and sustainable ways of organizing the production of software. Neither is blind destiny nor a determinative outcome of basic forces of industrial organization that are cleanly separable from the social conventions of intellectual property rights, policy, business models, and ideas in the popular imagination. It is impossible to know in the abstract which is "better," more efficient, more productive, or which would win in a clean competition. And of course there will be no clean competition between them, because extant market conditions, government rules, market power, perceptions, and other intervening variables are at play. In practice both forms of software production are likely to survive and coexist.

The Unix Crisis

By 1990 the proprietary Unix market, laboring under the weight of multiple incompatible versions of software and legal uncertainty, was in crisis. At the same time Microsoft was gaining market share across almost all segments of the software industry, from the PC desktop to enterprise-level server systems.

The various BSD releases appeared to be following the same path as commercial Unix, forking into separate and incompatible versions. BSD's fragmentation has been explained as a story of conflicting personalities and as a story of legitimate technological differences and sensible product differentiation.[4] Both explanations have merit. But the result during this time frame was the same—a fragmentation of developers' efforts and slow progress just when the open source process seemed most vulnerable.

Bill Jolitz's 386/BSD was the first Unix-based operating system for personal computers to be distributed over the Internet. In 1992 and 1993 Jordan Hubbard and several other developers who shared Jolitz's view that the Intel x86 architecture would advance rapidly in the market were working on an integrated patchkit for 386/BSD. Jolitz, meanwhile, had lost interest in the project. In 1993 he withdrew his approval for Hubbard's work, "without any clear indication of what would be done instead."[5]

This was essentially an invitation to fork the code base. Hubbard did exactly that by creating the FreeBSD project to optimize the software for Intel processors. In time, FreeBSD evolved into a stable and easy-to-administer operating system that would be used to run large-scale server operations (for example, Yahoo! runs on FreeBSD). It also evolved a development model much like the original BSD process, with 200 or so programmers ("committers") who can make changes to the code base and relatively little input from outside that circle. The interesting addition was a core team that is elected every two years to handle dispute resolution and the process of selecting new committers.

At the same time another group of programmers decided to take BSD in a different direction, optimizing the software not for a particular Intel chip architecture but instead for compatibility and portability to as many different hardware platforms as possible. This project became NetBSD; it runs stably in around fifty different ports.[6] NetBSD portrays itself as a research-oriented project, in contrast to FreeBSD's marketing of itself as "bringing BSD to the masses."[7]

This in effect was another code fork for BSD. The benefit was "product differentiation" in which different kinds of software were needed for different uses. The costs, however, came with the splitting of the development community's effort between different projects, with the attendant dangers of slower progress and incompatibilities that would prove difficult to fix. Fragmentation, even if it made some sense from a technical perspective, was exactly what the Unix market of the early 1990s did not need.

Unfortunately BSD was about to undergo yet another fork, and for reasons that had as much to do with personality differences as with technical differentiation. In the early 1990s Theo de Raadt, a talented developer with a famously sharp tongue, had been responsible for the SPARC port of NetBSD. In late 1994 the NetBSD core team took away de Raadt's privileges as a committer and asked him to resign from the core. The letter announcing this decision said:

> On December 20, Theo de Raadt was asked to resign from the NetBSD Project by the remaining members of "core." This was a very difficult decision to make, and resulted from Theo's long history of rudeness towards and abuse of users and developers of NetBSD. We believe that there is no place for that type of behaviour from representatives of the NetBSD Project, and that, overall, it has been damaging to the project.[8]

Although the letter goes on to praise de Raadt's programming skills and thank him for his substantial contributions to NetBSD, de Raadt was furious. This letter set off a back-and-forth email "flame war" that lasted almost seven months. De Raadt keeps a record of these exchanges on his website.[9] At the beginning both sides might have been trying to negotiate a solution; over time the tone got increasingly strident. In November of 1995, de Raadt started a new fork of the code, which he called OpenBSD. A code fork means little unless developers decide to work on the new project; and de Raadt soon figured out that specializing in security would be OpenBSD's magnet for developers. In fact this fork helped solve some important technical security problems that had been plaguing Unix-type systems for many years.

In a different market environment, the BSD forks might have been seen as a positive development. BSD was in effect differentiated into three usefully distinct and specialized products. It could recruit a larger pool of volunteer programmers as well. Those who wanted to work on security issues could go to OpenBSD, and those who wanted to work on portability could go to NetBSD. But in the market environment of the early 1990s, the fork was clearly a liability. The crisis was powerfully evident to Unix programmers, who watched with something close to horror as the overall market share of Unix-type systems slipped away, particularly in favor of Windows NT. In the autumn of 1993 Larry McVoy at Sun Microsystems captured the core of the problem in a memo called "The Sourceware Operating System Proposal" that he prepared for Sun CEO Scott McNealy. The memo began with the proclamation that "Unix is dying" because of duplication of effort around different implementations, leading to high prices; poor compatibility; and, worst of all, slower development as each separate Unix vendor had to solve the same kinds of problems independently. In McVoy's view, "Unix has become stagnant . . . [and] has ceased to be the platform of choice for the development and deployment of innovative technology."

McVoy made radical suggestions for a Unix resurrection. Sun should give away the source code for SunOS 4, its proprietary version of Unix, or simply drop the Sun operating system altogether and adopt Linux instead. The introduction of Linux into the discussion was probably premature—less than two years old at this time, Linux was in no shape to be a serious competitor at this level. But it served to underline McVoy's point about the importance of making source code available. By releasing its source code, Sun could hope to drive standardization out of an otherwise hopelessly fragmented Unix market. As important a goal was to recapture the inventive energy that developers had committed to Unix when it was an open, research-oriented operating system. In McVoy's view, Linux, despite its immature state, was garnering much of the attention from innovative code writers, attention that could otherwise flow to Unix. McVoy went one step further, to argue that this illustrated a broader problem in the relationship between hackers and the business community. He wrote, "for the business community to dismiss the hackers as 'nuts' is a disaster . . . it is far better to figure out a way to allow the business world and the hacker world to coexist and benefit one another."[10]

This was a prescient argument, but Sun was not ready to hear it. In fact Scott McNealy had already made the decision to drop SunOS and instead adopt AT&T's commercial Unix version, then known as UnixWare. McVoy's document was a rearguard action that failed to reverse this decision (although it did get the attention of software engineers and top managers at Sun). In retrospect, 1993 was either too early or too late for McVoy's message. The "free" software model that had flourished in the 1970s and early 1980s was mostly a memory; the

FSF seemed nostalgic to many commercial software engineers; and Linux had yet to prove itself as a viable alternative.

Evolution of Linux, Stage 1

The story of the Linux kernel began in 1991 (see Chap. 3). Because Torvalds could draw on extensive existing resources in free code (particularly GNU tools from the FSF), he made rapid progress early on and in less than six months had an early version of a working operating system, including a primitive kernel.

The kernel of an operating system is the base layer of instructions that control the key information processing and resource allocation functions that make a computer function. And although the kernel is generally a very small part of the software needed to run a machine, it is in some sense the most important because it is the foundation on which all utilities and applications rely.

Early on, Torvalds made an important decision about the size of the kernel that would have major implications for the future evolution of Linux. Some programmers feel that a kernel should be as large as it needs to be, so as to integrate all the major features of the operating system's foundation in a single body of code. This type of kernel, called a monolithic kernel, was out of fashion among programming theorists and academics in the early 1990s. They preferred microkernels, which are as small as possible, providing only the minimal functions for the core of the operating system and "outsourcing" the rest to many (sometimes hundreds) of small programs or utilities that run on top of the microkernel. The preference for microkernels came from the belief (and the experience) that more complex kernels are too hard to develop to the tolerance standards that modern computing systems demand. In principle it might be more efficient to integrate tightly all the tasks of an operating system in a monolithic kernel; but as kernels increase in size, they become more difficult to understand and produce bugs that are extraordinarily hard to unravel.

Torvalds overtly bucked the trend by writing a monolithic kernel rather than a microkernel. He thought a monolithic kernel would be easier to hack and tweak, consistent with his vision of Linux as a learning and research tool. But he also relied implicitly on the open source code model to compensate for the complexity that a monolithic kernel would entail. The bet was that free access to source code would allow developers to manage the intricacies of a larger integrated kernel, and to do so over time. Put simply, open source was supposed to reduce the intellectual and organizational costs of kernel complexity. Of course, none of this was explicitly theorized in 1991. Torvalds was too busy writing code, and no one outside the developers who joined him on the Linux mailing lists was paying much attention.

In autumn 1991 Torvalds released Linux version 0.02. The release notes for this software were appropriately modest—it was still a simple piece of code that had only limited use. And yet Torvalds's comments on the release show that he recognized an interest niche among developers for his experiment. Minix—the major alternative—was complete and available nearly for free, but it was also static. Andrew Tanenbaum (who saw Minix primarily as a teaching tool) had little interest in changing the software substantially or developing it further. On the other hand, the FSF's kernel project (HURD) was just a vague promise. The Linux kernel, albeit primitive, was running and ready for experimentation. Its crude functionality was interesting enough to make people believe that it could, with work, evolve into something important. That promise was critical and drove the broader development process from early on. Torvalds soon recognized this driver; by the end of 1991, his email posts no longer portrayed Linux as a self-indulgent hobby for himself but something of much wider interest to a broad community of developers.

In late 1991 the Linux software archive was "mirrored" at two important sites, one in Germany and one in Boston (where Ted Ts'o, who would later become a major Linux developer, was running an FTP site for Linux at MIT).[11] Increasing interest in Linux soon pushed Torvalds to reconsider his early decisions about licensing as well. Prior to version 0.12 (released in January 1992), Torvalds had his own peculiar license scheme for Linux, which prevented anyone from charging for distributing the code. This limitation became a serious constraint on distribution of the software. Mass access to the Internet was not yet available, so for many potential Linux users, the FTP site was not much help. Somebody had to copy code onto floppy disks (a slow and boring job) and then send the disks to others; but under the original license, the person doing the copying would have to absorb these costs. Many developers asked Torvalds to permit a small copying fee, "not because they wanted to make money but because they didn't want to lose money on making Linux available to others."[12]

Torvalds took the cue and in January 1992 decided to adopt the GPL as a standard license for Linux. This was a major decision that Torvalds says he made simply and pragmatically—the GPL was available to him, known and "tested" by the community, and apparently good enough. This decision did remove the restriction on charging for distribution costs, but it also invoked the GPL "viral" clause, which ensured that any new software built with Linux code would have to be released with source code under the GPL as well and would remain free code forever.

The growing interest in Linux did not sit well with everyone. Some developers on the email lists for Minix began to complain that most of the posts on their lists were about Linux. In January Andrew Tanenbaum weighed in on the discussion. In a post titled "Linux is obsolete," Tanenbaum criticized Linux for the use of a monolithic kernel, calling it a "giant step back into the 1970s." Among other complaints, he also belittled Torvalds's fascination with the Intel x86 chip architecture, arguing that Linux was far too tightly tied to a chip design that might be superseded in a few short years.

Within a few hours Torvalds responded, and forcefully. First was the issue of cost: "Look who makes money off minix and who gives out Linux for free." Second (but clearly more important) were the technical issues. Torvalds wrote about what he called "the brain damages of minix" and said of Tanenbaum's new research project that he hoped it "doesn't suck like minix does."

It is not surprising that this exchange set off a long and sometimes heated email debate.[13] But the vitriol slowly washed out of the language. Torvalds apologized for the tone of his first message, and Tanenbaum countered with his own semi-apology. At the same time both men stuck to their technical guns. Tanenbaum maintained throughout that a monolithic kernel was old-fashioned and dysfunctional. Torvalds admitted that Tanenbaum had a point but that his monolithic kernel design had advantages he wanted to keep. Ken Thompson (the originator of Unix) weighed in with his opinion that microkernels were the future and that monolithic kernels were easier to implement but were also more likely to turn into a mess as they were changed over time. The fight was never settled, but the technical positions were spelled out, leaving the stakes in the design decision more transparent to everyone than they were at the start.

This long exchange illustrates some of the distinctive characteristics of conflict in the open source process. It is carried out entirely in the open, with messages on email lists accessible to everyone in the community. Ultimately the discussions get down to technical issues, clarifying the trade-offs among design strategies and decisions that matter for the function and performance of software. Torvalds was forced to think hard about the limitations and problems with his design and justify a plan of attack to the community, which actively responded and prodded and pushed. And because all the communications were archived on the lists (they can still be read today, and often are), people were for the most part offering closely reasoned opinions that educated the community about the issues in play.

This interaction is in sharp contrast to the strangely antiparallel battle that was going on between AT&T and BSD at about the same time. The AT&T battle was not about technical issues; it was a legal crusade to claim ownership of code. It played out mostly behind closed doors and outside the scrutiny of the community of people who were writing the code. This legal battle pushed people away from BSD, but it wasn't just because the legal uncertainties inhibited investment of time and energy in the code. It was also an emotional response to a battle that seemed to belong to someone else.[14] In contrast, the Torvalds-Tanenbaum argument pulled people in toward Linux and excited their interest. It was a battle that the community owned and would fight on its own terms. Several key Linux contributors (including David Miller and Peter da Silva) made the transition from "interested bystander" to core participant in the Linux development process through their participation in this debate.[15]

Evolution of Linux, Stage 2

The organization and principles of decision-making for Linux work themselves out as the development process itself unfolds. If there is a de facto constitution for this "community of practice," it is one that gets "written" only as it needs to be, when development runs into new roadblocks and demands.[16] Several key events of 1992 illustrate this concept.

The user interface is the screen that a program presents to a user, and typically it provides a means of input so the user can tell the system what to do. Linux 0.12 had an extraordinarily primitive user interface. Rather than build it from scratch, Torvalds used a freely available GNU program called BASH as a bare bones shell for the operating system. BASH showed the user a simple DOS-like command line, familiar to many users of the first generation of PCs (C:>).

The Linux community wanted something more sophisticated and graphical. They wanted, essentially, a system of "windows" not for the sake of pretty icons and menu bars but because they wanted to be able to control several programs at once. Many developers wanted to use X, a basic but functioning windowing program familiar to Unix users. In early 1992 Orest Zborowski took on the project of porting X to Linux. Later others joined him and the X windows venture became an autonomous free software project, with source code available under a specially designed MIT X license.[17] This set an important principle for mass open source development projects: If there is something you want and others also want it enough to help you build it, go ahead and do it.

Torvalds's response to the X project established a second important principle. Torvalds did more than accept the new project and cooperate with the X windows developers. He made use of the X windows project as a way of stressing and testing the foundations of the Linux kernel in new circumstances. His philosophy was simple: Employ good utilities and application programs to test and illuminate weaknesses in the kernel, then fix the weaknesses. "Porting software to the kernel" became a process by which both sides moved toward each other rather than a one-way street.

Torvalds reworked parts of the kernel so it would function smoothly with X windows and, in May of 1992, released version 0.96a with support for X. These version numbers capture an extraordinary rate of evolution in the software. During this period there were updates and re-releases almost every couple of days. This furious rate of change was without precedent in the software industry at the time. Obviously it would have been impossible before the advent of Internet technology and the increasing availability of connections that allowed FTP file sharing. It's not surprising, then, that the next major challenge for Linux would center on how the operating system would connect effectively to the Internet.

Put simply, the Linux kernel needed state-of-the-art TCP/IP networking built in. This was not a trivial problem. Ever since Bill Joy wrote the reference TCP/IP stack for BSD in the early 1980s, developers had struggled with implementing temperamental and tricky code for this protocol in other settings. The problem was made harder by the ongoing AT&T lawsuit: Given the legal cloud hanging over BSD, the Linux community was wary of using any code (and particularly high-profile code like the TCP/IP stack) that they did not write themselves or that was unambiguously free (in the FSF sense of that word). So they started from scratch.[18]

Ross Biro, the original volunteer leader of this effort, produced some crude code that was later taken over by Fred van Kempen. Van Kempen had a grand vision for a sophisticated code architecture that would allow the Linux kernel to access networks other than TCP/IP.[19] The problem was that the style of development that went along with that vision did not fit with the evolving norms of the Linux community. Van Kempen kept things close to his chest, thereby breaking the key rule of open source development to "talk a lot." His own network link was slow and unreliable, which made it difficult for others to communicate with him and download the code he was writing. Most importantly, van Kempen was taking too long. The elaborate vision, exciting as it was, did not produce in a timely fashion usable interim code that "worked reliably and satisfied the 80% of users," which is what the Linux community wanted along the way.[20]

Pressure was mounting on van Kempen as lead developer. But because the community had no authoritative mechanism to "fire" or even to demote a leader, efforts were made to convince van Kempen to shift his plans. Torvalds soon took a more radical step. He sanctioned a parallel coding effort led by Alan Cox, a developer in England who proposed to take van Kempen's early code and debug it into something working and stable for that 80 percent, as quickly as possible. This decision produced a direct conflict between two strong-willed individuals, a conflict that was primarily over development philosophy. Cox's view, "make it work first, then make it work better," was put up against van Kempen's view, "throw away the old and write it all from the bottom up for a perfect grand vision."

Torvalds could adjudicate this conflict only in the sense that he could choose which code to accept into the official version of the kernel. In fact he accepted Cox's code and not van Kempen's. The risk, of course, was the explicit possibility of a major fork. Van Kempen was angry. He could have taken the Linux code base, put in his networking code, and started his own post-Linux project as a direct competitor. In fact van Kempen did continue his development effort for a while. But he gave up, mainly because the community of active developers stayed with Linux. The code did not fork in a meaningful way. And the development strategy of "make it work first, then make it work better" was strongly reinforced.

This series of events established a third principle of open source organization, more specifically the organization of decision-making in Linux. Torvalds's actions created a leadership role for Alan Cox. Cox was then the semiofficial "networking guy" and the community of developers began to send most communications or code patches having to do with network functions directly to him, rather than to Torvalds. The lieutenant model was born, along with the informal, pyramidal hierarchy that characterizes decision making for Linux. It was never decided *per se;* it simply evolved in practice. Torvalds endorsed and legitimized the practice when he starting sending networking code that was submitted to him down the line to Cox before Torvalds himself acted on it.[21]

Evolution of Linux, Stage 3

In March 1994 Torvalds released Linux 1.0. This next phase of maturation saw the porting of Linux to chip architectures other than Intel x86, the spread of "packaged distributions" of Linux with rudimentary business models around them, and innovation in the development and release strategy.

In 1994 a highly respected Unix programmer at Digital Equipment Corporation, John Hall (nicknamed "Maddog"), ran into Linus Torvalds at a DEC user meeting. Torvalds installed Linux on a PC and put on a demonstration that Hall found impressive. Hall went back to DEC and began to proselytize for Linux, telling his colleagues that this free software was nearly as good as DEC's proprietary version of Unix (called Ultrix). Hall then convinced Torvalds to work on porting Linux to DEC's new 64-bit Alpha processor, with help from some DEC engineers who were thinking about doing this as well.

This was a major move for Linux. Remember that Torvalds initially designed the system to run on the Intel 80386 chip for personal computers, and Linux was still tied to the Intel x86 architecture. The Alpha was in an entirely different league, a high-end chip processing 64 bits at a time (it would be a few years before Windows NT ran on 64-bit chips). DEC became the first major computer company to make a serious commitment to Linux. By supporting the effort with donated hardware and the dedicated time of some its top engineers, DEC was making a statement that it would work with Linux, not ignore it or oppose it.

For his part, Torvalds was making a high-visibility statement that Linux was no hobbyists' toy but rather a first-class operating system for advanced computing architectures. From a technical standpoint, this meant reengineering the kernel in ways that would enhance the portability of Linux to different architectures, thereby abstracting the code away from hardware dependencies. When Linux 2.0 was released in spring 1996, it would support the Intel and Alpha architectures and be close to official readiness for several other key ports, among them the Motorola 6800 series, the Power PC series, and MIPS r4000 systems. Three years later Intel would agree to support the porting of Linux to its Itanium chip, still under development as the successor to the Pentium.

At about the same time that Hall was pushing the Alpha port, a Rutgers student named David Miller with a part-time systems administrator job decided to try to port Linux to Sun's SPARC processor because he had some SPARC system computers lying around his office. What started as a hobby project soon became a major initiative for the community and a SPARC port of Linux was released in November 1995. This port put Linux into operation on the leading high-end commercial hardware platform. It is significant that Sun did not help the project; in fact, Sun was opposed to the Linux port, but there was nothing the company could do to stop Miller's efforts.

The second aspect of Linux's growing maturity in 1994 was the growth of software "packages" or distributions. Because Linux was written explicitly "by hackers for hackers," it was not a simple undertaking to get Linux running on any particular machine. A user would have had to find and assemble pieces of software, including the kernel, a set of utilities, the right drivers for the devices on the user's machine, and then configure these pieces to work together. Linux's design made this process possible, but it was certainly not easy, even for relatively sophisticated programmers. As interest in Linux grew, there emerged a demand for an external integrator of sorts—someone who would do the dirty work of putting together the right pieces of the latest code, configure them for a particular hardware setup, and make the whole package easy to install.

In late 1993 Ian Murdock, then an accounting student at Purdue, decided to try to build a coherent package through a voluntary distributed development process, much like the process he believed was working so well for Linux. With early support from the FSF, Murdock set up what he called Debian to define a set of standards for Linux distributions. Meanwhile, another Linux enthusiast named Patrick Volkerding saw a similar opportunity and built his own distribution called Slackware, which he sold more or less at cost. A new company, Yggdrasil Computing, went an important step further by dropping floppy disks and putting the software together on a newly popular storage media, the CD-ROM. Yggdrasil also began to build a rudimentary business model around this process. With the CD-ROM priced at $99, the company was charging not for the software, which anyone could download from the Internet for free, but for the convenience of a neat, coherent distribution.

Yggdrasil took another major and controversial step in its distribution strategy. Unlike Debian, which used only free software in building its distribution, Yggdrasil carried a programming tool kit for graphical user interfaces called Motif. Motif was expensive (about $150), but much more importantly it was a classic proprietary piece of software. It could not be copied and it could not be modified because it came without source code. For some within the free software community, the idea of distributing proprietary software for use with Linux was heresy. In the eyes of FSF, Yggdrasil had committed a sin. But for many software developers, it was simply an issue of pragmatism and opportunity. This group wanted to use Motif because they liked the tool kit and because it opened up for use on Linux a wide variety of Motif-based software. Codistribution of open source and proprietary software would become a major dividing line within the community later on, particularly as business interest in Linux grew; but the basic lines of disagreement were established quite early on in 1994.

Other commercial Linux ventures took slightly different paths.

Pacific HiTech (later renamed TurboLinux) packaged free software along with proprietary software that could render Japanese fonts for the Japanese market. SuSE, founded in 1992 to do Unix consulting in Europe, switched to Linux and soon became the dominant supplier of Linux consulting and customization services on the continent. In 1993 Marc Ewing launched Red Hat with the business model of making Linux installation and configuration easier for less sophisticated users. In 1994 Bryan Sparks launched Caldera (first as a project within Novell, and later spun off as an independent company). Caldera took perhaps the most baldly commercial path; its business model was to "surround" Linux with proprietary software products to increase the attractiveness of the package to businesses. Caldera did more than just bundle proprietary software with free software on a single CD, as Yggdrasil had done. Caldera integrated the proprietary applications in a way that made it hard to separate them out. This spawned some important licensing issues—if you couldn't isolate the free software from the proprietary software covered under restrictive licenses, you really couldn't make legal copies of the distribution or easily modify the source code or engage in the other freedoms that free software was designed to permit.

This was a challenging precedent for the open source community. The problem, at least for most open source enthusiasts, was *not* Caldera's commitment to deliver open source technology to the mainstream business marketplace. The problem was about the nature of the compromise with proprietary software that Caldera was willing to make. These kinds of decisions become key considerations in licensing schemes (see Chap. 6) and business models (see Chap. 7).

The third major step in Linux's maturation was an innovation in the development process in spring 1994. Right after the 1.0 release, Torvalds found himself spending a lot of time working on ports rather than on new features. This led to a slowdown in the outrageous rate of releases that Torvalds had managed in the prior year. Meanwhile an inherent tension was emerging between the most sophisticated developers (who continued to experiment at a breakneck pace with new ideas and features) and the increasing number of somewhat less sophisticated, nonhacker users, allied with the commercial distributors in some cases, who wanted a stable snapshot of the kernel with which to work.

Torvalds's idea was to create two distinct strands of releases. Even point numbers (1.0, 1.2) would be stable releases that had been deeply tested and promised reliability to users. Odd point numbers (1.1, 1.3) would be experimental releases, filled with new features and elements in the process of being worked out and debugged. The experimental versions at a certain point would become locked by agreement. At that point there would be no new features added; instead the community's energy would be redirected toward debugging the current code. When debugging was complete, the software would be released as a new stable version (debugging, of course, is never really complete, but adequate for broader use). Thus 1.1x would be frozen at a certain point, debugged, and then released as 1.2.0. At the same time, 1.3.0 would be started for new experimental code. This numbering system made it possible for the Linux process to more effectively engage with two different constituencies—the sophisticated developers who wanted a research project, and commercial or relatively less sophisticated users who wanted reliable software that they didn't have to update on a weekly basis.

Apache and the Web

A web server is the software that answers a query by returning a web page to the computer that asked for it.[22] In 1994 the most widely used web server was a public domain http daemon, which had been developed by Rob McCool at the National Center for Supercomputing Applications (NCSA) at the University of Illinois (in conjunction with Mosaic, the first widely used web browser).

It was still early days for the web, but the rate of experimentation was extraordinary. Developers were playing with the NSCA code to build primitive web servers and establish an early presence for their organizations on the web. When McCool left NSCA in the middle of 1994 and many of his collaborators went off to build proprietary (and very expensive) server software for a company called Netscape, development of the public domain server software stalled at NCSA. But it certainly did not stall out on the periphery, where webmasters were developing their own extensions, patches, and bug fixes to the NCSA code. Informal groups of webmasters shared patches among themselves; some sent their best code back to NCSA, hoping it would get incorporated into an official release. Unfortunately the remaining developers at NCSA were overwhelmed and dropped the ball.

Lack of responsiveness of this kind is a clear cue that leadership of an open source–style development process is failing and represents a de facto invitation to fork the code. That is essentially the origin of Apache, although not in a conscious sense.

Brian Behlendorf in 1995 was a student at Berkeley and an early employee of *Wired* magazine, where he was implementing a server that would allow people to download magazine articles over the web. He then moved on to putting up new content, or articles that were not in the magazine. This effort evolved into *Hotwired,* one of the first webzines, and Behlendorf was appointed chief engineer. He was using a patched-up version of NCSA server software to run the site and sharing fixes with friends and colleagues who were trying to do similar kinds of things at other companies.

Because NCSA had dropped out of the game, this group took their own initiative with the code. In early 1995, Behlendorf volunteered his server as a joint information space for the eight core developers with whom he was sharing code, and agreed to host a public email list for communication about the project. On the first day, around 40 developers subscribed to the list; three months later, there were nearly 150 subscribers.[23] The core developers decided to create a central committee for decision-making about the code, which they later called the Apache Committee. The first interim release of the Apache server came in April 1995. Robert Thau reworked much of the software to improve the modularity of the code so distributed development in an open source process could proceed more efficiently. Apache 1.0 was released in December 1995. It quickly came to dominate the market for web servers and continues to do so, serving as a major boost to open source. In short order an open source project had eclipsed proprietary alternatives and had done so in a mission-critical business application. In fact Apache was tightly tied to commercial use from its very beginnings. Many of the Apache developers were creating websites for companies, large and small. They were not concerned with ideology or morality; rather they wanted to build the best web server as quickly and cheaply as possible. This focus, along with the close ties that many of the developers had to Berkeley, is why Apache was released with a minimally restrictive BSD-style license rather than the GPL.

The Apache Group never had a single leader, charismatic or otherwise, as did Linux. As the software grew in popularity and the code base became more complex, the core developers found that they needed a concrete set of rules to govern decision-making. In fact the Apache group created a de facto constitution with a system of email voting based on a minimal quorum consensus, and a procedure for adding new members to the core committee of decision makers.

Apache was and is important not only because it dominates a major market. It also pioneered new ground in developing relationships between the open source process and traditional business structures. IBM would come to bet on Apache as the core of its future web business strategy. IBM became a member of the Apache Group in 1998. In 1999 the Apache Group incorporated as a nonprofit organization, the Apache Software Foundation, in part to enhance itself with a legal infrastructure that could manage patent and liability concerns. The foundation later began to serve as an organizational umbrella, networking several other open source projects together and providing them with shared institutional infrastructure.

A Community Cementing Its Identity

Linux 2.0 was released in June 1996. The operating system took several important technical steps forward. In addition to multiarchitecture support (Intel and Alpha, with more coming), 2.0 also offered symmetric multiprocessor support so it was capable of running on high-end computing systems that used multiple processors.[24] This was a clear signal that the Linux developers were aiming at the most demanding segments of the corporate computing market. The other important watershed in 1996 was Torvalds's move to the United States. In October Torvalds announced that he would take a job at a privately held technology firm in Silicon Valley named Transmeta. Torvalds decided not to join a commercial Linux venture, but rather to work for a company that promised him time to work on Linux.[25] Transmeta (although it was not known publicly at the time) was developing a new architecture for very fast and low-powered chips useful for mobile computers and smart devices, and it would later use modified variants of Linux to run some of those devices.

Some Linux developers worried about the future of Linux after Torvalds had taken a "real" job. Linux was becoming a major enterprise-level computing system with substantial commercial energy behind it, but the community that was building it still had the mindset of a hobbyist's club. Linux and the broad community of developers who contributed to it and other open source projects needed a new self-consciousness, a name, an identity, and a more clearly articulated mission, to take the next step toward maturity.

The Free Software Foundation would have been the obvious nexus for that evolution; however, it could not be in practice and mainly because of the ideological passion and dedication of Richard Stallman. Stallman was (and remains) an intensely moral and political voice in the free software world. He was and still is a force to be reckoned with in any discussion of what the battle over software is about. But ideological fervor in this community, as in most communities, has self-limiting aspects. Stallman marked out an ethical position on software with great eloquence, but it was still a position that many developers and even more users of software found to be extreme and uncompromising.

Stallman understood that most of his audience were pragmatists. He was trying to change that fact by illustrating the values he felt were at stake in their practice, and moving the entire frame of the discussion about software into the realm of ethics. For better or worse, he failed at that task. Pragmatism is still the prevalent "moral" stance among developers and users of computer software. And for pragmatists, what was at stake was a different kind of freedom than the FSF believed in, a freedom to express creativity and build great software and expand its use with an absolute minimum of restrictions. BSD-style licenses implicitly articulate a version of this philosophy. BSD after all was built out of AT&T code because it worked; BSD code was free for companies to take and commercialize (without releasing source code) if they wished; that was precisely what Bill Joy did when he joined Sun Microsystems in 1982. But BSD itself suffered from this laissez-faire attitude, in practice as well as principle. The development process splintered; much good code was done inside proprietary implementations and never released back to the community; some companies and people made money relying on the cumulative work of volunteers and gave nothing or almost nothing back to the community. If the FSF had "too much" philosophy to cement a community identity around, BSD arguably had "too little."

It fell to Eric Raymond, an accomplished developer with strong libertarian leanings and an amateur anthropological bent, to write the essay that would form the core of the debate about identity. "The Cathedral and the Bazaar," which Raymond first presented in early 1997 to a Linux Users Group, had a galvanizing effect because it articulated a clear technical and behavioral logic with which the open source community could identify. The developers were already doing all these things; what Raymond provided was a cogent story about what it was they were doing and why it seemed to work so well. He also provided a powerful image and an evocative metaphor, rendered in a concise way with clever language and memorable catch phrases. Linus's Law—"with enough eyeballs all bugs are shallow"—is an important example. This is not a criticism; all communities need slogans as well as deep understandings, and Raymond's essay offered both.

"The Cathedral and the Bazaar" is still the most common starting point for people who want to understand the open source phenomenon. Raymond's writing is clever, sometimes brilliant, and often controversial. Like many anthropologists, he is frequently attacked for seeing within the open source movement what he wants to see, the drivers of human behavior that fit his personal philosophy or experience. Certainly there has been a great deal of energy expended in discussion of Raymond's metaphors, in critiquing simplistic notions of self-organization and hierarchies, communism and libertarianism, free markets and so on. Some of this critique is a game played by outsiders, people who have wanted to use a metaphor of the open source community, to the extent that they understand it, to make a point about something else. A great deal of the discussion is, more interestingly, the guts of the process by which the community of developers carries out a dialogue about its identity, its goals, and its reason for being. Within that frame, whether Raymond was right or wrong is less important. What matters is that his essay put an intellectual stake in the ground for an explicit discussion of identity. For the open source movement, "The Cathedral and the Bazaar" clearly marks the beginning of a new phase of maturity, a joint, articulated, political self-consciousness around which the community could and did rally and argue.

But for all the focus that Raymond's essay provided, the community still lacked a coherent label or name. Stallman's eloquent explanations of what "free" meant aside, growing interest in the software was accompanied by growing confusion over what it was, where it came from, and what you could do with it. The proliferation of licensing schemes further clouded the issue. By 1998 the underlying tension between BSD-style thinking and GPL-style thinking was clearly more than an arcane philosophical difference among specialist communities. It was a roadblock to the progressive mainstreaming of the software into widespread use. Outside observers as well as some of the most "insider" developers began to agree that the confusion was a rate-limiting factor on commercialization of the software and was reducing its attractiveness to mainstream corporate settings. Free software may have been technically desirable; but from a marketing perspective, it was a disaster, in no small part because of the name.

Tim O'Reilly, a long-term advocate who had built a substantial business publishing technical-support books and hosting conferences for free software, understood the importance of having a straightforward story that the community could tell to the outside world. At his Spring 1998 freeware conference, he was hoping to put together a political consensus among major figures in the community to take things forward in that direction. While O'Reilly was planning this conference, Eric Raymond and others had been summoned to Netscape (in January 1998) to help that company think through its impending decision to release the source code for its browser. The discussions at Netscape convinced Raymond that, no matter how he tried to reframe it, the "free" label was getting in the way. At a meeting held at VA Linux in early February 1998, Raymond, VA Linux Chairman Larry Augustin, and John "Maddog" Hall came up with the more neutral-sounding term "open source," which the freeware summit went on to endorse in April.

The open source synthesis now needed a more formal definition and a set of boundaries. This meant confronting fundamental cleavages within the community, including the tension between BSD philosophy and GPL philosophy, between pragmatists and purists, between the moral arguments of Richard Stallman and the commercial desires of companies like VA Linux and Red Hat. Raymond pushed for an open source definition that could accommodate the GPL as a core but also other licenses that met a set of basic necessary requirements. Debian had already gone quite far in its thinking about this problem. Debian, now led by Bruce Perens, in 1997 had written and published a formal social contract with the free software community, spelling out the core values it was going to promote. The contract promised that the Debian distribution itself would remain 100 percent free software, but it also pledged that "we'll allow others to create value-added distributions containing both Debian and commercial software, without any fee from us. To support these goals we will provide an integrated system of high quality 100% free software with no legal restrictions that would prevent these kinds of use." The last article of the contract goes even further, saying, "although non-free software isn't a part of Debian, we support its use and we provide infrastructure (such as our bug-tracking system and mailing lists) for non-free software packages."

To support this contract, Perens also wrote a set of guidelines that are essentially a meta-definition for free software. The Debian Free Software Guidelines were adopted as the open source definition, minus the specific references to Debian. The definition requires free redistribution (that is, the license cannot restrict anyone from selling or giving away the software alone or in combination with software from other sources). Beyond this core element, the open source definition leans toward fewer restrictions so it can accommodate a variety of licenses, including both BSD and GPL.

The open source definition says that the program "must include source code and must allow distribution in source code as well as compiled form." It says of derived works that "the license must allow modifications and derived works, and must allow them to be distributed under the same terms as the license of the original software." Notice the use of "allow" in this statement, not "require." The GPL *requires* distribution of derived works under the same terms, which clearly fits the definition. But so does BSD, which allows a derived work to carry a BSD-style license, but also allows it not to do so.

The open source definition makes a clear statement as well about codistribution of free and proprietary software: "The license must not place restrictions on other software that is distributed along with the licensed software. For example, the license must not insist that all other programs distributed on the same medium must be free software." It specifically prohibits discrimination against any person or group of persons (including, obviously, for-profit corporations) and specifically prohibits restricting "anyone from making use of the program in a specific field of endeavor."

The Debian social contract and the open source definition that follows from it clearly prioritize the desires and needs of *users of software*. A community that was born in a self-centered mindset (think of Torvalds's description of Linux as a program "by hackers for hackers") was growing up in a different direction. This was a clear signal of technical maturity, but even more importantly of social and political maturation. It was also a decisive move away from the core arguments of Richard Stallman. To build the open source process around the goal of meeting the needs of users was a very different objective than convincing developers and users alike that fundamental moral issues were at stake.

This is not to say that creating the open source definition signed away anyone's belief in or commitment to the underlying "good" of the process. Many developers believe as strongly as ever that their values around cooperation and sharing in knowledge production are the fundamental reasons why they do what they do. But the open source definition makes a clear statement that the *community per se* will not define itself by those values or place restrictions on its activities and products in the interest of promoting a set of values. Pragmatism rules and the metric for success is now clearly laid down—it is about conquering the "market" by building software and software packages that meet the needs of users better than any alternatives. In short, a new production process with a very standard measure of achievement was established.

Does Linus Scale?

Success creates dilemmas for organizations of all kinds. In the summer of 1998 Linux was about to confront some of these dilemmas acutely. Major hardware and software companies were focusing on open source products as serious competitors or in some cases possible avenues for collaboration. Press coverage was heating up as Torvalds became something of a media star.[26] Meanwhile Torvalds had his job at Transmeta, a second child, and a rapid (and rapidly growing) Linux development process to manage.

Outsiders might say that the organizational capabilities of the Linux development process were coming under time pressure and the strain of divided attention. For insiders the observation was simpler: Their leader was failing to respond to them in an efficient and timely fashion. This led first to general frustration and then to a crisis that nearly resulted in a major fork of the Linux code. Instead the crisis was "solved" or managed through a combination of organizational and technological innovation that brought the Linux development process another large step forward toward maturity. The answer to the question of scaling was no; the response to that was to build elements of an organization that could scale, rather than to allow the process to break.

The crisis became acute in late September 1998, when it became clear that versions of Linux located on a particular mirror site called VGER, at Rutgers University, were out of synch with what Torvalds held as the official version of the code. A mirror site is simply a convenience, a copy of what is on another computer so data can be located closer to some set of users. Dave Miller, who had set up VGER, was accepting patches that Torvalds was not, and incorporating them into the code tree held on VGER. In effect, what was supposed to be a mirror site was on the verge of becoming an autonomous development site—a different code base, a de facto VGER Linux separate from Torvalds's Linux and thus a real fork.

Torvalds did not at first try to heal the rift, but rather lashed out in a series of angry emails about the "irrelevance" of VGER. This brought back from Miller and others the deeper story, of the frustration many developers were feeling at Torvalds's recent lack of responsiveness to their work. Martin Mares wrote, "Some time ago you promised you'll accept a single large video patch before 2.2 and I did send it to you, but I got ignored." Dave Miller picked up on this point: "Everyone who maintains the video driver layer is telling you look at Martin's patch, nothing more. If you continually ignore him, you are the road-block plain and simple."

Miller was warning Torvalds. Torvalds struck back, suggesting that the way to solve the problem was to shut down VGER. Ted T'so then stepped in with an effort at conciliation. He suggested that Torvalds should acknowledge a real problem, that he had simply not kept up with the flow of work, and that other developers were feeling ignored and frustrated. Perhaps what was happening at VGER was not the best solution, but clearly there was a problem that needed to be solved and Torvalds needed to help solve it. Torvalds grew angrier, demanding a public apology from Miller and writing this exasperated email:

Quite frankly this particular discussion and others before has just made me irritable and is ADDING pressure. Instead I'd suggest that if you have a complaint about how I handle patches you think about what I end up having to deal with for five minutes. Go away, people. Or at least don't cc me any more. I'm not interested, I'm taking a vacation, and I don't want to hear about it any more. In short, get the hell out of my mailbox.

All of this argument happened in less than two days and suddenly Linux was in crisis. Interestingly, it was Eric Raymond who took the first successful step in bringing down the level of emotion.

Raymond used his status as unofficial anthropologist of open source to depersonalize the situation and repackage it as an issue about organizational efficiency. According to Raymond, this was a test of the open source process under stress, not a personal battle between Torvalds and Miller or anyone else. The organization was being stretched to the limit and as a result people were showing signs of stress and burnout. Dropping patches should not be thought of as a personal insult—the problem was that it "degrades the feedback loop that makes the whole process work." In Raymond's words, "the effect of rising uncertainty as to whether good work will make it in at all is certainly worse than that. Anybody who starts to believe they're throwing good work down a rat hole will be *gone*. If that happens too many times, we're history." In this sense the open source production process was no different from any other: As the demands of the process bump up against its organizational limits, a new set of bargains needs to be configured. Technology is a facilitator. For this community in particular, the idea of a technological fix helped bring the parties together on common ground, but ultimately the solution was going to be a political one.

Larry McVoy suggested the technology fix. He proposed a blueprint for a new code management system called Bitkeeper. If "Linus doesn't scale," as McVoy said, then what the process as a whole needed was a new piece of software, a code management system designed specifically around the open source development process, organized in a way that would formalize and facilitate the pyramidal structure of decision-making.

At this point Bitkeeper was just an idea. Nobody really believed that source management software by itself would solve the problem, which was fundamentally one of workflow and organization. But the promise of a technology adjunct was enough of a nexus to encourage the political discussion necessary to prevent a major fork. The key players, including Torvalds and Miller, came together for a rare face-to-face meeting over dinner in Silicon Valley in late September 1998. Technology was the shared foundation for a discussion about how to relieve some of the pressure on Torvalds. Torvalds would reduce his exposure to the media, letting Eric Raymond take on the role of "minister of propaganda."[27] More importantly, the principals agreed on a somewhat more formal pyramidal structure for the flow of patches and software submissions.

These decisions were the mainstay of the evolving organizational structure for Linux decision-making. The process by which they were reached was at least as important as the outcome. The key players had, in effect, looked straight into the eye of a major fork and turned back from it. The heated conflict took place out in the open, on mailing lists accessible to the entire community. The resulting bargains and most of the negotiations were public. The vehemence of the conflict was de-escalated by a common language around technology. And the fight did not drag on forever; in fact, the acute phase lasted less than a week. The conflict management "system" of the open source process was becoming more defined.

Open Source to the Enterprise

Open source certainly captured the attention of the public during 1999, when Red Hat and VA Linux successively sold initial public offering (IPO) shares in what were two of the most spectacular stock openings in history.[28] Chapter 7 discusses the business models that lie behind these and other "open source" companies (more properly thought of as companies building profitable economic models around the open source process). But behind the sound and fury of fabulous IPOs, open source was making steady progress into mission-critical business settings. It was being adopted as the core of strategic initiatives by major software and hardware companies. And it was attracting serious attention from Microsoft and others as a real competitive force in markets, albeit one they didn't understand very well.

A major use of information technology within large organizations (apart from communications) is to put information in and take information out of large databases. In 1998, several major suppliers of enterprise-level database systems announced that they would port these high-end (and very expensive) packages to run on the Linux operating system. Computer Associates announced in April that it would port the Ingres II database to Linux. A few months later, Informix released a Linux port of Informix-SE; and at the end of the year, IBM released a beta version of the DB2 database for Linux. Probably the most important announcement came from Oracle in July. Oracle had run a skunk works project for about a year, to experiment with porting its 8i database to both Linux and FreeBSD. In July Oracle announced the port to Linux and went one step further by committing to set up a business unit to maintain and support 8i as well as some of their other major products on Linux.[29]

This was a major breakthrough in mainstream credibility for the open source operating system. It was reinforced still further when the German software firm SAP announced, in March 1999, that it would port its enterprise resource planning (ERP) suite R/3 to Linux. ERP software is used to run many of the most important backend information-processing tasks such as planning, manufacturing, sales, and marketing in large companies; nearly half of the Fortune 500 companies use R/3 for this purpose. Now R/3 would be available for Linux, with dedicated support from SAP.

A series of parallel announcements came from major hardware vendors in 1999. Hewlett-Packard led in January 1999, announcing an alliance with Red Hat to support Linux on the popular HP "netserver" machine (a computer optimized for use as a web server platform). A few months later HP created an open source solutions operation within the company to pull together a number of disparate initiatives, and in April the group announced that it would offer full-time support for several different Linux distributions, not only on HP hardware but also on hardware from Compaq, Dell, and IBM. Meanwhile Dell in February announced that it would offer servers configured with Linux. IBM announced first that it would support Red Hat Linux on its major servers and later other Linux distributions as well. Compaq, Silicon Graphics, and Gateway soon joined the rush.

By the end of 1999 a major business could choose Red Hat Linux on a Dell server, running an Oracle database, with full-time support from IBM global services. If the open source movement measured its success partly by whether it could achieve status as a competitive technological solution for mainstream business use, by 2000 that question was answered definitively in the affirmative.

Netscape and IBM

While many of these initiatives were happening behind the scenes, in at least two cases the move to make open source the core of a business strategy was visible and dramatic. Netscape shocked the computing world when, in January 1998, it announced that it would release the source code for its flagship browser product, Communicator 5.0, in the spring. This signaled the convergence of yet another part of the core technologies of the Internet with the open source movement (joining Apache, Sendmail, BIND, and Perl) as well as a major corporate strategy decision, to take what had been proprietary code and make it open source.

This decision had roots in events of late 1996. Until that summer, Netscape held a substantial lead in web technologies; its Navigator software dominated the market for web browsers and Netscape server software was selling rapidly and at a high price. Microsoft had been slow to understand the potential of the web. Until the end of 1995, the company focused instead on its proprietary MSN service, a "walled garden" with controlled access to the wider Internet. In 1996 Microsoft dropped that idea and moved aggressively into competition with Netscape. The company put huge resources behind the accelerated development of Internet Explorer (IE), Microsoft's web browser. Internet Explorer version 3 (released in August 1996) was a credible alternative to the Netscape browser. Microsoft gave its browser away for free and, more importantly, used all its market power and distribution channels to get IE onto people's desktops in lieu of Netscape.[30]

By late 1996 Netscape was losing market share and top decision makers at the company knew the firm was at risk. Eric Hahn (who would later become CTO) wrote a series of memos to top management with ideas about what Netscape could do to boost its chances. The "heresy documents," as they were called, suggested, among other things, that Netscape match the zero price of IE and then go one huge step further—give away the source code for the browser. If zero price were the best way to get the browser onto people's desktops, Hahn (who had been watching Linux) believed that giving away the source code was the best way to generate a surge of interest among software developers.

The open source proposal resonated strongly within the company, particularly among the small army of developers who were writing code for the browser. Jamie Zawinski, a highly respected developer within Netscape and a long-time free software advocate, quickly became a powerful promoter for the idea. Frank Hecker, technical manager for Netscape's government sales group, was also a strong supporter but realized early on that, as long as the developers were the only ones advocating open source, the idea would go nowhere. Someone needed to make a clear business case for the move, stressing the commercial not just the technical logic. Hecker took on this task in the summer of 1997. His memo "Netscape Source Code as Netscape Product" argued that the company should reconceptualize the source code as a product that it delivered to customers, and it proposed a set of plans for making money with that product.

The decision to open source the Netscape browser seems to have grown out of a fall 1997 meeting between Hahn, Hecker, Zawinski, and CEO Jim Barksdale. The formal announcement came on January 22, 1998, but it would be several months before the code was ready to be released. In fact there were substantial hurdles to be overcome. It wasn't like starting with a core code base that had been developed in the open source setting. Instead, the Netscape browser code was a huge and complicated patchwork that had been built in a quick and dirty way with inadequate documentation. The code had to be cleaned up and organized in a way that someone coming into the process could make sense of what was done before. There were legal concerns over third-party technology, pieces of code that Netscape had licensed from others and might not have the right to release as open source. Java components that belonged to Sun were an example.

Netscape needed also to develop an appropriate licensing scheme for the code. That job fell to Mitchell Baker, associate general counsel, who consulted with Torvalds, Raymond, Stallman, and others about the trade-offs. The GPL was impractical in part because of the way in which the browser software had to work in conjunction with other software that was not GPL'ed; it also was seen as commercially not viable for Netscape. At the same time the software engineers at Netscape wanted something as close to the GPL as possible to maximize the likelihood that developers in the open source community would contribute actively to the project over time.

The awkward compromise was the establishment of two licenses, the Netscape Public License and the Mozilla Public License (NPL and MPL). While the MPL was quite similar to GPL, the NPL was used for code that Netscape also used elsewhere in its product line and, crucially, for code that had been licensed to third parties. Under NPL, Netscape could give the code to third parties without binding them to any GPL-style provisions. Netscape could also include this code in other Netscape products, *without* making the source code available, for two years. The rationale sounded simple: Because Netscape contributed its source code to the community, giving away four years of very expensive and very sophisticated coding work, it had the right to ask for something in return—in this case, special privileges (but time limited) on the code that others would contribute.

No one knew if this "deal" with its peculiar terms of reciprocity would work. Clearly the company was trying to mobilize the energy of an open source process for the purpose of advancing its own interests, and it was relying heavily on developers' anti-Microsoft sentiment and the excitement of "helping the underdog win the browser war" to motivate contributors. When Netscape released source code at the end of March, the immediate response was indeed impressive—nearly 200,000 downloads of the code within two weeks and some important changes checked back in by volunteer developers. One very important contribution from developers in Australia and England provided cryptography elements that Netscape had to strip out of the source code release to comply with U.S. export laws at the time. This happened less than a month after the code release; these developers used a free software security library that had been developed outside the United States and thus could be distributed worldwide.

But early signs of success faded as the rate of external contributions declined over time.[31] The Netscape code, even after the cleanup operation, was a messy difficult-to-understand patchwork with many locked-in elements. Outside developers felt they were facing a project that was 90 percent fait accompli and that they could affect the evolution of the code only at the margins. Progress was slower than expected. The Netscape engineers had planned to stabilize the code as of September, which meant stop the development of major changes and new features and debug what they had in preparation for a stable release. The announced stabilization date came and went. In late October the Netscape engineers announced a radical decision: to junk the existing layout engine (the part of the browser that turns HTML code into a display on the user's screen) and start over with a new engine, called Gecko. This decision responded to the demands of web content authors, who wanted layout engines to be compatible with standards drawn up by the World Wide Web Consortium (W3C). (At this time neither Netscape nor Internet Explorer was fully compatible with W3C standards; as a result, web pages often looked very different when viewed on different browsers.) The content designers' preferences hadn't changed—they always favored W3C standards—but in opening up the source code to developers, Netscape had also de facto opened up the discussion about what would constitute a "shippable" product.

From a technical standpoint, this might have been a good decision, regardless of the business logic. But it did not mesh well with the logic of the open source process in two ways. It meant throwing away six months of work and postponing a working release for an undefined period. This discouraged developers both inside and outside of Netscape, including Zawinski, who resigned from the project at the end of March. In a public letter to the community explaining his decision, he proclaimed the failure of Mozilla: The project still belonged to Netscape; it had never really been adopted by the broader community as its own; and there was not sufficient promise of being able to ship a product in a timely fashion to change that.

It was never really clear to what extent the licensing issues or the practical issues of the code base were the problem, but the outside developer community never fully latched on to Mozilla. Volunteer developers drifted away to other, more promising projects. It was an important lesson about limits for the open source process. As Zawinski put it, "It is most definitely not a panacea. If there's a cautionary tale here, it is that you can't take a dying project, sprinkle it with the magic pixie dust of 'open source,' and have everything magically work out."

At about the same time the Netscape story unfolded, IBM was facing a very different challenge around open source technology. In 1997 IBM asked James Barry to make sense of the company's struggling web server business. Barry found that IBM had lots of pieces of the puzzle in different parts of the company, but not an integrated product offering for web services. His idea was to put together a coordinated package, which became Websphere. The problem was that a key piece of the package, IBM's web server software, was technically weak. It held less than 1 percent of a market that was dominated by Netscape, Microsoft, and mostly by Apache. The solution was to find a partner. IBM opened a discussion about acquiring Netscape and explored the possibilities of a partnership with Microsoft. Neither of these initiatives panned out. That left Apache—the most popular web server in any case—but to approach the Apache Group was not exactly like negotiating with a company. When Steve Mills, general manager in the software group, authorized Barry to talk to the Apache Group in March 1998, it was not clear what those negotiations would entail or what kind of relationship would be possible.

Under Apache's licensing terms, IBM did not have to make any particular kind of deal with Apache. IBM could have taken the Apache code, modified it, and released it under an IBM label (as long as a statement was made that the IBM version was derived from Apache). But that would have cut off IBM from the core Apache developer community and would have left it relying on its in-house resources—a bad bargain, even given IBM's considerable resources, if the possibility of building a supportive relationship with the Apache Group could be made to work.

Barry approached Brian Behlendorf and the two quickly discovered common ground on technology issues. Building a practical relationship that worked for both sides was a more complex problem. Behlendorf's understandable concern was that IBM would somehow dominate Apache. IBM came back with concrete reassurances: It would become a regular player in the Apache process, release its contributions to the Apache code base as open source, and earn a seat on the Apache Committee just the way any programmer would by submitting code and building a reputation on the basis of that code. At the same time, IBM would offer enterprise-level support for Apache and its related Websphere product line, which would certainly help build the market for Apache. This proposal took some organizational work at IBM. There were legal issues making it complicated for IBM employees to contribute code to another organization. And although both the IBM developers and top management supported the idea, there was considerable resistance among middle layers of management.

Barry's consensus-building task within the company was helped by the fact that IBM had other initiatives underway in open source software. As early as 1997, for example, IBM developers had been experimenting quietly with porting Linux to IBM's top-of-the-line mainframe, System 390. To open up the most sophisticated IBM hardware to non-IBM software would be a huge rupture with long-standing IBM tradition. This is exactly what Chairman Lou Gerstner did in December 1998 when he announced a company-wide strategic initiative to bet on open source software as a core part of IBM business strategy.

In this way IBM brought together its disparate projects around open source to create a broader and deeper relationship with the developer community. IBM released a Linux port of its DB2 database program, started shipping Linux on some of its PCs, and in January 2000 made the dramatic announcement that it would port Linux to its major server hardware lines. At first IBM simply released the code for running Linux on the System 390; a few months later, the company announced that there had been sufficient customer interest for IBM to offer enterprise-level support for Linux on the S/390. It would be hard to imagine a more powerful symbol than Linux running on the gold standard corporate mainframe, with full support from IBM.

Microsoft and the Halloween Documents

Not all the attention paid to open source software in the late 1990s was friendly. In August of 1998, Vinod Valloppillil wrote a confidential document for Microsoft management called "Open Source Software: A (New?) Development Methodology."[32] This document was later leaked and became known as the Halloween document. It is in many ways a remarkable piece, for its sharp analysis of aspects of the open source process and for the insight it provides into the mindset of senior players at Microsoft about the relationship between open source and proprietary models of software development.

The Halloween document described open source as a development process that was "long term credible" and a "direct, short-term revenue and platform threat to Microsoft." It confessed that "commercial quality can be achieved/exceeded by OSS projects" and that "Linux and other OSS advocates are making a progressively more credible argument that OSS software is at least as robust—if not more—than commercial alternatives."

These were competitive issues for Microsoft. But the more fundamental issue had to do with distinctive features of the open source process. Valloppillil wrote, "The intrinsic parallelism and free idea exchange in OSS has benefits that are not replicable with our current licensing model and therefore present a long term developer mindshare threat" and "the ability of the OSS process to collect and harness the collective IQ of thousands of individuals across the Internet is simply amazing. More importantly, OSS evangelization scales with the size of the Internet much faster than our own evangelization efforts appear to scale."

The Halloween document began to lay out ways of thinking about how Microsoft could learn from, compete with, and fight against the open source movement. Valloppillil recognized that this was not a straightforward task because "to understand how to compete against OSS, we must target a process rather than a company." Microsoft was one of the most profoundly successful organizations on the planet when it came to strategy. It had (and has) an extraordinarily well-honed system for managing its relationships with other corporations. It was just as expert and nearly as successful in managing its relationships with governments.

But the Halloween document betrayed the uncertainty that Microsoft faced when thinking about how to manage a relationship, even an intensely hostile one, with the open source software community. The Halloween document asked (in slightly different language), Is it possible for a hierarchically structured organization to import core elements of the open source process, without losing control? Can a hierarchy learn from the open source movement how better to capture mindshare of creative individuals, manage communication and complexity, and design social structures that robustly reward cooperative behavior? Alternatively (or in addition), can a hierarchy undermine the open source process by hiring away individual programmers, spreading "Fear, Uncertainty, and Doubt" about it,[33] and leveraging property rights through the legal system and otherwise, to lock out open source? What matters for the moment is simply that Microsoft was asking these questions in a serious way.

CHAPTER 5

Explaining Open Source: Microfoundations

Collaborative open source software projects such as Linux and Apache demonstrate that a large and complex system of software code can be built, maintained, developed, and extended in a nonproprietary setting in which many developers work in a highly parallel, relatively unstructured way. This chapter and the next make more explicit the puzzles that lie within this observation and then put forward solutions, which together constitute a multilayered explanation of the open source process.

A lot is at stake in this explanation, and not just for social science theories that may sometimes seem arcane. Open source is a real-world, researchable example of a community and a knowledge production process that has been fundamentally changed, or created in significant ways, by Internet technology. For all the ink that has been spilled about "virtual communities," online groups, and other forms of social interaction through packet-switched networks, we lack a good understanding of how these organizations or communities or networks are similar to or different from traditional social systems. The fact that we don't really know what to call them simply reinforces that point.

The stakes are high also for the open source community itself. As a vibrant social entity, the open source community is in the process of re-making itself on a continuous basis. And because its self-conscious self-identification as a distinctive community is relatively new, the debates that go on over questions like "who are we," "what are we doing, and "why" can be heavily charged with raw emotion. The narrative that open source developers tell about themselves is part of the glue that holds the community together. That is not special; every community depends in part upon the story it tells about itself.

What may be unusual is the rapt attention of outsiders focused on the open source community at an early stage in self-definition. There is an understandable fear that certain observations of the community risk influencing the direction in which the identifying narrative evolves. Someone going through adolescence under the unremitting gaze of a psychologist, an endocrinologist, a behavioral economist, and a sociologist would at some point scream in frustration, "You don't understand a thing about me." The resentment would come from the sense that the observers were trying to shoehorn the subject into their own framework, rather than seeing what was "really" there. I ask for some indulgence on the part of the people whose motivations, organizational structures, and behavioral patterns I am trying to explain. I do not believe the social science conceptual apparatus is sacrosanct; rather, it is a set of tools for constructing models. Here, as elsewhere, models depend on using language that is not native to the phenomenon at hand. Sometimes that language is software code or mathematical equations; sometimes it is economic or political concepts. The purpose of the model is not to represent reality; its purpose is to place in sharp relief particular elements of reality so we can look at the model from different angles, tweak it in various directions, generalize it, and then come back to reality with a deeper understanding of what happens there.

I am attempting to build an understanding that covers at least four different bases. A good explanatory story must be *social* because open source software is a collective phenomenon, the product of voluntary collaboration among groups of people. It must also be a *political* story because formal and informal structures and organizations function to allocate scarce resources and manage conflicts as well as promote certain practices and values. It must be a *technical* story because the core product of the open source process is software code. And it must also be an *economic* story, in a fundamental way. I do not mean that familiar notions of economic behavior like rent-seeking, opportunism, and even standard cost-benefit analyses need to be front and center. What I do mean is a more primitive version of economic reasoning. At the center of the open source process are autonomous individuals who make choices about what to do with their limited time and energy. To understand the reasoning behind their choices is to understand the microlevel economics of open source.

Political economy as a way of thinking covers most of these bases. And from a political economy perspective, the open source process poses two puzzles *a priori*. The first is about microfoundations. Why do individuals voluntarily allocate a portion of their time, effort, and mind space to the open source process, rather than to something else? The second is macro-organizational. How do these individuals work with each other, in a way that makes their contributions add up to a joint product?

In a few pages I will refine and focus these questions more tightly. First I want to dispose of two myths about open source that get in the way of moving toward analytically rigorous answers.

The first myth, surprisingly common in the general media, sees open source basically as amusement for enthusiasts; a game of fun among like-minded hobbyists.[1] Some people like to write code: Give them a platform for sharing and they will get together with similar folks and write code together. Imagine this analogy: If all the model train enthusiasts in the world could join their tracks together through the Internet, they would build a train set just as elaborate as Linux. Nobody has to tell them how to do this and surely nobody has to pay them; it's a labor of love. And because everyone feels the same way, there is nothing to argue about.

The macro part of this story is either unarticulated or naively wrong. Like-minded or not, participants in the open source process argue more or less continuously, and about both technical and organizational issues. As I described earlier, these arguments are often intense and emotional. If open source software were simply the collective creation of like-minded individuals who cooperate easily because they are bound together by hobby-love or semireligious beliefs, there would be little disagreement in the process and little need for conflict resolution among developers.

The micro part of this story then shades into assumptions about altruism. If there were no mechanism for conflict resolution, the "hobbyists" would have to be following motivations other than personal satisfaction. They would have to be acting in an explicitly pro-social way, and doing things that others want, for the sake of the other and the act itself. This would be altruism. To act selflessly in this setting would be to write and contribute code for no apparent compensation other than the personal gratification that comes from doing something that helps someone else.

But the evidence confounds any straightforward version of this argument. If altruism were the primary driving force behind open source software, no one would care very much about who was credited for particular contributions. And it wouldn't matter who was able to license what code under what conditions.[2] Certainly people help each other in open source for the sake of helping—as elsewhere, one of the ways people express their values is in the act of providing help. Richard Stallman's original manifesto likened the act of sharing code to neighbors helping each other to put out a fire. But neighbors know each other; they live next to each other over time; a fire next door to my house threatens my house directly; and I have reason to expect reciprocity from my neighbor at some time in the future. The geographical distribution and relative anonymity of the Internet makes altruism a dicier proposition. There is in fact important evidence against the prevalence of altruistic behavior on the Internet, even in settings (such as peer-to-peer networking) in which there are no or very small possible costs associated with making contributions.[3]

There is another, pragmatic reason to steer clear of altruism as a principal explanation. This has more to do with current discourse in social science, in which altruism is a highly loaded term. For better or worse, arguments about altruism tend to invoke an economics-inspired intellectual apparatus that places altruistic behavior *in opposition* to self-interest.[4] This can quickly become an unproductive discussion in which people argue about whether or when it makes sense to redefine self-interest so it can accommodate a desire to do something solely for someone else. In other words, should individual utility functions include a term for the welfare of another? These are important issues, but they don't need to be settled or even really engaged for the purpose of understanding open source. By sidestepping this particular aspect of the debate, we can focus more cleanly on what mix of individual motivations are at play, including (but clearly not limited to) a desire to do something that increases the "utility" or benefit to others.

The second myth goes under the heading "self-organization." In the context of political community, I am wary of this term and of the way of thinking it represents for two reasons. First, self-organization is used too often as a placeholder for an unspecified mechanism. The term becomes a euphemism for "I don't really understand the mechanism that holds the system together." That is the political equivalent of cosmological dark matter.

Better-specified notions of self-organization build on the notion that order arises organically or endogenously out of the local interactions among individuals. Here self-organization is being used in contrast to overarching authority or governance—a useful comparison. But that does not relieve the obligation to explain *how* those local interactions add up to "global" order. They do not always do so. We know from simple observation that not all groups of programmers self-organize into open source communities, and in fact open source communities still represent the exception rather than the rule. Neither the low transaction costs of a network nor the so-called law of large numbers can solve this problem by itself. There is something more than just the motivations and interactions of individuals, something else in the social structure that is autonomous and needs to be uncovered on its own terms to understand open source.

Second, I shy away from the heading "self-organization" due to the normative peculiarities of the discourse that it prompts. Self-organization often evokes an optimistically tinged "state of nature" narrative, a story about the good way things would "naturally" evolve if the "meddling" hands of corporations and lawyers and governments and bureaucracies would just stay away. Of course those non-self-organized organizations have their own narratives, which portray the state of nature as a chaotic mess.

To pose two state-of-nature narratives against each other creates a battle of assumptions, a tournament of null hypotheses, which is not productive. The underlying presumption—that there *is* in fact a state of nature without human agency—is even more damning to the discourse when we are talking about something like software code or knowledge production more generally. *There is no state of nature on the Internet.* Knowledge does not want to be "free" (or for that matter, owned) more than it wants to be anything else. Simply, it is people and institutions that want knowledge and the property rights around it to be structured in a particular way. We are going to be creating lots of new things in this technological space, and we can organize the creation of those things however we want. This is social constructivism at its core, pitting different social constructivist narratives against each other instead of against an imaginary state of nature. And this represents an important opportunity because a technologically created space like the Internet can make power easier, not harder, to visualize. Lawrence Lessig's gloomy perspective notwithstanding, I believe that code is in fact *more* transparent than lots of other "architectural" features that shape traditional political spaces.[5] The implications of what we build for power relations may very well be easier to analyze when it rests in software code than when it is buried in layers of tradition, language, historical practices, and culture. In that case we don't really need a mind as brilliant as Michel Foucault's for the Internet, because the architecture is more visible. To hide behind the notion of self-organization short-circuits that very important discussion.

Having disposed of the myths' more simplistic manifestations, I can set the problem of explanation more clearly, in the following four buckets:

- *Individual motivations.* Reasoning upward from the actions of the programmers, the question is, Why do these individuals voluntarily contribute to the collective provision of nonrival and nonexcludable goods?
- *Economic logic of the collective good.* Starting from the logic of the collective good itself and reasoning downward puts the same puzzle in a slightly different perspective. Open source software is aggressively nonexcludable at several different levels; in fact, that is its major differentiating characteristic. It is also nonrival in a profound way because it can be replicated perfectly an infinite number of times at zero cost. And it depends on joint provision for even a moderately complex program. What is the aggregate economic logic that frames individual decisions in one direction and the problem of bringing individual contributions together in the other? Because economics ultimately is a conceptual scheme that thinks about behavior in the face of scarcity, what exactly *is* scarce in the digital environment and how does that modify the economic problem?
- *Coordination.* Earlier I drew an analogy between software and collective poetry—the trick is not just to get contributions, but also

to coordinate those contributions so the joint product works. How and why do individuals coordinate their contributions on a single focal point? Authority within a firm and the price mechanism across firms are standard means of coordinating specialized knowledge in a complex division of labor, but neither is operating front and center in the open source process. Yet code-forking is the exception, not the norm. What sustains coordination in this setting?

- *Complexity.* Software is extraordinarily complex in many different ways. Even a moderately complicated program offers infinite possible paths through the lines of code. How has the open source process used technology and governance institutions to manage the implications of this kind of complexity among a geographically dispersed community not subject to hierarchical command and control?

The remainder of this chapter proposes answers to the first two buckets of questions. For the last two buckets, see Chapter 6.

Microfoundations

In 2000 three Kiel University researchers carried out an early, large-scale survey of Linux developers' motivations for contributing to open source software. Like any structured survey of motivations, the study has limitations. Among them is that respondents self-selected in the sense that they chose to take part in the web-based questionnaire. And because the researchers identified the target population for the survey through the Linux-kernel mailing list, there was already a built-in selection bias in the data. They could only sample among people who *do* participate in some way in the open source process, which makes it very hard to collect comparative data on the motivations of people who *do not* contribute.[6] The results naturally need to be interpreted with caution.

But caveats aside, the study did collect interesting data on the mix of motivations in this particular population, through over 140 responses from people in 28 different countries. And a rough picture of a motivational story does emerge. The modal Linux developer appears to be a person who feels part of a technical community and who is committed to improving his programming skills, to facilitating his work through better software, and to having fun along the way. This person recognizes the opportunity costs of open source programming (both time and money lost), but doesn't care that much—in fact, he cares somewhat less about the money than about the time.[7] He is optimistic about the future, expecting slightly more advantages and slightly fewer losses from his future participation. His own individual learning, work efficiency, and fun (rather than collective and pro-social motivations) are the main reasons why he would choose to contribute more time and effort in the future.

A 2001 survey by the Boston Consulting Group produced some additional insights by segmenting developers' responses into four characteristic groups.[8] About a third of the respondents to this survey were "believers," who said they were strongly motivated by the conviction that source code should be open. About a fifth of respondents were "professionals" who worked on open source because it helped them in their jobs. A quarter were "fun-seekers" who did it mainly for intellectual stimulation. And a fifth were "skill enhancers" who emphasized the learning and experience they got from open source programming. The survey also found that open source programmers seemed to cluster heavily in the Generation X age range (70.4 percent were between 22 and 37) with about 14 percent either younger or older. They were not for the most part novices: More than half were professional programmers, system administrators, or IT managers (only 20 percent self-identified as students).

Survey data, like any data, depends on the questions you ask and the way you ask them as well as on how the population that answers the survey is selected.[9] There are elements of individual motivation that can be picked up in questionnaires, and there are others that reveal themselves in interviews, in writings, and in the accumulation of anecdotes. And some elements emerge clearly only through deep interaction with the developer community—going to meetings, reading mailing lists, and talking with individuals. By combining these and other types of data, I propose a scheme that captures six kinds of motivations. The scheme is imperfect, with overlaps between categories and fuzz around the edges, but then again so are human motivations. Here are the categories, which I consider briefly in turn:

- Art and beauty
- Job as vocation

- The joint enemy
- Ego boosting
- Reputation
- Identity and belief systems

The fun, enjoyment, and *artistry* of solving interesting programming problems clearly motivate open source developers. Developers speak of writing code not only as an engineering problem but also as an aesthetic pursuit, a matter of style and elegance that makes coding an act of self-expression. There is an acid test for one kind of quality—code either runs or it does not run, it functions or it does not. But that is hardly the only kind of quality that matters. There are always several ways to solve an engineering problem, whether it is building a bridge across the San Francisco Bay or designing a new home or writing an operating system.

Solutions that work ("running code") range from clunky to clever to elegant. For many programmers, code is a core means of expression, an essential way of interacting with the world. There is a telling aesthetic vocabulary in use to describe different programs. People talk about "clean" code and "ugly" code rather than efficient and inefficient code, for example. Some programmers talk about a "Unix philosophy" that they describe in similarly aesthetic terms.[10] Torvalds has consistently said that his primary motivation for working on Linux is "the fun of programming," which he often equates with artistic creativity. Code that simply works is a product; code that represents an elegant solution to a complex problem is a thing of beauty that in the open source setting *can be shared with others*. Jeremy Allison captured this feeling when he spoke of the premium energy among open source developers for building "cool stuff."[11] One developer reminded me that Frank Gehry did not design the Guggenheim Museum in Bilbao to house art or to make himself more money.

Of course this kind of motivation operates at a basic level for proprietary developers as well. But these programmers typically have a boss that assigns the problems they must solve. And the solution is ultimately hidden from view. Open source developers voluntarily choose what problems to work on and show the results to any and all. It's a high-stakes game in a personal sense because free choice makes the effort self-consciously more than either a hobby or a job. Like a tenured academic who is free to write a book on whatever she wants, the result is then presumed to be that person's best effort. For people driven by creativity, this can be a good bargain. Open source lets you show the world just how creative you really are. It is the equivalent of putting your best work on display at the national gallery of art as compared to locking it in your basement. In the same way that J. D. Salinger's behavior seems peculiar to many other authors and to most readers, the open source process capitalizes on the creative person's drive to display her talent and share its fruits as an inherent part of the artistic endeavor.[12] Of course, having your code out there for all to see can also be a humbling experience in the same way that art criticism often is.[13]

To capture the artistic, creative motivation in standard economic discourse is not straightforward. It feels awkward to simply insert it as part of an individual utility function or to use euphemisms like "psychic reward" to make it fit. It doesn't matter how you prefer to think about artistry as long as you don't discount or underestimate it as an important driver of individual behavior in open source. The developers themselves emphasize its importance, and that is a piece of evidence worth taking seriously. In any case, human creativity is hardly confined to writing software code; we see this kind of behavior literally everywhere, *including* places where the economic stakes and opportunity costs are quite high. The hacker ethic described by Himanen and others is hardly unique to the Information Age.[14] What may be distinctive about the Information Age is what emerges when technology facilitates the connecting together of these people in real time and at near zero cost.

Creating elegant or clean code is part of the programmer's experience of *the job as vocation*. The idea of writing code to "scratch your own itch" is critical because it is a standard part of most software engineers' jobs. In practice, the vast majority of code is written internally—that is, customized within companies or by individuals who are trying to solve a problem. Getting something to work for your own use is a practical benefit. Sharing that solution with others and helping them to get their systems to work as well can often bring additional satisfaction, particularly if the cost of sharing is near zero. Programmers consistently describe this primarily as a feeling of efficacy rather than being about pro-social motivations *per se*.

If there is a common currency of feeling here, it is a shared sense that the programming world is full of intriguing and challenging problems to be solved. That has two interesting consequences. First is the powerful sense that it is not merely inefficient but downright stupid, almost criminal, for people to have to solve the same problem twice. There is just too much good new work to be done to waste the efforts of programmers in this way. Second is a deep frustration when people get things wrong or make "silly" mistakes. Open source programmers can be blunt to the point of brutality when it comes to criticizing sloppy reasoning by others. Asking a "dumb" (that is, uninformed) question on an email list can bring back a torrent of bitingly sarcastic criticism. To expend energy in this way (albeit negative energy) suggests strongly that programmers are treating their work as a vocation and are investing, in a sense, in the socialization of others to the same mindset.

Eric Von Hippel's work about the potential of user-driven innovation makes better sense in this setting. In 1988 Von Hippel made the argument for industrial products and processes that *users,* when they are empowered to do so by technology and by the legal and economic structures in which that technology is embedded, will innovate more quickly and effectively than will manufacturers.[15] The reasoning is straightforward: Information on users' needs and their preferences concerning complex trade-offs in product design is very sticky in the sense that it is costly to move it from the users' experience to the mind of the outside developer who sits in a factory hundreds of miles away. The manufacturer cannot easily know what a user wants to the depth and detail that the user does. And even if the manufacturer did somehow gain that knowledge, if it is dealing with a diverse set of users (as is usually the case), the manufacturer's incentives are to design products that are a close-enough fit for many users rather than the precisely customized product that a particular user really wants.[16]

The real promise of user-driven innovation for Von Hippel comes from the importance of what he calls "lead users" in fast-changing industries. Lead users face needs that will likely become general in the market, but they face them sooner than everyone else; and they are positioned to benefit in significant ways if they can obtain an answer to those needs.[17] The argument about benefits is based principally on Joseph Schumpeter's point about temporary monopoly rents that accrue to innovators. While this piece does not apply (at least not directly) to open source software, another less commonly cited element of Schumpeter's argument does apply, and strongly. While Schumpeter is often read as a story about economic rents, he also believed deeply in the emotional experience of creativity, the erotic satisfaction of making something new and making it work. Leaving behind the monopoly rents and emphasizing the erotic satisfaction in Schumpeterian innovation creates a setting in which innovators are deeply incentivized to share their work as broadly as possible with others. There is simply no cost, and considerable benefits to be had, by acting in this way. "Scratching your itch" then becomes a story about the satisfaction that comes with solving your own problem *and* solving someone else's problem as well.

For many open source developers, this experience is embedded in an ongoing battle with a *joint enemy*. Microsoft is the obvious villain, but in fact this single company acts as a proxy for a wide array of proprietary software developers. The texture of motivations here is subtle. It combines issues about business practice with a technical aesthetic. The Boston Consulting Group survey found that only 11.3 percent of respondents said that "to beat proprietary software" was a principal motivation for their work.[18] BCG concludes from this (narrowly, in my view) that hackers are not strongly motivated by a joint enemy. They are certainly right to suggest that most open source developers are happy to use proprietary software when it is technically desirable to do so; the open source initiative is built around this idea. However, 34.2 percent of respondents chose "code should be open" as a primary motivation. This could in principle reflect an ideological commitment on the lines of Richard Stallman, but that interpretation is inconsistent with the relative weakness of the Free Software Foundation and with the observed practices of most open source users. The simplest interpretation of this statement is to take it as a functional and pragmatic assessment of development practices. Code should be open not for moral reasons *per se*, but because development processes built around open source code yield better software. The "enemy" is not an ideological villain; it is a technical and business practice villain and that is what the conflict is about. Microsoft is the exemplar because this company is seen as sacrificing a technical aesthetic to ruthless business practice aimed at gaining market share and profits.

This interpretation of the survey data tracks more comfortably with the overwhelming (albeit anecdotal) evidence one picks up in interviews, at meetings, and on the email lists devoted to the "battle" with proprietary software. It is important because a joint enemy (or at least, target) helps to frame a culture of generalized reciprocity among open source developers. People work with open source code to solve their own immediate problems and to enhance their own skills, but also because of a distinctly positive valence toward the community of hackers of which they are a part. Torvalds said that the decision to release Linux "wasn't some agonizing decision that I took from thinking long and hard on it; it was a natural decision within the community that I felt I wanted to be a part of."[19] In the BCG survey 41.5 percent strongly agreed and 42 percent somewhat agreed with the statement "hackers are a primary community with which I identify." Generalized reciprocity is a firmly established norm of organizational citizenship within this community. Contributing code and helping others is a sign of "positive regard for the social system in which requests for help are embedded," a manifestation of pro-social behavior observed in other technically oriented settings as well.[20]

Individual *ego-boosting* is a powerful motivating force for open source developers, but it is not a simple one. For the developer's self-recognition, there is a consistent finding across surveys that the challenge of programming in the open source environment is a source of satisfaction (63 percent of respondents in the BCG survey said of their open source work, "this project is as creative as anything I have done"). Within the community, ego as a driving force is openly acknowledged and accepted. In trying to create a legacy as a great programmer, many developers believe deeply that "scientific" success will outstrip and outlive financial success. As they put it, the truly important figures of the industrial revolution were not Rockefellers and Ford, but Einstein.[21] Yet there is a strong countercurrent against overt *egotism*. Self-recognition and self-satisfaction are important, but the hacker is not supposed to self-promote at the expense of others; in fact, the norm is to be externally humble and (humorously, if possible) deprecate yourself. Bragging is off-limits: The norm is that your work brags for you. The model of ego-boosting at play here is curiously reminiscent of ideals of medieval knighthood: As Mark Stone puts it, "Behind shield and visor, and upon adopting a particular set of heraldic emblems, a knight took on a kind of persona, creating a public identity that might be quite different from his private identity . . . the good knight adhered to a code of behavior . . . to be humble, to regard himself at the service of others, yet to be judged by his prowess at his trade. . . ."[22]

The complicated part of ego-boosting is that it is not always in practice an individual experience and it does not only ratchet upward. Criticism stings in the open source world, just as it does in any creative endeavor, including science. The norm in the open source community is to criticize the code, not the individual who wrote it, which may reduce a little bit how badly it hurts.[23] But because code is precisely identified with an author, a virtuous circle of ego-boosting can easily become a much messier status competition, in which one person's ego boost becomes another person's insult. In a competition for status, the opinions of leaders carry extra weight, which confers on them real power. In a practical sense, what happens to a Linux developer's ego when his code is rejected by Torvalds? Or when someone else's code replaces his own? If egos can be boosted, they can also be damaged, which raises the question of what kinds of behavior will follow. The person with the hurt ego has choices: She can leave the project, she can fork the code, she can retaliate against the leader or against other developers. It's not possible to rule out any of these dysfunctional responses through the logic of ego alone; if they are rare, then that is a problem for macro-organization to solve.

Related to but separable from ego-boosting is the issue of *reputation*. A reliance on what others think of the quality of your work is not always a sign of unhealthy emotional dependence on external evaluation. In the case of complex knowledge products with aesthetic as well as functional value, it can also be a necessary cognitive component of concrete feedback. The author is too close to the work and needs external measures of quality in order to know whether the work is good and how to improve it. In this sense reputation is simply an adjunct (although a necessary one) to the primary motivation of artistry and ego. This logic should be familiar to many academics and artists.

But there is also a concurrent story about a proto-economy built on reputation, what Steven Freedman calls "reputonics" or what Josh Lerner and Jean Tirole labeled "the simple economics of open source."[24] Lerner and Tirole portray an individual programmer as engaged in a straightforward, instrumental cost-benefit analysis that goes like this: Ego gratification is important because it stems from peer recognition. Peer recognition is important because it creates a reputation. A reputation as a great programmer is valuable because it can be turned into money in commercial settings—in the form of job offers, privileged access to venture capital, the ability to attract cooperation from other great programmers.

The key point in this story is the signaling argument. The incentive to prove your worth shifts to the side of the developer. As is true of many technical and artistic disciplines, the quality of a programmer's mind and work is not easy for others to judge in standardized metrics. To know what is really good code and thus to assess the talent of a particular programmer takes a reasonable investment of time. The best programmers, then, have a clear incentive to reduce the energy that it takes for others to see and understand just how good they are. Hence comes the importance of signaling. The programmer participates in an open source project as a demonstrative act to show the quality of her work. Reputation within a well-informed and self-critical community becomes the most efficient proxy measure for that quality. Lerner and Tirole argue that the signaling incentive will be stronger when the performance is visible to the audience; when effort expended has a high impact on performance; and when performance yields good information about talent. Open source projects maximize the incentive along these dimensions, in several ways. With open source, a software user can see not only how well a program performs. She can also look to see how clever and elegant is the underlying code—a much more fine-grained measure of the quality of the programmer. And because no one is forcing anyone to work on any particular problem in open source, the performance can be assumed to represent a voluntary act on the part of the programmer, which makes it all that much more informative about that programmer.

The signaling incentive should be strongest in settings with sophisticated users, tough bugs, and an audience that can appreciate effort and artistry, and thus distinguish between merely good and excellent solutions to problems. As Lerner and Tirole note, this argument seems consistent with the observation that open source generally has had more of an impact in settings like operating systems and less in end-user applications. And the signaling argument might also help explain why open source tends to attract some of the most talented and creative developers to work on challenging and complex projects. It suggests a mechanism for self-selection, because it is clearly the best programmers who have the strongest incentive to show others just how good they are. If you are mediocre, the last thing you want is for people to see your source code.

The Lerner and Tirole argument is easy to nail down in traditional economic terms, but that doesn't necessarily mean it is the most important driver of individual behavior. Both the survey data and interview and anecdotal data suggest that it is not the most important conscious consideration for developers.[25] While reputonics may be a plausible framing for an extremely narrow bandwidth world, it is not so for a world in which measures of value can be and are much broader than price (see Chap. 8). And the simple, behavioral fact is that most code—as long as it works—does not get widely read, which undermines the claim that people write it to boost their monetizable reputations. As Paul Duguid describes practice, "If the code breaks and you have to hack it, you read it and deplore it. If it compiles and runs, let it be."[26] This suggests that reputational signaling may not be quite so significant except in exceptional cases. And the sectoral evidence is confirming—open source reputation has not become a conventional part of the career ladder toward highly paid commercial software development jobs.

In any case, the reputonics argument leaves several things unexplained and creates problems of its own, such as the following very important puzzle. If reputation were the primary motivation, we should be able to tell some version of this kind of story: Assume that project leaders like Torvalds receive greater reputational returns than general programmers do. Then programmers should compete to become project leaders, particularly on high-profile projects, of which there are a limited number. This competition could take at least two forms. We would expect to see a significant number of direct challenges to Torvalds's leadership, but in fact there have been few such challenges. Alternatively, we could see "strategic forking."[27] A strategic forker would fork a project not for technical reasons, but rather to create a project that he or she could lead. The problem of how to attract other programmers would be managed by credibly promising to maximize other programmers' reputations on the new project—for example, by sharing some of the gains with anyone who joins. In that case, a new programmer would be motivated to join the forked project rather than Linux.

The problem with this kind of story is that it simply hasn't happened. There are no significant examples of this kind of behavior in the Linux history. And given the story-telling culture of the community, it is certain that any such story would have become part of the general lore. Nor does it seem that the "system" or perhaps Torvalds has anticipated this kind of pressure and preempted it by strategic behavior, because the logic here would drive a leveling of reputational returns throughout the community. The bottom line is that there is not as much strategic behavior in reputation as the reputonics story would expect.[28]

Part of the counterpoint to a competition in reputation comes from strong elements of shared *identity and belief systems* within the community of developers. Steven Levy in his 1984 book *Hackers* chronicled the development of hacker culture around MIT in the early 1960s.[29] Levy described the following key tenets of that culture, which continue to characterize the open source community to a surprising degree:

- *Access to computers should be unlimited—the so-called hands-on imperative.* This notion was considered radical before the 1980s spreading of personal computers, when "computer" usually meant a single mainframe machine controlled by a technical priesthood that rationed time and access to officially sanctioned users. Today the idea of access seems obvious to just about everyone when it comes to hardware. The open source community shares the belief that the same should be true of software.
- *Information should be "free."* Richard Stallman would later become the most vocal champion of the principle that software, as an information tool that is used to create new things of value, should flow as freely through social systems as data flows through a microprocessor.
- *Mistrust authority and promote decentralization.* In the 1960s it was not Microsoft but rather IBM that was the icon of centralized, hierarchical authority relations in the computing world. Hierarchies are good at controlling economic markets and more importantly computing power. Control stifles creativity, which is ultimately what information-processing ought to be about.
- *Judge people only on the value of what they create, not who they are or what credentials they present.* This is the essence of a relatively pure meritocracy—anyone can join and be recognized for the quality

of their work, regardless of age or degree status or any other external sign. There are costs involved because credentials often act as proxies that save time and energy spent evaluating the substance of an individual's capabilities. But there are also benefits: More energy goes into creating code and less into self-promotion and bragging because your work brags for you.

- *People can create art and beauty on computers.* In the hacker community, software took on the status of a precious artifact or work of art that was valuable not only for what it allowed a user to do but also for its own intrinsic beauty.

- *Computers can change human life for the better.* There is a simple and familiar instrumental aspect to this belief—that computing takes over repetitive time-consuming tasks and frees people to do what is more creative and interesting. There is also the broader notion that cultural models and practices learned in working with information systems could transfer, for the better, to human systems. This belief obviously varies in intensity among developers—as I said earlier, the Open Source Initiative has worked to downplay the explicit political agenda that is central to the Free Software Initiative. But the political message comes through, at least implicitly, in almost any interview and causal discussion with open source developers. With different degrees of self-consciousness, these individuals know they are experimenting with economic and social systems of production and that the results of these experiments *could* have ramifications for how people relate to each other beyond the realm of computer software.

There are other important elements of shared belief clearly visible by observation within the open source community. A simple but foundational one is the notion that personal efficacy not only benefits from, but positively requires, a set of cooperative relationships with others. The popular image of an open source hacker as a lone ranger emphasizes the self-reliant attitude that is certainly present but misses the deep way in which that self-reliance is known to be made possible through its embedding in a community. The belief is that the community empowers the individual to help himself.

A related shared belief is that experimentation is the highest form of human behavior. To try new things that challenge one's skills and the skills of others is not just a tool for individual learning and development; it is a contribution to the community. As Eric Raymond put it in the primer "How to Ask Questions the Smart Way," "good questions are a stimulus and a gift."[30] Because pragmatism is the highest virtue, both experiments and questions should be laid out the same way—with simplicity, precision, and cleverness—all of which add up to a problem-solving perspective.

Finally there is an explicit recognition that these elements of shared identity and beliefs do not maintain themselves. Rather, "community standards . . . are maintained by people actively applying them, visibly, *in public*."[31] This both explains and justifies the public mailing list displays of criticism that are leveled, sometimes cruelly, at newcomers (and not-so-newcomers) who break the norms. Open source developers come to expect this—"How to Ask Questions the Smart Way" tells them, "get over it. It's normal. In fact, it's healthy and appropriate." In practice there is an implicit sense of obligation on the part of long-standing community members to "enforce" these norms against violators, even if it would be simpler and easier to ignore the violation by not responding.[32]

Adding together these elements of individual motivations yields a pretty compelling story about why some individuals, under at least some conditions, would contribute time and energy toward writing code for open source software. If you now say that the extremely low transaction cost environment of the Internet allows these people to find each other easily through a soft version of the law of large numbers, you might be tempted to accept the notion that individual motivations are all you need to explain the outcome. And of course microfoundations are a critical part of explaining any human phenomenon. After all, theorizing about collective action is not a matter of trying to decide whether behavior can be labeled as "rational." It is a matter of understanding first and foremost under what conditions individuals find that the benefits of participation exceed the costs. This means, of course, understanding a great deal about how people assess costs and benefits. But microfoundations are often not a sufficient or full explanation. For a complex social and technical system like open source software, there are several important puzzles that remain. Consider the politics that still need to be explained.

Open source developers are certainly much like artists in the sense that they seek fun, challenge, and beauty in their work. But artists typically don't give away their art for free and they do not show everyone how they make their art. More importantly, artists are not typically thought of as successful collaborators in large multifaceted projects that move forward without authoritative direction. The *Orpheus* symphony, which works without a formal conductor, is the exception, not the rule. And Jutta Allmendinger estimates that *Orpheus* musicians spend three to four times as many hours rehearsing per hour of performance time as standard orchestras with authoritative conductors.[33] If the cost-benefit calculations that drive people to play musical instruments are simple, the politics that keep them together as an orchestra are extremely complex.

Some developers emphasize the importance of a shared commitment to slay a dragon, or oppose Microsoft. Clearly Microsoft evokes strong feelings. But it is not at all clear that open source development is the best way to fight Microsoft. And hatred of Microsoft (even if shared) by itself does not explain the extensive coordination that has produced software like Linux, rather than a diffuse spray of anti-Microsoft efforts. This should sound familiar—after all, the majority of revolutionary movements fail precisely because they do not focus the antiestablishment energy into a coherent political challenge.

A high-intensity race for ego-boosting certainly explains some of the energy that developers devote to open source work, just as it explains some of the energy behind most scientific communities. But it does not explain at all the coordination of that work in open source. As I argued above, human ego is a very tricky thing to handle precisely because it can be hurt as well as boosted. And damaged egos are difficult to manage even in a hierarchical corporate setting. Inflated egos can make collaboration just as difficult. Why don't people try to promote themselves at the expense of others? A reputation for greatness is not typically abundant, because standards of "greatness" are themselves endogenous to the quality of work that is produced in a particular population. If there is a normal distribution of quality, and the bell curve shifts to the right, what would have been thought "excellent" in the past would then be merely good. The tails of the distribution define excellence in any setting, and they remain small. Ego-boosting can easily take on the characteristics of a rival good.

The Internet *is* a wonderful physical infrastructure to support large numbers of weak ties, in the sense that Granovetter used that phrase. The "strength of weak ties" is that someone with very different experiences, connections, and information sources than you will have the knowledge and expertise to solve the problem that you can't.[34] But it's not a simple situation from an individual perspective. You as a seeker of help have no direct way of assessing the provider's reliability, expertise, and motives. The provider knows very little about you—what are you really trying to learn, and what do you intend to use that information to do? This lack of knowledge could easily lead to adverse selection or (just as bad) the suspicion of adverse selection. Why not believe this: Strangers who can offer high-quality help would have no reason to do so and would see it as a costly expenditure of time and energy, while strangers with nothing better to do, or with mischievous motives, would be more likely to offer their low-quality help. Without a social structure of some sort to prevent that kind of unraveling, weak ties on the Internet could as easily become a market for lemons as anything else.[35] Even without adverse selection *per se*, there is still the risk of associative sorting—that weak ties are not really as weak as they seem, and that like-minded people who know the same things (and are thus likely to make the same mistakes) are more likely to be offering their help to you. "More eyeballs" might then only compound and deepen errors rather than correct them.

Finally, reputonics by itself does not solve the coordination problem. It creates conflicting incentives for the individual. Consider these possibilities. You might try to enhance your reputation by gravitating toward a project with the largest number of other programmers (because this choice increases the size of your audience, the number of people who would actively see your work). This would be inefficient on aggregate: Open source projects would then attract motivated people in proportion to their existing visibility and size, with a winner-take-all outcome. Or you might migrate toward projects that have the most difficult problems to solve, believing that you cannot make a reputation working on merely average problems (even for a big audience). But this choice would progressively raise the barriers to entry and make it difficult for new programmers to do anything valuable. Or you could engage in strategic forking—creating a new project for the purposes of becoming a leader and competing for the work of other programmers by distributing out the positive reputation returns more broadly within the community. There are examples of some of these kinds of behavior in the open source community, but none of them is common or prevalent.

The summary point is that individual motivations do not make up anything like a full explanation for the success of open source. Individual decisions to write open source code may be "simple" from an economic standpoint—once you have a rich understanding of the ways in which individuals really think about the benefits and costs attached to different possible courses of action. But the organization of the community that provides a necessary macrostructure to the open source process is not so simple. The next sections of this chapter explore the economic and political bases of that structure.

Economic Logic(s)

At a high level of abstraction, there are really two distinct ways to frame an inquiry into the basic economic characteristics of open source. One framework builds on a story about *abundance*. Another (more conventional, for economics) perspective builds an argument around *scarcity*. I treat them separately here because they are, in fact, incommensurable framings, and because the implications for starting points of arguments over how open source works that follow from these core perspectives are profound.

In his essay "Homsteading the Noosphere," Eric Raymond introduced the idea of a "gift culture" or "gift economy" into the narrative of open source.[36] The central notion of a gift economy is simple: Status, power, and "wealth" are a function not of what you control but of what you give away. An economic structure could certainly form around this notion, in a conceptual sense. Gifts bind people together; they create an obligation to give back; the artifact being gifted is not just a functional widget but carries with it some of the giver.[37] As Ralph Waldo Emerson put it, "Rings and other jewels are not gifts, but apologies for gifts. The only gift is a portion of thyself."[38]

Lewis Hyde argues that gift economies are prevalent in creative aspects of human life, and are in some cases necessary for generating the inspiration from which creativity flows.[39] Others have made similar arguments about academia and particularly about basic science.[40] But it is clear from casual observation that much art, academic knowledge, and basic science are created in the context of traditional exchange settings that have no notion of "gifting." Think of commercial graphic designers, contract research services, professors who move between universities to raise their salaries, and Xerox Parc. The question then becomes, Under what conditions do we observe gift economies to emerge in practice?

Raymond answers that "gift economies are adaptations not to scarcity but to abundance."[41] There is an unspoken element of Maslow's hierarchy in this reasoning—once the survival necessities are met, human beings move their competition to other realms (in Maslow's view, higher realms) such as creativity and status. Thus "gift economies arise in populations that do not have significant material-scarcity problems"—for example, aboriginal cultures living in mild climates with abundant food, as well as the extremely wealthy in modern industrial societies. Abundance "makes command relationships difficult to sustain and exchange relationships an almost pointless game." When you are this far out on a curve of diminishing marginal returns to owning something, what makes sense is to give things away (and gain status) instead.

The cultural characteristics of open source do bear some surface resemblance to this picture of a gift economy. The open source movement seems to bind people together, it encourages diffuse reciprocity, and it supports emotive feelings of stewardship for the "gift" that is both taken and given in return. It hardly seems to matter that the community is geographically distributed and in a sense impersonal, because the Internet can carry gifts from one participant to any number of others with almost perfect efficiency. The gift culture logic might work particularly well in software (as it seems to in certain kinds of artwork) because the value of the gift is hard to measure in concrete, replicable terms. Rather it is dependent on assessment by other members of the community. A complex technical artifact needs peer review not only to improve its function but also to get reasonable assessments of how fine a gift it really is.

Yet there is a key flaw in the gift economy argument. What, exactly, is the nature of abundance in this setting? Of course there is plenty of Internet bandwidth, disk space, and processing power. Moore's Law and Metcalfe's Law capture the feeling of an incredibly positive vector on these important resources—and both imply that the magnitude of abundance will be increasing and at an increasing rate over time. It is easy to get distracted by that unprecedented abundance. The problem is, computing power is simply *not* the key resource in this ecosystem. In part because of its abundance and cheapness, it is increasingly devalued. When anyone can have a de facto supercomputer on her desk, there is very little status connected to that property. And the computer by itself does nothing. It cannot write its own software (at least not yet) or use software by itself to produce things of value.

These are the things that produce meaning and value in any economy, gift or otherwise. *Meaning and value depend on human mind space and the commitment of time and energy by very smart people to a creative enterprise.* And the time, energy, and brain power of smart, creative people are not abundant. These are the things that are scarce, and in some sense they become scarcer as the demand for these talents increases in proportion to the amount of abundant computing power available. Here is a crude but useful analogy: Canada has plenty of trees and anyone can put a stack of paper on his desk for a very small price. That does not translate directly into an abundance of great writing. There are only a few people who can turn paper into literature; their hours are scarce; their energy is limited. That remains true no matter how abundant and cheap the paper becomes.

This moves the discussion back into a scarcity framing, a more comfortable place for customary economic thought. The starting point for thinking about the economic logic of open source then becomes a version of standard collective action analyses.[42]

The baseline is simple. Open source software is the epitome of a nonexcludable good, because no one is prevented from consuming it. It is also entirely nonrival in the sense that any number of users can download and run a piece of software without decreasing the supply that remains for others. This presents a straightforward economic puzzle of an essentially pure public good.[43] Put simply, the problem facing each rational self-interested actor is the opportunity to free ride. Whether or not you as an individual donate to public radio, the station will continue to broadcast the same signal and you are free to enjoy it, without diminishing in any way the enjoyment of others. Of course, if each individual acts in this narrowly rational fashion, the station will never come to exist in the first place. The public good will be underprovided.

More than a quarter century of economic, sociological, and behavioral research has explored the conditions under which this dilemma can be ameliorated, managed, or superceded, but it has not made the underlying problem go away. The successful provision of a public good is something to explain. And the situation with open source software ought to be at the worse end of the spectrum of public goods because complex software depends as well on voluntary collective provision. The world did not begin with a supply of open source software; it has to be built.[44] No one can force you to write code. And open source software would not exist without contributions from large numbers of developers. Yet for each developer, there is the problem of insignificant effect. A pledge of $100 to public radio represents a significant bite out of my monthly income, but it is barely a drop in the bucket for the budget of the station. It seems like a bad trade; why should I bother? Because every individual can see that not only her own incentives but the incentives of other individuals are aligned in this way, the system ought to unravel backward so no one makes meaningful contributions and there is no public good to begin with.

Part of the solution to this puzzle lies in individual motivations, some of which go beyond the narrow version of rational utility calculations that generate the baseline dilemma of collective action. But there is also at play a larger economic logic in the system as a whole that subtly but importantly reframes the problem of collective action in the context of open source software.

Rishab Aiyer Ghosh took a major step toward explicating that logic.[45] Using the image of a vast tribal cooking pot, he tells a story about collective action in which one person puts into the pot a chicken, another person puts in some onions, another person puts in carrots . . . and everyone takes out a bowl of fantastic stew. Nonexcludability would normally be a problem here because, if anyone can take stew out of the pot without putting anything in, there might be nothing left for those who did contribute and thus they are unlikely to put anything in themselves. But what if the cooking pot were magically nonrival? That is, if the production of stew simply surged to meet consumption without any additional expenditure of ingredients. Then everyone would know that there would always be stew in the pot. Even if people who didn't put anything in take out some stew, there would still be plenty left for those who did contribute. In this setting an individual would face a slightly different calculus. As Ghosh puts it, "You never lose from letting your product free in the cooking pot, as long as you are compensated for its creation."[46]

The Internet makes a digital product like software "magically" non-rival. Essentially this is a cooking pot that does create as many bowls of stew as there is demand. That is well known. The question now is, How are you going to be compensated for creating your product? In the digital environment, this too seems nearly straightforward, although slightly more subtle. When I put my product into the cooking pot, I am giving away a thousand, a million, or really an infinite number of copies of that product. However, in my own private utility calculations, multiple copies of this single product are not valuable. In fact the marginal utility of an additional copy, *to me,* is zero.

But single copies of multiple other products are, *to me or any other single user,* immensely valuable. In practice, then, I am giving away a million copies, each of which is worth nothing to me, for at least one copy of at least one other thing that is worth something to me. That is a utility-enhancing trade for anyone who makes it. And thus lots of people should make it. Ghosh puts it this way, "If a sufficient number of people put in free goods, the cooking pot clones them for everyone so that everyone gets far more value than was put in."

This is an attractive argument, but it too has a hole. Nonrivalness does not by itself make the challenge of joint provision go away. The missing piece in Ghosh's argument is that it does not explain the "trade." What is the underlying story that accounts for an exchange relationship here? In fact, no trade is necessary. It is still a narrowly rational act for any single individual to take copies of multiple products from the pot without contributing anything at all, and thus free ride on the contributions of others. The collective action problem is still fundamentally in place. The system would unravel not because free riders use up the stock of the collective good or somehow devalue it, but because no one yet has any real incentive to contribute to that stock in the first place. The cooking pot will start empty and stay that way.

I believe the solution to this puzzle lies in pushing the concept of nonrivalness one step further. Software in many circumstances is more than simply nonrival. Operating systems like Linux in particular, and most software in general, actually are subject to positive network externalities. Call it a network good, or an antirival good (an awkward, but nicely descriptive term). In simpler language, it means that the value of a piece of software to any user increases as more people use the software on their machines and in their particular settings. Compatibility in the standard sense of a network good is one reason why this is so. Just as it is more valuable for me to have a fax machine if lots of other people also have fax machines, as more computers in the world run a particular operating system or application it becomes easier to communicate and share files across those computers. Each becomes slightly more valuable to existing users as each new user enters the picture.

Open source software makes an additional and very important use of antirivalness, in maintenance and debugging. Remember the argument that there exist an infinite number of paths through the lines of code in even a moderately complex piece of software. The more users (and the more different kinds of users) actively engage in using a piece of software, the more likely that any particular bug will surface in someone's experience. And once a bug is identified, it becomes possible to fix it, improving the software at a faster rate. This is hugely important to the economics of software users, because customization, debugging, and maintenance usually accounts for at least half (and sometimes considerably more) of the total cost of ownership of enterprise software.

The point is that open source software is not simply a nonrival good in the sense that it can tolerate free riding without reducing the stock of the good for contributors. It is actually antirival in the sense that *the system as a whole positively benefits from free riders*. Some (small) percentage of these free riders will provide something of value to the joint product—even if it is just reporting a bug out of frustration, requesting a new feature, or complaining about a function that could be better implemented. In fact one wonders if it makes sense to use the term "free rider" here. Regardless—the more "free riders" in this setting, the better.

This argument holds only if there are a sufficient number of individuals who do not free ride—in other words, a core group that contributes substantially to the creation of the good. I have outlined a set of motivational drivers that, taken together in different proportions for different individuals, might inspire their active contributions. What makes this important in the large-scale and anonymous Internet setting is the heterogeneity of potential contributors.[47] A heterogeneous group has within it, out on the tails of distribution of interests and resources, people who (through some combination of micromotivations) will contribute to the joint product. The more heterogeneous the group is, the larger the proportion of people who sit out on the tails of the distribution. This might be true of many different kinds of collective action problems, but open source is different in these two essential ways. The transaction costs involved in connecting these people out on the tails is almost zero. And the people in the rest of the distribution are not really free riding in the sense that their behavior detracts in any way from the collective good. As I argued previously, they generally make some positive contribution. This explanation is consistent with the evidence concerning the 80–20 distribution of effort in large open source projects; it also helps explain why the 20 percent does not see any reason to try to exclude the 80 percent or put them in a formally different category of access to the joint good.

This dynamic yields a twist on conventional collective action arguments, where large groups are *less* likely to generate collective goods. The conventional view coming down from Mancur Olsen is that the larger the group, the smaller the fraction of total group benefit any person acting in the group can expect to receive, so that person gains more on the margins by allocating her effort toward a selfish pursuit. Second, the larger the group, the less likely there will be oligopolistic interaction that might help obtain the good—because any particular small group that wants to cooperate will again get a smaller fraction of the benefits.[48] And finally, the larger the group is, the greater the costs of organizing it in a way that can compensate for either of those problems.

The twist is this: Under conditions of antirivalness, as the size of the Internet-connected group increases, and there is a heterogeneous distribution of motivations with people who have a high level of interest and some resources to invest, then the large group is *more* likely, all things being equal, to provide the good than is a small group.

This recasts the nature of the problem that governance structures for open source need to solve. In fact analyzing the open source process through the lens of collective action begins to look subtly misleading. Contributions are not so problematic in this setting. The challenge is to *coordinate those contributions on a focal point,* so what emerges is technically useful. In simpler language, the problem is not to make something; it is to make something that is useful. The third and fourth steps in explanation then are to make sense of the social and political structures that establish and maintain coordination, and manage complexity, in the system. That is the subject of Chapter 6.

Explaining Open Source: Macro-Organization

Chapter 5 took on individual motivations and the economic logic of the good, which together make up the microfoundations of open source. This chapter focuses on macrolevel organization. There are two related issues to solve. First, how do individuals coordinate their contributions of specialized knowledge on a focal point in the absence of both authoritative command and the price mechanism? Second, what governance institutions manage the implications of complexity in the division of labor that result?

Coordination

The key question to answer about coordination is at one level simple: Why don't open source projects succumb regularly to code forking, which means the development of inconsistent versions of a code base that lead a software product to branch off in different and usually incompatible directions. It is the technological equivalent of speciation in genetics, when evolution changes the DNA of an organism sufficiently that its offspring constitute a different species.[1] The beauty of the genetic code is precisely that it does "fork" as much as it does. Life is a real economy of abundance, in the sense that there are almost infinite ecological niches to fill, and the demise of any particular individual is for most purposes nearly costless to the overall ecology. But this is obviously not acceptable for a human product like software that exists in an economy in which effort, intelligence, and energy are scarce. Remember as well that evolution is incredibly expensive and messy, leaving dead bodies and wasted resources (or at least resources that take a long time to recycle) everywhere. It is also incredibly slow.

Like speciation, there is not a sharply defined boundary for what is a code fork but rather a continuum. The notion of a discrete species does not exist in nature; it is a cognitive construct and so is the definition of a software fork. There are always different versions of software floating around, particularly with open source software because individuals are explicitly empowered to modify code. Linux has two official up-to-date versions, a stable release and an experimental release that in some sense constitutes an officially sanctioned fork. Samba forked in 2000 into a standard version and a next-generation version that took different engineering paths toward a slightly different set of desired functionalities. This kind of forking can be seen as desirable variation, experiments that make sense within a system set up for distributed innovation. Some developers consider it quite normal. The same thing happens in proprietary software projects. The difference is that in the commercial software world, authoritative decision-making within corporate boundaries cuts the forking process off before it goes too far. When synergies are lost, when individual developers and teams of developers are building pieces of software that are inconsistent and incompatible, and a new developer entering the project then has to make a de facto choice about whether to work on project A or project B, then in functional terms a fork has occurred. There are now dozens of incompatible proprietary versions of Unix. Developers and users recognize that Unix is heavily forked.

Why don't open source projects generally suffer the forked fate of Unix? As a null hypothesis, they probably should and for several different reasons. When developers disagree over how to move forward with a project, they are free to take the code and go their own way. They could also fork the code because of competitive issues—for example, if they believe that a subset of developers in the project is benefiting disproportionately from the work of the group as a whole. They could fork because of concerns about restrictions on use—for example, if a developer wants to use code for a purpose that is not allowed under an existing license. And of course they could fork for purely personal reasons—anger or frustration at the decisions or simply the behavior of a project leader.[2]

Albert Hirschman's classic argument from *Exit, Voice, and Loyalty* is a useful metaphor here. While the open source *process* certainly encourages the use of voice, open source *licenses* are designed explicitly to empower exit rather than loyalty as the alternative when voice fails.[3] The core freedom in free software is precisely and explicitly the right to fork. All of these driving forces are present in the open source process, and they are embedded in a culture that encourages intense and vehement disagreement. What holds the process together? In an abstract sense, the answer must be some combination of loyalty and raising the perceived behavioral costs of exit high enough that people put real effort into voice and stay with it long enough to solve coordination problems. More precisely, a combination of individual incentives, cultural norms, and leadership practices make up the solution.

Coordinating through Individual Incentives

Open source developers perceive themselves as trading many copies of their own (single) innovation for many single copies of others' innovations. To stay with the analogy, the size of the "marketplace" within which people trade then becomes important, just as in a stock market. Traders want the most liquid and diverse market possible. And they want anything that they trade for in that market to fit seamlessly within their portfolio (in other words, interoperate with their software). Forking would only reduce the size and the liquidity of the market.

A cultural framework rather than a precise economic definition of "trading" embeds this perception. The same framework generates some characteristics of an iterated game around reputation. If you as an individual developer choose to fork code, you may very well gain some additional control over your own contributions and hence your reputation. But if others do what you did and fork *your* code, and develop it further without your input, then you could be exposed to reputational risk that would be difficult for you to control. A forked code base for Linux that ran into severe development problems would exact a cost on Torvalds's reputation as well as on the reputations of other prominent Linux developers. This is neither rational nor efficient, but it almost certainly would happen anyway. As the "shadow of the future" gets longer for participants in this iterated game (as it should with the growing prominence of open source), this disincentive to forking becomes more compelling.[4]

A third piece of this puzzle follows from the mildly counterintuitive relationship between leaders and followers in open source. In any significant software project, a potential forker cannot achieve what she might want to achieve by herself. Regardless of the reason for forking, the leader of the fork will need to attract followers, additional developers who prefer to work on the forked code base rather than on the original. Robert Young has taken this point, combined it with the observation that maintaining software code is generally much more expensive than writing it, and reasoned to the conclusion that it will almost always be more economical for a potential forker to try to get the technical changes he wants incorporated into the existing code base when the community is committed to maintaining the software, rather than to split off and try to create a new community.[5]

Young's argument can be broadened by focusing on the power asymmetries at play. The potential leader of a forked code base is not in a powerful position, at least to start. Because the leader depends on followers more than the other way around, asymmetric interdependence favors the potential followers, who will make a free and voluntary choice about where to invest their work. The dynamic plays out in an interesting way: The more open a project is and the larger the existing community of developers working on it, the harder it is to attract potential followers to a fork. This is true for several reasons. It becomes very difficult for a renegade to claim credibly that she, as a fork leader, could assemble and hold together a bigger and better community of developers than is already working on the main code base. A forked minority code base could not then promise to match the rate of innovation taking place in the primary code base. It would not be able to use, test, debug, and develop software as quickly. And it could not provide as attractive a payoff in reputation, even if reputation were shared out more evenly within the forked community.[6] If innovation slows, the pie shrinks. And reputation depends at least in part on the number of people who know of your repute—which means the larger the audience, the more reputation you receive in return for any particular innovation. Forking would split the audience.

These individual incentives to coordinate differ somewhat, depending on the precise license under which a project is organized. They also create a degree of winner-takes-all dynamics within certain kinds of open source projects, with both positive and negative effects.

Coordinating through Cultural Norms

A distinct set of culturally based norms support and enhance the logic of these individual incentives. Norms can be notoriously slippery things in social life. Precisely because they usually lack the formal structure of laws or rules, and because (like laws and rules) they are not universally obeyed, people disagree over what a norm is and how we know when we have them. I am not going to solve those debates here or even engage them in a serious way, other than to note that the case for the presence of operative norms in the open source community is at least as strong as it is in many other communities in which social scientists comfortably invoke the concept. In an important book *Order without Law*, Robert Ellickson lays out three criteria that make up a plausible negative baseline, arguing that a norm should be said *not* to exist if:

- Close-knit participants do not punish persons whom they know have violated the norm.
- Ordinary behavior is mostly not in accordance with the norm.
- Group members' aspirational statements are inconsistent with the norm.[7]

If this is a reasonable argument (and I think it is), the case for the presence of at least three specific coordination norms in the open source community is strong.

"Ownership customs" make up the first core set of norms. Keep in mind that the question of who owns what in the open source economy is a separate question from the bundle of rights that ownership confers. Ownership in the open source community is fundamentally a grant of certain rights to distribute rather than the right to exclude. Who, then, has that right and how does she get it? Because the formal license structure essentially allows anyone to redistribute open source code, the question about norms of ownership becomes a question about who has the right, *recognized as legitimate by the community as a whole,* to redistribute modified versions of the software.

There are three typical ways in which someone (or some group) in practice acquires this kind of "ownership."[8] The first simply is to initiate the project. As long as the founder is actively engaged in the development process and is responsive to the community's questions and submissions, that person is the clear owner. The second is to have ownership passed on to you, explicitly and publicly, by the existing owner. There is an important "subnorm" in this process, centering on the notion that the owner has not just the right but the responsibility to bequeath a project to a competent successor when he is no longer willing, able, or interested in performing that role. The third way to acquire ownership is to pick up a project that appears to be abandoned—that is, when the presumptive owner has disappeared from the scene without passing on the mantle. Someone who wants to revive a project in this way is supposed to make substantial efforts to find the owner and wait a reasonable period of time for reaction from the community to any proposal to take over the project before claiming new ownership. It is also generally recognized that ownership acquired in this way is probationary and not fully legitimate until the new owner has made substantial improvements to the project and brought them out to the open source community.

Raymond makes an interesting observation about these customs. They bear a striking resemblance to the Anglo-American common law about land tenure that John Locke systematized in the late 1600s. According to Lockean property theory, there are three ways to acquire ownership of land. You can homestead on a piece of frontier territory or receive title from a previous owner. Or, if the title is lost or abandoned, you can claim the land through adverse possession by moving onto the land and improving it.[9]

This uncanny resemblance suggests the possibility of a parallel causation or at least a common logic. The plausibly shared functional story looks obvious: Customs like these are relatively efficient in settings in which property is valuable, there is no authoritative allocation, and the expected returns from the resource exceed the expected costs of defending it. We know that the first two of these conditions (valuable property, no authoritative allocation) hold for open source projects, but the third is problematic. What, indeed, are the expected returns from owning a project and how could anyone know *a priori* that they exceed the costs of defense? This is not a simple question in the abstract, and it is not simple in practice either, particularly when we see the extraordinary amount of time, energy, and emotion that breaks loose on email lists and newsgroups when ownership norms are threatened or breached. The point is that ownership customs do not arise spontaneously, even if they may be relatively efficient. And successful collaboration is not in any way determined by Lockean-style property customs even when they do arise. After all, even when these norms were widely accepted, the frontier was not a particularly peaceful place. And for collaborative engagement to provide more complex collective goods (the organization of towns, for example), typically authoritative institutions grew up on top of (and sometimes replaced) the common law regime.

There is a second core set of norms around decision-making roles that support ownership customs. The question these norms answer is, Who has the legitimate right to make decisions about which pieces of code are included in public distributions of the software? For the vast majority of open source projects, this is straightforward. When there are just a few developers working on a project, the right to make decisions about code is coterminous with ownership. For medium-sized projects, the norm is somewhat subtler: Authority follows and derives from responsibility. The more work an individual contributes and the more she takes responsibility for a piece of the project, the more decision-making authority she gains. This norm is backed up by an auxiliary norm that seniority rules in disagreements over who has responsibility for a piece of code.[10] There is a notable difference here with norms in academia, where formal seniority is proxy-measured by what degrees you have, where you got them, and what rank you have achieved in the professoriate (and at what university). The open source community places these formal credentials far below demonstrated coding ability and level of effort as a measure of seniority. It is hard to think of a comparable profession in which formal credentials are less important.[11]

Decision-making norms become more complex and interesting in the (relatively small number of) large-scale open source projects. Linux, for example, took on a formal differentiated role structure for decision-making as the project grew in size. In the mid-1990s Cox and T'so became recognized lieutenants to Torvalds. Each focused his efforts on a particular piece of the kernel and by his level of activity in the mailing lists became the most visible player in that space. Torvalds gradually reduced his own attention to those specific areas. And other developers started submitting bug reports to the lieutenants rather than to Torvalds, in practice recognizing their decision responsibility.

The final de facto "grant" of authority came when Torvalds began publicly to reroute relevant submissions to the lieutenants. In 1996 the decision structure became more formal with an explicit differentiation between "credited developers" and "maintainers." Credited developers make substantial contributions of code and are listed in the credits file. Maintainers (listed separately in a maintainers file) are responsible for shepherding the development of particular modules of code. They review submissions of code for that module, build them into larger patches, and submit these upward to Torvalds for final review. If this sounds very much like a hierarchical decision structure, that is because it is one—albeit one in which participation is strictly voluntary.

A particular form of "technical rationality" makes up a third set of norms in which the other norms are embedded. Open source is first and foremost an engineering culture—bottom up, pragmatic, and grounded heavily in experience rather than theory. There is a strong sense among developers that disputes can and should be resolved "objectively" and that the best dispute resolution mechanism is simply to "let the code decide." Of course code does not by itself decide anything and the notion of objectivity draws on its own, deeper normative base. Like all technical rationalities, this one exists inside a cultural frame. The cultural frame is based on shared experience in Unix programming, reflecting both the historical roots of open source and the aesthetic of many of the developers who participate in it.

Technical rationality starts with the foundational assumption that there exist technical solutions to technical problems. This may sound banal or naïve, depending on your viewpoint; but it sets an important tone for the way people fight out their disagreements. Naïve, uneducated, or even highly imaginative but undisciplined opinions are extruded from the discussion. Logical arguments made on technical grounds are the primary currency of debate. How to do something is a more important contribution than the idea that it should be done.

The technical rationality of open source is deeply embedded in the "Unix culture" in which creativity, cleverness, and engineering skill are demonstrated through elegance read as simplicity.[12] The core idea is modularity and flexibility: Write small programs that do one thing well, design them to communicate easily with other programs, keep everything transparent, and get things working first before you try to optimize anything. Central to this culture is the idea that code should be fun to work with. That is not self-evident—working on many complex programs can be frustrating to the point of exasperation ("like kicking a dead whale down the beach"). And fun is not an adjective this community takes frivolously. "Fun is . . . a sign of peak efficiency. Painful development environments waste labor and creativity; they extract huge hidden costs in time, money, and opportunity."[13]

The Open Source Initiative partially codified this philosophical frame by establishing a clear priority for pragmatic technical achievement over ideology (which was more central to the culture of the Free Software Foundation). A cultural frame based in engineering principles (not anticommercialism *per se*) and focused on robust, high performance products gained much wider traction within the developer community. It also underscored the rationality of technical decisions driven in part by the need to sustain successful collaboration, legitimating the focus on maintainability of code, cleanness of interfaces, and clear and distinct modularity. The core statement of the Open Source Initiative reflects the explicit victory of technical rationality: "We think the economic self-interest arguments for open source are strong enough that nobody needs to go on any moral crusades about it."[14]

But technical rationality does not mean technocratic determinism— far from it. In some fundamental sense the code may decide, but there are always many different ways to solve a problem in code and more than one will work. Raymond places this proclamation squarely in the center of the Unix philosophy: "Distrust all claims for 'one true way.'"[15] Technical rationality in this sense is deeply connected to the social organization of the community that enacts it. When people talk about clean code, they are making statements not only about some distinct characteristic of code but also about the way in which the technical artifact can interface with and be managed by an organized community. Many technical decisions about the direction of software development imply procedures that will need to be carried out by groups of people—thus, these "technical" decisions also reflect beliefs about effective ways to organize the community. In fact, technical discussions on how things should be done are intimately and often explicitly related to reflections on social practices and organization.

This creates a complex and volatile mix, even within the bounds of shared philosophy. Yes, there is a technical baseline that grounds the discussion. But the level of emotion betrays the importance of what still must be decided. The mailing lists on which these battles are fought show two distinctive characteristics about how technical rationality shapes the arguments. First is record-keeping. Because the email lists archive all communications, everything that everyone says in this setting is de facto for the record. People know this, and they know that others will often go back to read the email archives with care. Developers are not bashful or inhibited in using language, and they do not refrain entirely from personal attacks. But for the most part they do get down to technical issues and offer closely reasoned opinions that in effect educate each other (and lurkers who read the lists) about the issues at play. Second is the conspicuous energy that people devote to making their email posts clever, literate, and witty. Email lists (as opposed to the web) are built out of text and not images; coders spend much more of their lives interacting in text than anywhere else. Like a debate club, the cleverness and conciseness of your text carries weight in an argument—but because there is no physical presence, the text carries even more weight than usual. Technical rationality in this setting is also, then, a story about smart, precise, and witty language to carry the technical points home in the debate.

Leadership Practices

How important is the role of the leader in coordination? For small projects, leadership is again essentially the same as ownership. The leader/owner typically starts the project by articulating a goal, writing some code that demonstrates promise and viability, and inviting others to join in the work. If a leader/owner abnegates his responsibility, the presumption is that someone else will pick up the project if indeed it is worth picking up. This is a difficult proposition to test empirically because the parameters (did the leader do a good job? was the project really worth doing?) are ambiguous and subjective, and because for many projects the number of people who have to make those assessments is so small.

The question of leadership becomes more complex and interesting in large projects such as Linux. It is clear that leadership played a critical early role in getting the project started, setting an initial focal point, and maintaining coordination on it. Torvalds wrote the first substantial block of code largely by himself. It functioned as a focal point because—simplistic and imperfect as it was—it established a plausible promise of creativity and efficacy. Potential contributors looked at the code and saw the possibility that it could develop into something useful. The project contained and could be seen to contain interesting challenges and programming puzzles to be solved. Together these characteristics attracted developers, who, by investing time and effort in this project, were placing a bet that their contributions would be efficacious.

Torvalds's leadership helped to maintain the calculations behind this bet. An important part of this lies in his role first as the articulator and second as a continuing reinforcer of the community's cultural norms. Torvalds provides a convincing example of how to manage the potential for ego-driven conflicts among very smart developers. In a peculiarly charismatic way that combines self-deprecating wit with clear responsibility for decisions, Torvalds makes a point of consistently downplaying his own importance in the Linux story. He acknowledges that his decision in 1991 to release the code was an important one but characterizes it as a natural, almost instinctive act rather than a calculated part of a strategic plan.[16] While he is not shy and does not deny his status as leader, he does make a compelling case that he was not and is not motivated by fame and reputation. The documented history, particularly the archived email lists, support him on this point. He continues to emphasize the fun of programming and opportunities for self-expression and claims "the feeling of belonging to a group that does something interesting" as his principal motivation. While leaders of other large projects have different personality traits, they do tend to share an attitude that underemphasizes their own individual importance in the process. And they share, more importantly, a commitment to invest meaningful effort over time in justifying decisions, documenting the reasons for design choices and code changes in the language of technical rationality that is the currency for this community.

I emphasize the potential followers' calculations as a "bet" because the open source process is truly a voluntary association. Because anyone can join and leave at any time, the leader is in a real sense more dependent on followers than the other way around. The core question about leadership then becomes, How can a leader fail his followers?

The simple answer, which captures the unusual power dynamic, is "lack of responsiveness to those led."[17] In practice there are several related ways in which that can happen (and has happened). The shared core is a failure to act as an effective moderator. Just as the price mechanism for coordination requires a marketplace, coordination through talking requires a moderator for the discussion. A moderator can fail because of personality issues—when the leader doesn't have the right style, doesn't make contributors feel good about their work (even when it is rejected), or otherwise exacerbates the underlying potential for ego-based conflict. Some of the BSD forks of the early 1990s are an example, and there have been more such conflicts within the BSD communities. Torvalds has several times come close to failing as a moderator because he was dropping tasks and not responding in a timely and serious way to submissions. A leader can fail by making a series of design decisions that followers find faulty. More abstractly, a leader can fail by not setting realistic interim as well as long-term goals for a project, goals that can be achieved in a reasonable time frame and thus validate the efficacy of voluntary efforts. Some developers feel strongly that this has been the weakness of Richard Stallman, particularly in regard to the GNU kernel.

Of course, even a proficient and respected leader may at some point develop fundamentally different technical visions for the future of the project than some subset of followers holds. In that case, the issue is not really leadership failure but the technical direction of the project. Forking can occur for technical reasons rather than a breakdown of leadership *per se*. And that is not always a bad thing, nor does the open source community always perceive it as bad.

The Samba fork, which developed over about two years between 1998 and 2000, is a vivid example. Samba is an open source implementation of CIFS (Common Internet File System), a file-sharing protocol developed by Microsoft for Windows. Samba runs on Unix machines but speaks to Windows clients like a native. It allows a Unix-style system to interface seamlessly with a Windows network—an essential function. With Samba, if you have a machine running Linux or BSD somewhere in your network along with Windows machines (as many individuals and companies do), the Unix-style machine talks to the Windows network and everyone can share files and printers and communications and authentication and all the other services that run over the network.

The history of Samba development goes back to 1991, when Australian graduate student Andrew Tridgell wrote a simple protocol on his PC to read and write to a disk on a Unix server. Tridgell released his code under the GPL and within a couple of years attracted hundreds of developers to the project. In 1998 and 1999, a group of developers working on the Samba implementation for Windows NT began to express their frustration with the main Samba code branch—which (in part because it was so widely used) was on a relatively stable but also conservative development path. These developers had a more ambitious and radical development plan that would use architecture substantially different from that in the main Samba code. What started as a developmental code branch soon became de facto a code fork, called Samba TNG (the next generation).

The email lists show that this forking did not happen smoothly. Heated technical and personal arguments with allegations of improper leadership and lack of responsibility flew back and forth for several months, particularly in the fall of 2000. But in October 2000, Tridgell wrote an open letter giving his official blessing to the fork:

> Everyone pretty much knows now that the Samba codebase has forked, with the TNG branch being split off into a new set of releases. Despite some hilarious reports, this is actually a good thing. . . . As the original author of Samba I am delighted that this split has occurred. Many of the design decisions in Samba are showing their age . . . with a new project developers have a lot more freedom to try innovative solutions to problems without any concern about stability. While we don't yet know how the TNG project will work out, it will certainly teach us something about how their proposed approaches work when they are given the chance to be fully tested. I look forward to seeing more development in TNG now that the developers are not constrained by the more conservative elements of the Samba team (such as myself!) and I will be delighted to see the project flourish.[18]

I quote at length because Tridgell so eloquently captures the subtleties of coordination in the open source process. Forking, like speciation, is an essential source of variation and ultimately of radical innovation.

Too much forking would undermine the open source process in the obvious ways that people worry about all the time—scattered efforts, duplication of work, incompatibilities, and so on. But too *little* forking (in other words, too much successful coordination) would be as dysfunctional in a different way. Success (particularly in the marketplace) creates a demand for stability, which inhibits certain kinds of innovation. Debugging is important, but at a certain point it may be more sensible to junk the code base and rewrite from scratch rather than patch an obsolete system. No matter how much you love your old car, one day you stop replacing parts and buy a new (or newer) car because the core underlying systems are much more up-to-date and can be improved much faster and more efficiently.

Too much coordination can get you stuck working in an old and inefficient architecture, the equivalent of a local maximum in an ecological terrain. Most of the time in biological systems, evolution keeps you there through a process of stabilizing selection.[19] Coordination in the open source process does the same thing, and it is also usually desirable. Of course, biological systems can escape these local maxima—for example, when they are geographically isolated or when they undergo radical speciation (usually through mutation in a regulatory gene). In principle, proprietary software projects should be able to escape local maxima when a corporate manager makes a strategic decision that the time has come to do that. In business practice that is actually a very hard decision to make, because it means placing at risk all sorts of sunk costs and existing competitive advantages.[20] These corporate pressures may not be a major factor in the open source process. But the open source process also lacks an authority that can command the development team to make the radical and risky jump when someone or some powerful group decides that "jumping" is the efficient thing to do. Instead, open source relies on precisely the messy kind of communication and consensus-building that the Samba story illustrates.

The overall predisposition against forking, which is the outcome of the coordination mechanisms I have described in this chapter, holds things together in an imperfect way. The fundamental right to fork keeps the pressure on that bargain at all times. The balance between these forces is an emergent rather than an engineered property of the system, and it is being tested in practice. A system that has strong winner-takes-all, positive feedback forces embedded in it has definite advantages for coordination on a focal point, but it also has limitations. The core limitation is how much complexity the system can manage.

Complexity

Software is an extraordinarily complex artifact. Depending on precisely how you count and what you include, the Linux kernel now contains upward of 2.5 million lines of code; a full distribution of Red Hat Linux 7.1 (which includes some basic applications) runs to over 30 million lines of code.[21] Brooks's law captures some of the reasons why constructing an effective division of labor around software engineering at this scale of complexity is so difficult. Standard arguments in organization theory predict that increasing complexity in a division of labor leads to formal organizational structures.[22] In contrast to both Brooks's Law and the organization theory arguments, much recent literature on the Internet and the "new economy" argues that Internet technologies radically undermine organizational structures because they reduce the costs of communications and transactions toward an asymptote of zero. This is supposed to enable the formation of "episodic communities on demand," so-called virtual organizations that come together frictionlessly for a particular task and then redistribute to the next task just as smoothly.[23]

Each of these arguments has a point. Internet technology does reduce communication and transaction costs in many situations, sometimes radically. And this does affect in demonstrable ways existing boundaries of organizations and industries—sometimes in a revolutionary way.[24] Joseph Schumpeter in *Capitalism, Socialism, and Democracy* used the phrase "creative destruction" to describe this kind of process. It is an apt and evocative phrase. The problem is that many of the contemporary Internet arguments have picked up only half of it, concentrating on the destructive part and what is being left behind while paying much less attention to the creative part, the new organizational structures that arise to manage reconfigured and complex productive processes. I have argued at length that "self-organization" as a concept by itself can't fill this gap. The Internet does not solve foundational political problems of organizing complexity. It does not create working divisions of labor. Reducing or even removing the costs of geographically widespread and time-dependent collaboration is important, but that effort still leaves other collaboration costs unsettled—decision-making, human emotion, resolution of technical uncertainties, and so on. In principle, the Internet can increase these difficulties because it can be set up (and in the open source process, is set up) to be non-excludable.

These issues of complexity need to be managed by some means. Formal organization is one such means, but it is not the only one, and formal organization can take many different forms. When I use the term "governance" in this discussion, I am using it in the way it is used in international relations. In that context, "governance" is not government, it is typically not authoritative, and in fact it is not about governing in a traditional sense as much as it is about setting parameters for voluntary relationships among autonomous parties. Given that perspective, the central question becomes, How has the open source process used technology along with both new- and old-style institutions of governance to manage complexity among a geographically dispersed community not subject to hierarchical control? The answer has four elements: technical design, sanctioning mechanisms, the license as explicit social structure, and formal governance institutions.

Technical Design

The key characteristic of technical design for managing complexity is "source code modularization." Recall that a major tenet of the Unix philosophy is to keep programs small and as simple as possible ("do one thing and do it well"). A small program has far fewer features than a large one, but it is easier to understand and to debug. Small programs can be combined to enable more complex functionalities. The Unix philosophy is to build complex integrated applications by constructing them piecemeal; a large program works by calling on relatively small and self-contained modules.

Good modular design requires limiting the interdependencies between modules. Think of it as the engineering corollary to what organizational theorists call "loose coupling."[25] Or call it permissive coupling. Ideally, modules would generate discrete outcomes and communicate with each other through standard interfaces. Effective source code modularization means that a programmer working on one particular module knows two important things. The output of the module must communicate cleanly with other modules; and she can make changes in her own module without requiring a downstream ripple of changes in other modules, as long as she gets the communication interface right.

Source code modularization obviously reduces the complexity of the system overall because it limits the reverberations that might spread out from a code change in a highly interdependent and tightly coupled system. Clearly it is a powerful way to facilitate working in parallel on many different parts of the software at once. In fact parallel distributed innovation is nearly dependent on this kind of design because a programmer needs to be able to experiment with a specific module of code without continually creating problems for (or having always to anticipate the innovations of) other programmers working on other modules. One of Torvalds's most important decisions, to redesign Linux's early monolithic kernel into a set of independently loadable modules for Linux 2.0, is notable in this regard. Torvalds originally built a monolithic kernel because it was easier to start and he thought that Linux would be a learning and research tool for a fairly limited audience. As it grew into a very large project involving hundreds of developers, the core bet behind that decision—that free access to source code would allow developers to manage the intricacies of a large and integrated kernel over time—began to look wrong. The size of the program and just as importantly the size of the community working on it demanded a modular redesign. As Torvalds put it, "Managing people and managing code led to the same design decision. To keep the number of people working on Linux coordinated, we needed something like kernel modules."[26]

Torvalds's implicit point is simple and crucial: These engineering principles are important because they reduce organizational demands on the social and political structure for managing people. This is a goal toward which all software projects, open source or proprietary, aim. But achieving a good modular design, maintaining it in the face of ongoing change, and protecting it as the system scales or evolves toward major new functionalities is a very tough problem.[27] The structure of conventional software tends to deteriorate over time because of deadline constraints, demands for new features and functions, and the introduction of multiple loosely coordinated changes that don't share the same vision of how to evolve an existing structure. Without command and control authority to mitigate some of these pressures, the baseline expectation should be for open source projects to suffer even more severely. But major open source projects (Linux and Apache in particular) tend to do better than one would expect—both have maintained a high degree of modularity in the face of incremental changes and the introduction of radical structure changes to meet new functional demands (such as support for symmetric multiprocessing, a way to speed up performance by making multiple processors available to complete individual computing tasks simultaneously, in Linux).[28] This is a significant puzzle. The answer, I believe, lies in the way in which the open source process makes transparent the pressures and the costs of not meeting them, thus pressing the trade-offs out into the open where developers are forced to deal with them in a self-conscious way.

The theoretical background for this answer is simple. Technical rationality in practice is linked closely to the shape and structure of the organization that is trying to implement it. And so technical decisions implicitly reflect beliefs about effective ways to organize development. The more complex the collaboration, the more deeply technical discussions on how things should work and how they should be built are linked to beliefs about and reflections on social practices. In 1968 Melvin Conway made an argument about this relationship that software developers now call Conway's Law. This is the idea that the structure of the (technical) system mirrors the structure of the organization that developed it. According to Conway, it is first and foremost a consequence of the communication needs of the people building the system. The computer scientist David Parnas takes this argument a step further by defining a software module as "a responsibility assignment" for a piece of an organization first, and only secondarily as a subprogram.[29]

The open source process relies on a foundational consensus around technical rationality—that is its stake driven firmly in the ground. It is actively evolving organizational structures around that stake. Thus open source developers really are forced to live by the lessons of Conway's Law. The architecture of the technical system drives the organization, rather than the other way around.

The reason Conway's Law actually works in favor of the open source process is that early architectural formulations are approximations and are almost always unstable. The formal hierarchical organizations that enclose proprietary software development are resistant to change and often end up driving the technical architecture (the dysfunctional flip side of Conway's Law). In the ideal case the organization should follow this evolution rather than lead it. Open source developers know intuitively and experience on a day-to-day basis the fact that their informal and voluntary division of labor is extremely incomplete. The coordination problems raised by that fact are front and center in their discussions, and the architecture is designed accordingly. Torvalds learned this principle through experience with the 2.0 version of the Linux kernel, and it is now part of community practice. Obviously it doesn't work perfectly and considerable costs remain, but the management of complexity in open source does benefit from transparency of those costs.

Sanctioning

As a political scientist, I am innately pessimistic about the stability of communities. When a complex political system seems to operate effectively, it is never sufficient simply to explain success. What you have to explain is the lack of failure, which is subtly different. The challenge is to assume that there are individuals somewhere in the system who, if given an opportunity, will act opportunistically, take advantage of situations in which others play by the rules, exploit trust, and act in similar ways that benefit the "cheater" in the short term but pose a threat to the aggregate good. The mindset is just like that brought to bear on software security issues—a good programmer assumes that a clever opportunist will try to exploit vulnerabilities in any code. But the solution has to be different. Human systems have mechanisms to exact costs on people who try to break the rules and norms of a community. If a developer working in a company is not following the rules, he will be fired. In that case, he cannot take his code with him because the company owns the rights to it. Obviously these sanctions (along with others) loom in the background and act as a deterrent to antisocial behavior within a proprietary production process. The question then becomes how does the open source community, which cannot fire people or deprive them of access to code, sanction rule- or norm-breakers whose actions might place at risk the sustainability of the process?

"Flaming" is the most visible form of sanctioning in open source.

Flaming is public condemnation (in the sense that email lists and the web are public) of people or companies that violate norms. Flamefests can be quite fierce, but they also tend to be self-limiting for several reasons. First, developers understand the adage about sticks and stones when it comes to breaking bones or in this case changing behavior. Flaming might make a person uncomfortable; and there are costs in that, but not necessarily decisive ones. Second, there is a constraint on the use of flaming that arises from the foundational consensus on technical rationality. Developers flame each other when they have ideological disputes, disagreements about the norms of behavior in the open source community itself, or sometimes for extreme personal issues. They do not flame each other in the same way over technical issues. When the dispute is about code, you criticize the code and not the person who wrote it. Unlike many academic disciplines, you cannot enhance your reputation in the open source community by attacking the competence of another developer. Third, because flaming happens in archived text that everyone in the community can read, developers with less of a stake in the dispute tend to keep a finger on the pulse of important flamefests and intervene to stop them when things go too far.

What makes flaming effective—its very public nature—is what gives the broader community de facto oversight of just how long it is permitted to go on. The public context also enhances the way in which flamefests serve as a means for discussing, deconstructing, and reconstructing the normative consensus around what are acceptable and unacceptable behaviors within the community. Because the lists are archived, they also serve a valuable education and socialization function for new developers who are just starting to work within open source. But flaming by itself would not be effective in constraining a determined opportunist or for that matter a stubborn developer with very strongly held beliefs (and there are plenty of these). The more important form of sanction in a functional sense is "shunning."

To shun someone—refusing to cooperate with them after they have broken a norm—cuts them off from the benefits that the community offers. It is not the same as formal excludability in economics jargon. Someone who is shunned can still access any open source code that he would like and can still do anything he wishes with that code. The cost of being shunned is behavioral—the target will find it much harder to gain cooperation from others. The threat of shunning is to be left on your own to solve problems, while a community that shuns you is drawing on its collective experience and knowledge to do the same.

Doing the work on your own can represent a huge cost when it comes to goods that require customization, tacit knowledge, and experience to optimize—as do almost all knowledge goods. Any auto mechanic can buy a manual that covers my 86 Saab. To figure out a tricky problem in the car, though, she is more likely to call a friend who is an expert on that particular model than to try to track down the answer in the "open" documentation. Lawyers and veterinarians operate similarly. There is no proprietary "code." The law is freely available to everyone and so are books on cat diseases. But when lawyers and vets face unusual cases or diagnoses, they call their friends and colleagues to ask about precedents and experience with treatments. The point is that a lawyer or a veterinarian who could not access their communities easily, quickly, and at low cost would soon fall behind the curve and end up considerably less competent than the norm.

The situation is similar and probably more pronounced with complex software. Developers and users of software depend on a network of interdependencies that goes far beyond the source code itself. They need design and implementation advice, about the specific code and about how to relate a piece of code to their existing code base. They need help with development sticking points, which are often time-urgent. They need help with characterizing bugs that appear in their particular implementation of the program. And if they develop patches that solve their own problems, they have substantial incentives to get their patches adopted into the standard code base to avoid having to maintain them in sync with new releases.

No one can be excluded from access to the code itself, but to be excluded from access to the support of the community is a substantial penalty. The shunned person will have to run faster and faster just to stay in place while the community moves forward more or less without him. A very similar set of incentives faces small companies that use open source code—they too want to be able to get improvements adopted into the core code base so they can share debugging and maintenance in both directions with the broader community.[30] A very large company might be able to go it alone, but the costs (essentially to reproduce the open source community's expertise in-house) would be

substantial, along with the risk that competitors might end up controlling some key technology. Large companies have a different and more
attractive opportunity to influence the direction of open source software development, in a positive sense. They can contribute at a large
scale, both by offering code and by paying developers to write code for
the project.

IBM's relationship with Apache illustrates the upside. An example
of the potential downside—that is, the costs of a company being
shunned—is the story of SSH Communications. SSH is a widely used
set of tools that encrypt commands and data sent between servers
and PCs.[31] A large and diverse community of developers, led by Tatu
Ylonen, built the first version of SSH under an open source license
in the mid-1990s. The problem began when Ylonen in 1995 quietly
changed the terms on the license for release 1.2.12, restricting commercial distribution and asserting a trademark on the name SSH.
Ylonen then started a company, SSH Communications Security, to sell
a version of the software to commercial users. The company filed for a
trademark on the three letters "ssh."

The open source community saw this as a betrayal—not because
Ylonen was trying to make money from a commercial version of the
software, but because he was trying to restrict the freedom of others
to do the same thing. The community responded by taking the last
version of SSH code that was fully open source and starting a new project, OpenSSH, to develop and extend the open source version. The
OpenSSH project developed in close connection with OpenBSD (the
security-specialized version of BSD); it is now essentially a drop-in replacement for the proprietary version and in many situations outper-
forms the commercial product. In February 2002 SSH Communications released a letter to the open source developers threatening a suit
for trademark infringement, but it is not clear what the company
could gain from bringing formal legal action. SSH is widely used as a
standard and as a label in much the same way as people use the word
"band-aid" to refer to plastic bandages. In fact Ylonen promoted the
SSH name in this way and only later tried to restrict its use. The
OpenSSH developers are not engaged in any commercial gain, so
a trademark action would be problematic. Most importantly, whom
would SSH Communications sue? It would have to sue developers scattered around the world, because OpenSSH maintains no formal orga-

nizational structure. And if the company were to win its suit, what kinds of damages could it extract? It is difficult to see how SSH Communications would come out ahead of the open source community in any reasonable scenario for how this conflict will be resolved.

License as Social Structure

Open source licenses are legal-style documents that spell out terms of use for the software they cover. Around a dozen open source style licenses are in general use, and many more are used only occasionally. Some of these licenses are very carefully crafted with extensive legal expertise; others are slapped together by engineers. In either case the formal legal status of these licenses is not entirely clear. There are reasons to think that even the most meticulously crafted licenses like the GPL may not be fully enforceable in the courts. Much of the literature analyzing open source licensing has focused on this question of legal status, and it is an important one. Yet there is another way to see the license, as a de facto constitution. In the absence of hierarchical authority, the license becomes the core statement of the social structure that defines the community of open source developers who participate in a project. One way to manage complexity is to state explicitly (in a license or constitution) the norms and standards of behavior that hold the community together. This is the significance and purpose of the open source license that I explore here.

The core constitutional message of an open source license is fashioned as a statement to the developers. And the foremost statement is that they will be treated fairly if they join the community. At that very general level, the statement is partly a result of the open source process itself. In practice, most developers who participate in open source expect to be on both sides of a license—that is, acting at different times as licensor and licensee. This naturally produces an internal balancing of interests when it comes to developers thinking about the structure of the license; the process is one step removed from the usual legal dynamic of adversarial interests in which each party is trying to get the most advantageous terms that he can for that particular side.

But the core notion of fairness is also a self-conscious piece of the open source community's self-image. When Bruce Perens in 1997 crafted a statement about this self-image, he began by calling it the Debian social contract.[32] This was a contract made "with the Free Software Community" that committed developers working on the Debian distribution of Linux to a clear set of constitutional principles: Write free software only but do not discriminate against users who want to run nonfree software; make public any problems, including all bug reports; and prioritize the needs of the users while protecting the interests of the free software community.

The general principles here are simple and significant. There are three explicit in the document and one implicit. The explicit principles are:

- *Freedom*—to give away or sell the software, as well as to modify it, through access to source code.
- *Nondiscrimination*—no discrimination against a person or a group of people (for example, a company or a country); or against a particular field of endeavor (for example, using open source software for nuclear weapons tests simulation or genetic research).
- *Pragmatism*—users may wish to access both open source software and proprietary software for different purposes, and Debian should not restrict that.

The implicit principle is *meritocracy*—in this community, developers are given equal opportunity to succeed (or to fail) based on how good they are as coders. This is an important principle precisely because it is difficult to implement in practice. The owner of software code in the commercial world obviously has substantial special rights—she decides when to hire and fire developers, how to share out the wealth that is generated, what the future direction of development will and will not be. The "owner" in the open source world also has special rights. The open source process does not completely eliminate the gap between privileged and nonprivileged players, so it cannot promise a perfect meritocracy. What it does do is minimize that gap in several ways.[33] Eliminating license fees and royalties from the equation means that the privileged person cannot get direct monetary gain from the work of others. More importantly, by creating the right to fork code, the open source process transfers a very important source of power from the leader to the followers. The privileges that come with leadership then depend on the continuous renewal of a contingent grant from the community. This comes as close to achieving practical meritocracy as is likely possible in a complex governance situation.

Within the broad landscape of the open source definition, crucial variation exists among specific licensing schemes. The most important difference from a political standpoint lies between BSD-style licenses and GPL-style licenses. The BSD license has relatively few constraints. It is a very short document, usually just a page or so, with three basic provisions. BSD grants explicit rights to unlimited use of software in source *or* binary form (that is, without source code), with or without modification. It requires that the developers' copyright notice be retained and reproduced in redistributions (thus giving credit to the original authors of the code) but prohibits the use of the developers' names as endorsements or for advertising of a derivative product unless the developers explicitly grant that permission. Lastly it includes an "as is, no warranty" provision that protects the developers (and the institution, like UC Berkeley in the original case) from any legal liability that might be associated with use of BSD code in any setting.[34]

This is a very permissive set of licensing terms. The BSD "community" logic reflects its heritage as a byproduct of university research, particularly during a certain era of thinking about how university-based research ought to relate to the larger technological community, including corporations. The license serves to credit the researchers, protect them and the university from liability, and then let people do what they want, as they see fit, with the product. In principle the academic background conditions invoke an auxiliary set of norms for the community—for example, universities have their own general principles about how faculty and graduate students ought to relate around issues of who is credited for what work under what conditions. In practice, the looseness of the license and the ambiguity around some of the auxiliary norms has caused problems and dissension about what is legitimate behavior. When Bill Joy left the CSRG at Berkeley and took his BSD code to help build Sun Microsystems, he was acting entirely within the boundaries of the formal BSD license provisions. At least some of his colleagues felt, however, that he had broken the norms of university research behavior. That feeling obviously got worse with Sun's extraordinary commercial success in the 1990s and was not helped by Sun's ambivalent and reluctant relationship with the open source community during much of the 1990s.

The General Public License (GPL) is considerably more detailed, more constraining, and more explicit about the political and social principles that underlie its structure.[35] The GPL is about ten times as long as the BSD license. It includes a substantial preamble (labeled as such) that states the underlying principles of the license and why it is structured the way it is. The preamble explains, much like a constitution really, why the license must place certain constraints on peoples' rights, in order to protect the more important core rights that "really" matter. The language and the underlying argument is Lockean: "To protect your rights, we need to make restrictions that forbid anyone to deny you these rights or ask you to surrender the rights. These restrictions translate to certain responsibilities for you if you distribute copies of the software or if you modify it." Working with GPL software means accepting this social contract and knowing that you have in fact accepted it.

The GPL is designed to try to keep developers from "hoarding" software code under any conditions. The community's products are open for the taking; but if you take, you must give back essentially anything that you do with the product. To "enclose" GPL code is not allowed. To use GPL code to build proprietary products is not allowed. These restrictions are a broad statement about what the world of software ought to look like (and thus go way beyond the pragmatic "use it any way you want" attitude of BSD). Even if the term "viral" has negative connotations for some, it does describe the practical effects of the political agenda motivating the GPL—it wants to spread its vision of ownership and sharing. It implements that agenda by requiring:

- That GPL code must be distributed without license fee and with the source code.
- That derivative works of GPL code must also be licensed under GPL. To repeat the point, the distinguishing feature of the GPL is that this is not simply allowed, it is *required*. The restriction covers a broad definition of a derivative work—not just modified GPL code but also a program that uses pieces of GPL code or that statically links to GPL libraries.

The broad definition of "derivative work" is an essential part of the GPL political logic, but it causes practical complications. The technical distinction between dynamic linking and static linking of two pieces of software is not a clean one.[36] Of course software programs

need to work together and share inputs and outputs. In most computing environments, a user might very well want to work with GPL software and proprietary software at the same time. When a GPL program
links dynamically to a proprietary program (for example, a GPL program uses existing system facilities like a graphical user interface library), the GPL license does not require that the proprietary library
disclose source code. That makes good pragmatic sense in terms of
getting people to use GPL programs without having to give up using
other software that they own.

But when a proprietary program is doing the primary work and it
wants to link dynamically to GPL code to use GPL'ed resources to
carry out its task, the situation is more ambiguous. At that point, GPL
software is essentially being used to facilitate and further the functionality of proprietary software. Richard Stallman's intention in crafting
the GPL clearly was to try to prevent this scenario (in other words, that
a developer would use GPL code to link dynamically with a proprietary
program for the purpose of making a better proprietary product). The
foundation of the social contract is that no one should be able to take
nonreciprocal advantage of the community's joint efforts, by using
GPL code to build non-GPL software. But the distinction between dynamic and static linking, as well as the issue of which program is doing
the primary work and thus gaining the benefits of linking to the other,
is often a judgment call.

Stallman later wrote a secondary license called LGPL (library GPL)
that was an imperfect attempt to clean up some of the ambiguity.
LGPL explicitly permits proprietary software to make calls to GNU libraries, and declares that the proprietary program can do so without
being considered a derivative work. The intention was to increase the
market penetration of some GNU libraries, making it clear that people
could and should use them with both free and nonfree software. But it
is not a perfect solution by any means, and Stallman himself has since
become skeptical of the LGPL (he now refers to it as the "lesser GPL"
and advices against using it frequently).[37]

The GPL clearly is an incomplete contract, like any real contract.
One of the advantages of incompleteness is that the contract can be
modified to try to preserve the core values in unexpected situations as
they arise. Netscape's debate over licensing the Mozilla project is a
good example. Netscape really was the first company to write an open
source license designed explicitly to make the community structure

compatible with the needs of a large, for-profit corporation. The Netscape answer was both creative and awkward—two separate licenses with different provisions. The MPL (Mozilla Public License) expanded the GPL by including more explicit definitions of what is a derivative work that must itself then come under MPL. It also allows MPL code to be combined with separate proprietary code to make a "larger work" that need not be MPL'ed. Yet it requires that anyone using MPL'ed code in this way keep the proprietary code in separate files and open source the APIs (application programming interfaces, the means by which the MPL and the proprietary code interface), so anyone who wants to create alternatives to the proprietary code can do so. The second half of the answer is the NPL (Netscape Public License), which grants Netscape special rights on particular parts of the code. Netscape can use NPL code in other products without that code itself having to be NPL'ed for a period of two years; and NPL code can be relicensed to third parties not on NPL terms. Netscape did this to preserve control and greater pricing power on some of its code, as well as to manage the consequences of having some original source code licensed to other companies under terms that would preclude subsequent free release. Netscape justified the NPL privileges by arguing that, in donating a huge amount of code to the open source community, it had the right to ask for something in return.

Although the Netscape solution was not very successful in practice, it did establish the basic principle that companies could themselves use hybrid open source license schemes to maneuver between the social structure of the open source community and the needs of large companies. Sun Microsystems has struggled visibly with this issue, arguing in very detailed justificatory documents that its "community source" (SCSL) license would "take the advantages from each of the proprietary and open source models and eliminate the disadvantages."[38] The core SCSL idea is to create an open source–like community among individuals and organizations who want to extend and build applications on top of a common infrastructure (Java, for example). Anyone can join the community and easily gain access to the source code for research use, with a click-through agreement. If you agree in addition to conform to tests and specifications that ensure compatibility with the standard core infrastructure, you can step up to an "internal deployment" license that allows limited distribution and testing in anticipation of a product launch. If you then want to market your product, you step up to a commercial license, which requires that you pay a fee to Sun for having built the core infrastructure on which your product rests. All along the way, developers are required to give bug fixes back to the community, but they explicitly are *not* required to share other modifications such as performance enhancements or platform adaptations (these can be kept proprietary if the developer wishes, although the APIs have to be open).

Sun was betting that this combination of structures would foster a community in which "the developing organization has sufficient motivation to invent and innovate [while] for participating community members there are incentives to invent in the marketplace and protections for those inventions within the community."[39] It sounds reasonable enough, but the open source community has in practice been ambivalent about SCSL and its progeny. They are responsive because of Sun's canonical status and because many of the core technologies (like Java) are quite good, and at the same time they are reluctant because of uncertainty about the effects of the considerable proprietary privileges in the SCSL and about the need for the license in the first place.[40] For its part, Sun recognizes that it is finding its way through uncertain territory; Gabriel and Joy explained, "In defining the Sun Community Source License, Sun has tried very hard to get it right, but maybe it isn't perfect . . . right now, in the context of an industry rapidly changing, it's our best attempt—it's a work in progress."[41]

This kind of serious experimentation with licensing should be expected because what is at stake here is not simply a set of legal definitions and restrictions. Rather, the license represents foundational beliefs about the constitutional principles of a community and evolving knowledge about how to make it work. The social structure of the open source community, then, is not invisible and it is not mythically self-organized; it's just constructed formally in an unusual fashion. Open source licenses are a major expression of the creative side of creative destruction. Unconventional formal organization is another important expression.

Formal Governance Structures

Most open source software projects are small and have no formal governance structures. This was true of Linux in its earliest days, when Torvalds ran the project and made unilateral decisions. As Linux and the community of developers working on it grew, the practical demand for an organizational structure to manage flow of communications and decisions grew as well. The Internet modifies demand for formal organization but does not erase it. Torvalds can communicate instantly with as many Linux developers as he wishes. Code management systems can help him keep track of newly written patches. But the time and energy available to make thoughtful decisions and justify them to the community is still quite limited. As the developers put it, "Linus doesn't scale" and this creates a demand for governance structures.

All complex production processes need governance mechanisms to make them work. Two things about governance structures in open source are distinctive. The first is the need for an organizational form that supports (or even better, takes advantage of) asynchronous communication. The larger open source projects involve developers from all over the world. They don't meet face to face; just as important, they don't work at the same time of day or, for that matter, in many cases at predictable times of the day or even at regular intervals. The second is a slight twist on the notion of hierarchy. That there is no hierarchy for the division of labor—that is, assigning tasks to particular individuals—lies at the heart of the open source process. There can be a hierarchy of decision-making, for vetting and incorporating the results of distributed work, yet participation in that decision-making hierarchy is voluntary and remains voluntary for any individual developer, because it is always possible to exit and fork. These features can be dealt with and combined in different ways.

The formal governance of Apache is one distinct example. Starting with just eight people in early 1995, the Apache Group grew quickly to several dozen core developers working with a penumbra of hundreds of other developers who occasionally contributed ideas, code, and documentation to the project. The core developers made up a geographically diverse group—based in the United States, Britain, Canada, Germany, and Italy—and each had a full-time job (in most cases related to web services; indeed, that was the source of their interest in building Apache). Decisions early on were made by informal email-driven consensus; but that informal system came under pressure with increasing numbers of participants, and with the "burstiness" of participation (developers might be doing something else for a week before they could come back to their Apache work, but the project as a whole could not wait for everyone's bursts to coincide). Apache needed a mechanism for gauging group consensus using asynchronous communication and some set of rules for dealing with bursty input.

The answer in practice was a system of email voting based on a minimal quorum consensus rule. Any participating developer can express an opinion by casting a vote on any issue facing the project, but only the votes of the Apache Group members are binding. Code changes require a minimum of three positive votes and no negative votes (there is a unit veto, although vetoes are expected to carry with them a convincing explanation). Other decisions require a minimum of three positive votes and an overall majority in favor. Election to the Apache Group is roughly meritocratic by peer review—if you do a lot of good work on a piece of the code, you may be nominated by a member of the Apache Group and added to the Group by a unanimous vote of existing members.[42] Like all voting systems the Apache consensus procedure is not perfect; it seems to work less well during periods of rapid, intense development than for incremental change.

In 1999 the Apache Group formally incorporated as a nonprofit corporation, The Apache Software Foundation.[43] It now serves as an organizational umbrella for a range of web-relevant open source projects (including the original Apache web server as well as Jakarta, Perl, TCL, and others). Each has its own project management committee that is roughly analogous to the original Apache Group, including a set of committers who make day-to-day decisions and can write changes to the code base, a set of credited developers who make contributions to the project, and a larger circle of users. The organization is roughly like a set of concentric circles that overlap with each other at the center, where an Apache Software Foundation board of directors is responsible for overall direction, coordination among the different projects, legal issues, and other kinds of "central services" that benefit the individual projects.

Linux, as it expanded, developed a semiformal organization for decision-making about code. The term "hierarchy" is misleading if it carries with it a connotation of authority; "pyramidal flow" is more descriptively accurate. There exist clearly differentiated roles within the Linux community. The organic result is what looks and functions very much like a hierarchical structure where decision-making flows through a fairly well defined pyramid. Over time the differentiated roles within that structure took on more formal characteristics.[44] Linux 1.0, released in 1994, had an official credits file listing 80 developers and describing their contributions to the program (this replaced the simple and informal acknowledgments that Torvalds had previously written). In February 1996 Torvalds added a maintainer's file to parallel the credits file, formally acknowledging a higher status of decision-making for the developers who owned responsibility for particular modules. The first maintainer's file had three names; now there are well over a hundred. Torvalds sits atop the pyramid as essentially a benevolent dictator with final responsibility for managing decisions that cannot be resolved at lower levels.

The Linux pyramid works imperfectly. In fact there have been recurrent crises of decision-making capacity, one of which I described in Chapter 4. In 2002 essentially the same issue—how does Linus scale—came back to the fore. The issue became acute, interestingly, when Torvalds stepped outside the normal flow of decision-making and unilaterally replaced a significant piece of code managing virtual memory in the 2.4 kernel (a stable release, whose maintainer at the time was Torvalds's most trusted lieutenant, Alan Cox). What made it worse was that the problems in the original virtual memory code, according to some developers, arose mainly because Torvalds did not keep up with the flow of patches that were being submitted to him through normal channels.

Once again it seemed that Torvalds was responding to time pressure by simply "dropping patches on the floor."[45] And once again major figures in the Linux community talked openly of rebellion against the leader. But in a sure indicator of organizational maturation, the main energy soon moved toward finding an institutionalized solution. Alan Cox acknowledged in an interview that overthrowing Torvalds was not the answer: "A simple replacement of Linus has the same problems the original did, coupled with probably having poorer taste and less people skills."[46] Torvalds showed his responsiveness by stepping back from early and emotionally charged responses on the mailing list and announcing that he would make changes to his work flow patterns. Raymond generalized the situation as a need to find "some way to institutionalize and distribute the leader's role."[47] Whether this took the form of a "patch penguin" (a deputy to Torvalds who makes sure patches don't get lost) or some enhancement to the roles or capabilities of individual maintainers was less important than that the decision-making system was evolving through trial and error toward greater scalability.

The open source process is an ongoing experiment. It is testing an imperfect mix of leadership, informal coordination mechanisms, implicit and explicit norms, along with some formal governance structures that are evolving and doing so at a rate that has been sufficient to hold surprisingly complex systems together. There is no off-the-shelf template for coordination and nonauthoritative governance of complexity in the open source setting. What this chapter demonstrates instead is a diverse set of experiments, a challenging environment that brings out the "bugs in the system," and an imperfect but recursive and self-conscious error-correcting mechanism that is trying to find solutions that work. Writing computer code is not the same as writing a constitution, and formal governance is still a secondary piece of how open source manages complexity. But the norms and behavior patterns that have made the open source process a technical success are showing promise as well as a means of evolving the governance mechanisms for the process itself.

CHAPTER 7

Business Models
and the Law

Software does not exist in a vacuum. To be useful, a program must be compatible with a broad set of technologies—it has to share data and communicate with other programs and with the hardware on which it runs. Compatibility often is tricky, even when it is just about technology. For open source, the problem of compatibility is broader because open source software is not just a particular technology. It is a way of building things that enters an ecology densely populated by institutions that make and do things slightly differently. Open source diverges from the conventional organizational logic of a business; it relies on an idiosyncratic twist of legal structures for its principles of ownership; and it makes use of some economic principles and practices that are different from those of most of the institutions around it. Yet the open source process needs to interact deeply and effectively with each of these existing structures. The two most important are business and the law.

The business model problem recognizes that there is no such thing as a freestanding "open source economy," any more than there is an "information economy" or an "internet economy" that somehow stands alone. The legal principles that surround open source are similarly in contact with conventional rules of law. Compatibility at the points of contact allows the open source process to coevolve with these extant institutions. This chapter focuses selectively on parts of the interaction that bring open source software into close and challenging kinds of contact with basic principles of capitalist business organization and modern legal institutions of property. And so the first caveat: This is not a chapter about specific corporate strategies, an exhaustive study of businesses that rely on open source technologies, or a primer on how to make money with open source. And it is not a comprehensive analysis of the extraordinarily interesting legal questions that open source has raised (and can raise in the future). For example, is source code protected speech under the first amendment? A second caveat is that there is nothing strange, magical, or impossible about open source from a business model or legal point of view. It is not an oxymoron to build for-profit organizations around free software or to protect open source code with copyright law. But it is challenging to do so, and the experiments thus spawned may have broader consequences for information-era business models and law.

Underlying Business Logic

Conventional business models for proprietary software have a simple core logic. A company typically sells to a customer the right to use software but does not transfer full ownership of the product. This is a key distinction because what is essentially a right-to-use license can and does place restrictions on what the customer may do with the software. In practice, right-to-use licenses are customized in limited ways—I can sell you a license that allows a single person to use the software, or a license for multiple users within an organization; I can sell you a license for using software in support of a particular project with different costs and terms than a license to use the same software for a different purpose. In essence these are differential or segmented pricing schemes analogous to what airlines do by selling seats to different kinds of customers (with different needs for advance purchase and so on) at different prices.[1] In addition to the right-to-use license, you might also want to buy support, consulting, and systems integration services to help you use the software to do the things you want it to do.

This logic creates a market for information technology where power lies more with the suppliers than with the customers. The customers want solutions to practical problems, and they express those desires, imperfectly, as demand for software. The suppliers in principle build software to meet the demand. But the demand function is complex, fragmented, rapidly changing, and highly granular because it depends on the very specific circumstances of particular users. So in practice software development companies build products based on (imperfect) feedback from their largest customers, and on the skills that they have internally and can easily access. The result is often a kind of least-common-denominator solution—like broadcast television, just good enough to attract a large segment of users, without being optimized for anyone. The users are then stuck with the problem of trying to use and integrate these least-common-denominator pieces of technology (sometimes from different suppliers) to get some part of the functionality that they really wanted. This task can be exceedingly difficult and expensive; without access to source code, it is often impossible to do well.

But control of the source code is the foundation of this business model. Source code is conceptualized as the key basis of competitive advantage that a proprietary software company truly controls.[2] Protecting that advantage (that is, retaining control) is paramount. The simplest way to retain control is to give only the binary executable codes to the customer. If parts of the source code are shared (for example, with collaborating developers or with large customers), tight legal constraints on what can be done with the source code are necessary to retain control.[3]

The open source process undercuts the conventional business logic. The GPL does more than just release control of the source code; it explicitly establishes a situation in which *no one* can control the source code. This forces a dramatic shift in the underlying structure of the software market.

The obvious point is that suppliers cannot generate significant income from selling undifferentiated copies of open source software (freedom of redistribution would move the market price toward the marginal cost of reproduction, which is asymptotically zero). The more important point is that power in this market shifts away from software suppliers and toward the customer or user of software.

With access to source code, users can choose functional software pieces that best meet their needs, customize the pieces to a much greater extent, and more easily solve the otherwise obstinate problem of making the pieces work together. Customers become independent from any specific IT supplier because, when you have the source code, you can plug your own security holes, fix your own bugs, write your own (better) documentation—or hire a third party to do any of those things for you. From an overall industrial organization perspective, open source dramatically reduces the potential for supplier lock-in. This solves what is otherwise a huge problem of potential opportunism on the part of suppliers, who (by controlling source code) in effect create the setting for "asset-specific investments" by customers and use those investments to lock their customers into a dependent relationship.[4] Indeed that kind of opportunistic behavior is really at the heart of the proprietary software business model; and while it predictably provides huge profits for IT vendors, it is clearly inefficient from an aggregate market perspective. Access to source code opens up the market in similar ways on the hardware side as well, by enabling customers (or independent developers) to port software from one hardware platform to another, including older hardware architectures, less popular ones, and hardware components or whole systems from competing suppliers. Power in the market shifts to the consumer.

This market shift creates a major challenge for business models. The generic question is, What within this newly configured market is not a commodity; what can generate sustained economic returns? This is a tricky problem, but it is not an impossible one. The key is to remember that software, even with source code included, is less like an airplane seat and more like a complex recipe for a very sophisticated restaurant dish. Provide infinite free copies of airline seats, and it would be nearly impossible to run an airline in a capitalist economy. In contrast, Alice Waters publishes her best recipes but that has not shortened the lines or driven the prices of a meal at her restaurant Chez Panisse to zero.

Abstractly there are two general ways to approach this problem. The first is to focus on what you can protect through legal restrictions that remain even after the source code is free.[5] Brands and trademarks, for example, are not trivial things in complex markets in which the quality of the good or service is hard to measure without substantial investment. Certainly I can use Alice Waters's recipes in my new Berkeley restaurant; but if I were to call that restaurant Chez Panisse, I would soon be facing (and losing) a lawsuit. The Chez Panisse brand is a valuable proxy for a promise of quality performance. In some sense, giving away the recipes may actually enhance the value of the brand by raising people's awareness of just how complex the process of bringing that meal to the table actually is.

The second way to approach the problem is to focus on the accumulation of sticky, hard-to-communicate, tacit knowledge that is needed to turn source code into a practical solution to an information-processing problem. Here what cannot be commoditized are practical experiences of problem-solving, familiarity with the code base, and the cumulative learning that can be maximized if you set up your feedback loops just right. Torvalds's "competitive advantage" in Linux is fundamentally the fact that he knows the code better than anyone else.[6] Years of experience playing around with a code base, customizing it for different settings, figuring out how to make it work in diverse environments, is in practice a real barrier to competitive entry. A company that organized itself to boost the rate at which that kind of knowledge grew among its employees would have, in effect, created a business model that was quite viable in, and familiar to, capitalist economies.

At an abstract level these are not new ideas. Yochai Benkler, among others, characterizes the economics at play here as "indirect appropriation," but that is a peculiarly conservative view that tries to preserve the notion of source code as the "real" source of value from which direct appropriation would otherwise occur.[7] Often this is a social myth, as in the case of the argument that professors engage in indirect appropriation because they get paid as teachers but gain their position as a result of their research. The story can be told more cleanly by simply saying that professors engage in direct appropriation—they get paid for their scholarship and provide teaching as an auxiliary service.[8] (You may not hear this argument often, however, because it challenges public understandings of what a university is and why it ought to exist as a core institution in modern society.) Once you take this discussion out of a space that is morally charged, it becomes extremely easy to see. If you instead use the indirect appropriation idea and protect common understandings, you end up supporting the notion that software is somehow "naturally" built within a proprietary, closed source structure because that is the only way to "directly" appropriate value. Instead, I think it makes more sense to redefine direct appropriation in practice and let the institutional cards—in other words, the firm and its strategy as dependent variables—fall where they may.

The pragmatic question, and the essence of creativity in the business model problem, is figuring out how to put into practice permutations of these ideas. Of course creativity and experimentation with business models are also not new. Organizations in the 1980s and early 1990s had to construct new business models around processes like lean production. Some of these business models succeeded; others failed. Open source drives the same kind of exploration (and certainly will have the same mixed results). The next sections chart some of the interesting experiments and consider some implications of the innovations.

Generic Business Models for Open Source

Frank Hecker and Robert Young have each written generic descriptions of basic business model templates for open source software.[9] I use their labels to map the space, and then explain the core logic behind these templates and discuss several examples of companies that have built practical operations by combining particular elements.

Support sellers package and distribute open source software on convenient media (like CD-ROMs), and offer a set of technical support and customization services to users. Why would someone pay for this function when she could download all the software from the web, configure it for her systems, install it herself on a set of machines, write her own documentation for particular uses within her company, and provide her own support and continuous updates? Phrased this way, the question answers itself: It is almost always more efficient to outsource these functions to a specialist who achieves economies of scale by performing these tasks for many companies.

Technical support is the most obvious way to make money "on the edge" of open source. Stallman's GNU manifesto explicitly recognized this possibility quite early on; one of the first (and most successful) open source companies—Cygnus Solutions—implemented it by supporting GNU tools and, most importantly, the GNU compilers. Linuxcare tried to establish itself as the "800 number" for Linux, the company you call no matter what distribution you are trying to run on whatever hardware you happen to be running it. Such a business model is not easy. There is often strong price competition around the distribution itself (because anyone can copy it) and the technical support function is incredibly labor and knowledge intensive, making significant economies of scale difficult to achieve in practice.

Loss leaders give away open source software as a way of generating demand and seeding a larger market for a linked commercial product. The commercial product is often a different piece of software. For example, an open source product can be used to build the software vendor's reputation, make the commercial product more useful, or expand the community of developers who build new applications and improvements for the commercial product.

The *sell it, free it* model takes the loss leader idea and extends it through time. The core idea here is that a company would first sell its software under traditional commercial terms and then, at some point later in the product life cycle, release the code as open source. That point would be reached when the benefits of an open source development process are believed to outweigh the proprietary licensing revenues. The open source product would then function as a loss leader for the next-generation commercial product. And depending on the specific licensing provisions, what is learned in code development for the open source product could be incorporated into a next-generation commercial product (this is essentially what Netscape tried to do).

The linked commercial product in a loss leader model could just as easily be hardware (Hecker and Young call this model *widget frosting*). A company that makes money from hardware might use open source to build software drivers, compilers, or applications and even operating systems that customers need to make effective use of the hardware. If the open source process produces software that better (and more cheaply) enables the functionalities promised by the hardware, then the hardware itself becomes more valuable and the market for the hardware should expand.

Accessorizing is the idea of selling physical accessories that make it easier to use open source software. The most common accessory is a book, a manual, or some other documentation that helps developers and users get the most utility out of their software. The outstanding example is O'Reilly & Associates, whose core business is publishing what are considered gold-standard books and technical manuals that document and explain various open source software packages.

Service enablers distribute and support open source software primarily to generate traffic to other revenue-generating services. Hewlett-Packard, for example, in 2000 released the source code and set up an open source development process for its e-speak software. This is a program that provides a set of standard communication tools and an open environment for "collaborative commerce," the creation of new business relationships across different industries through the discovery and interaction of web-based services.[10] By open sourcing e-speak, HP hoped to benefit from the contributions of freelance developers—but just as importantly the company was making a firm commitment not to "slant" what is essentially a neutral platform in favor of any privileged partners (or itself). If e-speak improves more quickly and its market share expands to become a de facto standard for collaborative commerce platforms, these trends would certainly expand HP's position in the market for the products and services it does sell.

The logic of *branding* in open source software is familiar. The company owns the brand, not the source code, by retaining exclusive rights to its product trademark. If someone else wants to make a software product from the open source code, they can do so but they cannot label the new product with the "brand name" (unless the branding company sells the right to do so, for example, by franchising). The question of why customers would pay for a branded open source product is essentially the same question as why people pay for branded commodities in any part of the economy. The brand has a perceived value that often reflects some "real" value (perhaps the branded product undergoes additional testing, perhaps the customer has increased confidence that the branding company will be around a few years later, or perhaps the brand is part of the "experience" that the customer is willing to pay for in buying a product).

Business Experiments in Open Source

The business model concepts I've discussed so far are ideal types. Most companies that rely on open source software combine elements of at least two of these concepts. To give a sense of the possibilities for experiments and innovation, I will point out some of the more prominent examples.

BITKEEPER. As a technical solution to the "Linus doesn't scale" problem, Larry McVoy wrote Bitkeeper, which has evolved into a very sophisticated code base management tool, a scaffold for development teams that work with a continuously changing base of code, patches, and updates. McVoy's company, Bitkeeper.com, has a "stated goal of all free software projects using our system."[11] Accordingly, the software for Bitkeeper is freely available along with the source code. The license allows for modifications of the code but with a key restriction: Modified versions must pass a regression test to demonstrate that they are compatible. Many other open source licenses (for example, for Perl) require regression tests, but a modified version that fails the test simply loses the right to use the original name. If a modified version of Bitkeeper fails the test, it may not be used at all.[12]

This licensing provision protects a critical part of the Bitkeeper system, which lies at the core of a clever business model. Bitkeeper has a logging feature that keeps track of all changes to the code base and logs these changes onto a central server. That log is openly available on the web so anyone can see precisely what is happening with any development project that is using Bitkeeper to handle its code. That presents no problem for open source projects; in fact, it's an advantage because it simplifies communication among developers. The trick is that proprietary software development projects would also like to use Bitkeeper because the technology is good. But a proprietary software company is not going to want to have its change logs open on the web for anyone to read; that would almost be the equivalent of giving away source code. Here is the innovative business model idea: Bitkeeper offers a commercial version to any company that wants to pay for it. The commercial version keeps the change log private and thus protects the secrecy of the development process. The model is sometimes called commercially crippled software—if you want to use the code for commercial software development, you have to pay for the privilege.[13] One purpose of the license restriction is to protect this feature: The regression tests check to make sure that no modifications are made to the logging feature.

The commercially crippled business model combines elements of the loss leader, service, and sell it, free it ideal types in an interesting way. The core idea is to build a fantastic product that everyone wants to use, and then find in that product a feature that benefits the open source community but is a liability for non–open source users, such that the latter group would pay to remove it.

VA LINUX. Founded in 1993, VA Linux had the core idea of using open source software to anchor sales of integrated web business infrastructure, combining hardware and software. The company had three arms. The "systems" division built servers and storage systems and other pieces of hardware, optimized for use and delivered in an integrated way with Linux and other major open source software packages. The consulting division sold a typical range of services—integration of hardware and software, porting open source software to particular hardware configurations, troubleshooting, and support. And OSDN (Open Source Developers Network) ran a series of websites (including SourceForge and Slashdot) and conferences that became the meeting places, communication tools, and collaborative work platforms of choice for many programmers.

The underlying experiment was to capitalize on synergies between the three arms of the business. A customer would be able to turn to VA for a complete Linux-based solution—VA servers running customized software, supported by expert consulting services, and with the underlying foundation of OSDN's development capabilities and proselytizing of the open source model. OSDN was in a real sense the glue that held the strategy together. To keep the open source community on board and supportive of what VA was doing, OSDN was designed explicitly to maintain the "brand" identity of the developers and engineers who wrote the software, rather than VA's brand *per se*. To the extent that OSDN could provide useful tools to software developers and enhance their reputational payoff, VA would benefit from the overall growth of the market in open source solutions. It made sense for the same reasons for VA to hire and pay a number of prominent open source programmers (including Jeremy Allison and "Maddog" Hall).

RED HAT SOFTWARE. In 1995 Marc Ewing and Robert Young founded Red Hat Software to make Linux easier to install, use, and maintain for systems administrators. To start, they packaged a Linux distribution with some additional applications and good documentation, offered initial technical support, and sold the whole thing for about $50. In part because of the auspicious timing (they got started just as the popularity of Linux was about to explode) and in part because the Red Hat package was technically good and really was easier to use, the company quickly became the leading Linux-based operating system supplier. This early success allowed Red Hat to expand its business model by taking advantage of its clear market leadership. But the form of that advantage was distinctive. Because all the software that Red Hat sells and writes is licensed under the GPL, Red Hat does not in the traditional sense "own" any intellectual property. Red Hat has became a de facto technology standard, but not because it can exclude other companies or individuals from appropriating its technology. Instead, Red Hat has become a standard by virtue of its brand. The value of the brand is partly like the value of any other brand in a commodity market: It promises reliability, extensive testing, ongoing support, and confidence that when you "call the 800 number, someone will answer the phone." The brand has also some particular self-reinforcing advantages to Red Hat. By scaling quickly—expanding the market and taking a small amount of revenue from a large number of transactions—Red Hat can (and does) earn funds to invest in new open source software development, which it gives back to the community under the GPL. This is part of an explicit strategy to maintain a synergistic relationship with the open source community. Red Hat funds the salaries of several top-tier Linux developers. This is obviously a way to ensure the health of the underlying intellectual property foundation.

But it is also partly a branding strategy in and of itself. For many corporate customers in particular, Red Hat has become the de facto institutional "face" for open source software. When in early 1998 Intel started getting requests from some of its high-end customers for porting its key chips' math libraries to a "new" operating system (Linux), Red Hat emerged quickly as the partner of choice. In September 1998, Intel (along with Netscape and two major venture capital firms) made a large strategic investment in Red Hat.[14] Success built on success, as is often the case with brands. When Dell, Compaq, and IBM decided to offer Linux on some of their mainstream hardware systems, Red Hat was their obvious partner. The same was true when Home Depot, Toyota, and Fidelity decided to switch to open source software for key enterprise applications.

It is easy to understand Red Hat's business model in semitraditional terms. Red Hat takes a free operating system and enhances it with tested, compatible middleware applications to create what IT users sometimes call a single stack solution to a core business function. As an assembler, integrator, and supporter of freely available components, Red Hat originally got paid as a more efficient outsourcer for things that a customer could in principle do on its own. Red Hat is now moving some of these core functions into an online service model, mimicking the move that other software vendors are making away from selling discrete products and toward selling software services over time. At the same time Red Hat is customizing versions of Linux to run on new client platforms, such as small Internet appliances and next-generation cell phones.

But there is something else to the Red Hat business model, harder to define in traditional terms and less immediately important to large corporate customers but essential to Red Hat's position. If Red Hat Linux makes it on to the PC desktop of individual users in a significant way over the next few years, it will not be simply because the Red Hat Package Manager makes Linux easier to install, or because Red Hat Linux is "better" for the individual user than Windows XP. It will be in part because of symbolism, the feeling and experience that people get (and pay for) when they buy Red Hat. In this manifestation the brand is not just about selling software; it is about selling a certain experience, a virtual ticket to the open source revolution. In this sense a Red Hat T-shirt is not just an advertising gimmick but also an essential part of the experience, the sense of belonging to a movement. If this sounds somehow "fuzzy," simply transpose the story onto a luxury good like a watch, designer blue jeans, or high-end automobile. In fact, selling something as a branded experience is an increasingly common source of value in modern economies. Software may very well have been a laggard in this sense up until now, because it didn't function well enough for anyone to worry about the fuzzier elements of the "experience" (the customer was happy if the software did what it was supposed to do most of the time). As the technology improves, the experience becomes more important relative to the core functionality.

APPLE COMPUTER. This company's newest desktop operating system, OS X, is built on top of two key open source systems.[15] The core of OS X, called Darwin, combines code from the Mach 3 microkernel developed at Carnegie Mellon University, and FreeBSD 3.2. Both are open source programs, and Apple has released Darwin as open source under a BSD-style license as well.[16] Why the break with Apple's tradition of developing its own operating system software and keeping the code secret? In fact the old Macintosh operating system, visually elegant as it was, lacked two essential modern capabilities—protected memory and preemptive multitasking—both of which were present in open source Unix-style systems.[17] Steve Jobs, who returned to Apple as interim CEO in 1997, brought with him engineers from his previous company NeXT, who had built that company's operating systems (Openstep and Nextstep) around 4.3BSD. When this group started to think about designing a next-generation operating system to fuel Apple's revival in the marketplace, they turned to open source as the "most natural way to do things" (though it certainly was not "natural" for Apple).[18] Apple moved decisively to build a cooperative relationship with the BSD community by releasing its source code modifications (not necessary under BSD-style licenses, of course). It hired Jordan Hubbard (a major open source developer and a cofounder of FreeBSD) to work on OS X and manage the relationship with the BSD community. And it promoted OS X to that community as a "great example of BSD running on the PowerPC platform."[19]

Apple has not released proprietary higher-level software that runs on top of Darwin (such as the Aqua graphical user interface) as open source. Hubbard has argued explicitly that Apple should do so—in fact, that it should open source its entire operating system.[20] The logic of the argument is that Apple could leverage its customer loyalty and the tremendous amount of good will it would generate among developers to seize technological leadership in desktop operating systems and break open the dominance of Microsoft at the same time. Here is the positive scenario: Application developers switch from writing for Windows to writing for Mac OS because they have full access to the source and greater confidence that market share will be there; volunteers step up to port Mac OS to multiple hardware systems (including, of course, the Intel chips that run Windows); Apple continues to sell OS X with a newly enhanced brand along with leading-edge applications and elegant, beautifully designed hardware to run OS X; and the Windows market share shrinks over time in favor of Apple. This would be a revolutionary move, particularly for Apple, and the company does not officially acknowledge that it is under consideration. But the logic of such an experiment makes sense from the perspective of an innovative open source business model.

IBM. IBM at the start of 2000 announced a major integrated strategy initiative around open source software, pulling together elements that had been developing within different parts of the company. IBM's commitment, on the order of $1 billion over several years, represents a bet that Linux (as a discrete technology certainly, and as a representative of a process of development most likely) is fundamentally disruptive to the computing industry, possibly as disruptive as the Internet. IBM's commitment to open source now stretches across the company. In addition to porting Linux onto its major mainframes and servers, IBM now offers all of its major enterprise applications built around a Linux platform. The key middleware for web-enabled business, including advanced databases, web services, e-commerce, infrastructure management, security, and so on, run as a portfolio on IBM machines on top of Linux. IBM is leading a major technology initiative around grid computing, using open source software as the key technology engine. (Grid computing is an old idea for harnessing shared computer resources around the Internet to handle extraordinarily demanding processing tasks.[21] The SETI@home program, which uses distributed computing power sitting in millions of desktop PCs to process data from radio telescopes, is one example.) The company is trying to build an open source development process around software for web services along with a wide variety of partners to compete primarily with Microsoft's .Net initiative.[22] And it has invested heavily in a Linux technology center, an Open Source Development Lab (in collaboration with other IT vendors), and competency centers for Linux, all in the interest of expanding the size and expertise of the pool of developers who write for open source projects.[23]

SUN MICROSYSTEMS. This company, despite its strong roots in BSD Unix, for many years had an ambivalent relationship with the open source community. Integrity of source code has been a key issue, in particular after Sun sued Microsoft for breaching a 1996 deal on the use of Sun's JavaScript code within Internet Explorer (Sun accused Microsoft of manipulating the source code in an attempt to "embrace, extend, and extinguish" the developing standard around Java).[24] Nonetheless, Netscape and Novell as well as other companies that saw themselves as fighting the dominance of Microsoft put increasing pressure on Sun to make public the source code for Java, as a defense against Microsoft's efforts. Key people at Sun (including Bill Joy) were open to the idea, while concerned about the complexity of managing

Sun's existing licensing agreements and the possibility of losing control over the integrity of the code.[25] Meanwhile the Free Software Foundation was aiming to produce an open source clone of Java (which turned out to be a very difficult project).

From mid-1998 on, Sun struggled to find a "third way" for open source through which it could maintain control over the code base and capture royalties from the resale of programs based on Sun software even after it released the source code for those programs.[26] In the summer of 1998 Sun published the source code for Jini (a communications standard for devices of various kinds) while retaining copyright and royalty privileges from third-party resales. At the end of 1998, Sun announced that it would do the same for Java 2.0. And in January 2000 Sun released the source code for its operating system Solaris 8 with modified restrictions: Sun eliminated end-user license fees but retained control over redistributed code. In other words, source code was free to customers and could be modified for their internal use, but Sun did not include the right to redistribute modified source code outside the enterprise. The open source community was ambivalent in return and sometimes openly dismissive of this strategy.

Evolution of Experimentation

For much of 1999, American venture capitalists and the NASDAQ market acted as if open source were a guarantee of financial success. Reality set in slowly. The fate of Netscape's Mozilla initiative was an important psychological watershed. When Jamie Zawinski resigned from Mozilla exactly one year after Netscape released the source code, he wrote in a widely read letter that "the project was not adopted by the outside." Only about thirty outside contributors joined the hundred or so Netscape engineers working on the project. The source code, in a significant sense, kept them away—because the original code was written under intense time pressure in a proprietary setting, it was too complicated and full of shortcuts and holes, even after much of it was cleaned up for the open source release. The licensing issues turned out to be harder and more awkward than expected. The technology progressed slowly. Zawinski expressed a worry that other developers felt as well—the project might never really gel into anything other than a series of imperfect beta releases. Although Zawinski and other

Mozilla employees joined many commentators within the broader open source community to make the point that this story should not be read as a more general failure for open source (and in fact they had good arguments behind that point), that is precisely the way many outsiders interpreted it.

And then, of course, the broader market bubble burst. Sky-high valuations for open source companies like Red Hat and VA Linux crashed down to earth as investors recalibrated their expectations about the potential profitability of these business models (and, importantly, the time frame within which profits could be realized). If 1999 was the year that open source could do no wrong, 2000 was the year in which open source could do nothing right, at least in the eyes of investors.

The real story became more interesting in 2001 as open source companies shifted strategies and built new experiments that pushed the possibilities of their business models. In many instances this had the effect of bringing the community of developers into closer and more intricate interaction with traditional economic structures, along with standard measures of investment, expenditures, and profits. MandrakeSoft began to sell a software subscription service for regular updates. Turbolinux pushed higher-level customized applications at a higher price. And VA Linux began to sell proprietary software along with its open source offerings.[27] At the same time, open source continued to find its way more deeply into large established companies, in part via the migration of young programmers from failed startups who often brought with them some piece of the open source gospel.

Several developments illustrate the evolution of open source business models in this direction. The first was the increasing importance of powerful database programs in open source, most notably MySQL. MySQL is a sophisticated open source database server that competes with products like Oracle, Sybase, and Informix database systems to run the backend of data-intensive websites, data warehouses, and other mission-critical business applications. MySQL AB, the Swedish company that owns the source code and the trademark, offers a dual licensing scheme: The software can be downloaded freely under the GPL or purchased under a commercial license (for users who do not want to be bound by the GPL.)[28] Although MySQL was somewhat slow to incorporate support for new advanced features (transactions across different servers, user-defined functions, and other changing market demands), it is a fast, stable, and extremely efficient mainstream database for most information and content storage applications. Yahoo, Motorola, NASA, and Texas Instruments top the list of MySQL's approximately 2 million registered installations.

The second important development was the growth in value-added resellers (VARs) and integrators who specialize in supporting and customizing open source software for small- and medium-sized users (not just the largest end-user companies, which tend to have relationships with the major Linux distribution vendors like Red Hat). VARs are specialists; some support very small end users; others focus on a specific market niche with a vertically integrated set of functions. A more developed market ecology would have the largest distributors and support vendors backstop the smaller VARs by providing them with pooled technical assistance and marketing support, in return for fees and for gaining access to information about a much broader group of users than the big vendors can access directly. Caldera and Red Hat began to move in this direction during 2001.

Third was increasing and broader interest in using the open source process for developing new software applications. Collab.net, a company started by Brian Behlendorf, Tim O'Reilly, and others in 1999, experimented with different ways to play the role of an intermediary in this process. The original idea behind Collab.net was to create a liquid market for open source programming skills, called Source-Xchange. A company wanting a particular piece of software written would post a request for proposal (RFP), which developers would then bid on. Code would be peer reviewed; skills inventory and rating systems for developers would emerge over time; and a body of code would be built up as a feedstock for reuse and innovation, presumably lowering development costs for companies in the market. Source-Xchange didn't attract enough attention to generate the liquidity that would have made a market like this viable. The idea was modified into Sourcecast, a collaborative software development platform that can be used internally by companies to mimic key elements of the open source development process in a controlled space (or "walled garden"). Collab.net offered in addition specific consulting services aimed at training leaders and "communities" within corporations in the skills and norms of the open source process. In practice, Collab.net was experimenting with the boundaries of how far principles of open source collaboration could be extended into core practices of the enterprise.

Fourth was the changing attitude of Sun Microsystems toward open source. In early 2002 Sun significantly eased licensing rules on Java, in a clear bid to attract open source developers to a standard that could counterbalance Microsoft's effort to dominate web services through .Net. In February 2002 Sun announced an important broadening of support for Linux, particularly for embedded systems and edge servers, which provide lower-end and less complicated services than Sun's high-end hardware running its proprietary Solaris software. Sun decided also to port many of its key software application packages to run on Linux, to enhance Linux application compatibility in Solaris, to invest in several Linux technology companies, and to extend contributions of source code to open source projects like GNOME, Mozilla, Apache, and others.[29] In summer 2002 Sun released its first server with Linux as an up-front choice of installed operating system (as well as its proprietary Solaris system). In effect, Sun was acknowledging and hedging against the possibility that even the most complicated enterprise computing tasks would soon be manageable on clusters of Intel-based servers running Linux.[30]

Legal Structures

The legal structures that impinge on the open source process cover as broad a range of issues as do business models. We are still at a very early stage at which the most significant points of contact between open source and the law have arisen over basic questions about protection. The important questions are about different ways people think about "protecting" intellectual products—what there is to protect, what protection means, and why a legal structure is a sensible way to provide protection. Notice that I did not say "intellectual property." I take that term to be a legal construction rather than a natural or given state of affairs.[31] At a deeper level, the legal debates that use the term "intellectual property" are embedded in notions of human and organizational motivation connected to particular notions of property. They are also embedded in core beliefs about effective strategies for managing conflicts of interest and values, conflicts that are almost an inevitable part of the creative-economic process.

To track what the courts are saying about a particular case at a particular time would guarantee the obsolescence of this book on the day it was published, because many of these cases are live and evolving. Instead, I focus on two concepts of intellectual property under which arguments in the literature and cases brought before courts are visibly starting to sketch out the contours of how legal regimes interact with open source. These are copyright and patent law.[32]

Copyright at its core is a legal mechanism granting an exclusive bundle of rights to the creator of an original work. The bundle includes the right to make copies, to authorize others to make copies, to create certain kinds of derivative works, to perform the work publicly, and so on. The partial monopoly granted by copyright is limited in time and scope. The U.S. Constitution instructed Congress to create laws that would incentivize the creation of new works; but the framers and later legal theorists understood well that creativity depends on access to previous works. Hence the logic of fair use (limiting the scope of the monopoly) and of a copyright that expires after some specified period of time. Courts constantly reinterpret the precise terms, but the core of the bargain remains anchored in the idea that some balance needs striking between exclusive rights provided to incentivize creativity and the freedom of others to build on what an artist, scientist, or author has created.

Copyright law has typically been the favored means of legal protection for software. The logic of using copyright is linked to the distinction between "expressions" (which copyright protects) and "ideas," which it does not. This dichotomy is often difficult to apply in practice; it has many complications and subtleties that provide a continuous stream of case law and interpretations marking out the precise boundary. Is the presentation of data in overlapping windows on a computer desktop an idea or an expression?[33] But in its abstract articulation, copyright does make sense for software. Many of the tasks that software allows computers to do are not really new ideas—for instance, filing data in a retrievable form, or moving words in a document from one place to another. The expression of those ideas in software code is a demanding, creative act. As Eben Moglen argues, computer programs take more space and effort to explain to humans what they are doing than they do to instruct the computer what to do.[34] Programming thus has several important elements of expression within it. And copyright seems a sensible means to manage the balance between incentivizing an author to create new code and ensuring that others have free access to the underlying idea and can make fair use of what is created.

Open source licenses generally depend on copyright law for their claim to enforceability. The rationale for this use is simple and exceedingly clever. Copyright, by default, does not allow redistribution (nor even use) of software. The copyright holder grants specific permissions when he or she licenses the software to a user. The license can require the redistributor to fulfill certain conditions. Typically those conditions reserve certain rights for the original author. The GPL uses the same mechanism but twists it to ensure that redistribution remains free. The GPL offers to the user permission to copy, distribute, modify, and redistribute software code, but only under its specific conditions—that is, the inclusion of source code and the transfer of the GPL to derivative works. A breach of these licensing provisions would presumably constitute copyright infringement. And because the Free Software Foundation encourages authors of GPL code to assign their copyright to the Foundation, there would presumably be an aggrieved party with the standing to bring suit against a transgressor.

The GPL has not been fully tested within the courts and opinions range as to its legal enforceability (though they weigh heavily toward a positive view on that question).[35] In practice the GPL "works" in the sense that people generally comply with it. And in cases in which there have been questions, the Free Software Foundation has brought possible violators into compliance with the threat of a lawsuit. Probably because enforcement has taken place in the form of bargaining outside the courts, many of the operational complexities of "copyleft" have not been worked out in a generalizable way. For example, the practical distinction between static and dynamic linking of code is often fuzzy, and there are real arguments over what constitutes a copy of a software program. But there remain also fundamental questions about how the GPL copyleft "regime" will interact with a legal system built around a different and increasingly more restrictive notion of intellectual property. Two central issues here are the significance of anticircumvention provisions in laws such as the Digital Millennium Copyright Act and the standing of non-negotiated licenses.

The delicate balance of copyright depended in a peculiar way on the physical difficulty of replicating and distributing intellectual products. The containers that held the intellectual product (physical books, vinyl records, and so on) were difficult and expensive to copy. Digital technologies upset that balance in several ways, by making it possible to produce a perfect replica of the content, to make an infinite number of such copies, and to distribute them across a network instantaneously at nearly zero cost. What in the past might have been a noncommercial act of infringement (making a bootleg tape) now poses a disproportionately large threat to the fundamental logic of the copyright regime, because the impact of a single violation could in principle be exponentially greater.

The U.S. 1998 Digital Millennium Copyright Act (DMCA) was a major effort to recapture the core logic and "make the digital environment safe for the sales of copyrighted works."[36] It is an enormously controversial effort that has been criticized from all sides. But the strategy behind the DMCA is clear: The law essentially tries to constrain technologies that are thought to pose a threat to the copyright regime, rather than punish conduct in violation of copyright *per se*. The justification for this idea is the necessity of preemption: The nature of digital technology demands technical incapacitation of possible violators before they act, instead of relying on the threat of liability after the fact as a deterrent.

One of the DMCA's most important provisions is the anticircumvention clause, which prohibits decryption of copyright-protection measures with only a narrow set of exceptions. Thus, if I deliver to you an encrypted DVD, it is illegal for you to decrypt the protection because doing so creates the possibility (although not necessarily the conduct or even the intention) of copyright infringement. What really poses a problem for the open source process is the part of the law's provision that goes a step further and prohibits the creation or distribution of utilities or tools for this type of decryption, and apparently without exception. Put simply, if I place a digital lock on a copyrighted work, it is not only illegal for you to break that lock but also illegal for you to build or distribute a piece of software that is capable of breaking that lock. These restrictions hold regardless of your purpose or intention.

In principle, the DMCA gives copyright owners a strong claim on the right to define and enforce exclusive intellectual product rights that extend far beyond the standard copyright bargain. A number of cases have been brought before the courts in efforts to clarify just what this anticircumvention provision means in practice.[37] One of the most controversial cases (and one of the most significant for the open source community) is the so-called DeCSS case. CSS (content scramble system) is an encryption scheme that restricts the playback of DVDs to machines that are equipped by the manufacturer with a CSS unscrambler. In October 1999, a 15-year-old Norwegian named Jon Johansen posted on the Internet source code for a program (DeCSS) that allowed the playing of an encrypted DVD on a player without CSS.[38]

DeCSS was originally designed to let programmers create a DVD player that could be used on computers running Linux. It could thus have a perfectly legitimate use—for example, if I owned a DVD movie and wanted to watch that movie on my laptop computer that runs Linux as its operating system. But under the DMCA, the potential for illegitimate use of DeCSS to crack an encryption scheme created grounds for a lawsuit, which the Motion Picture Association of America brought in 2000 against an online magazine and other websites that linked to the DeCSS code.[39] In November 2001 the Second Circuit Court of Appeals upheld a lower court decision that found the posting of or linking to DeCSS code in violation of the DMCA. That decision has so far stood.[40] A range of issues is at stake here, including the question of how web hyperlinks can be used, a watershed issue for the future of the web. But for the open source community the anticircumvention issue is critical, if the DMCA can be used to stop open source programmers from building systems that provide the functionalities of proprietary systems but in open code. By some reckonings, the DMCA and related laws could be used as well to limit public release of information about bugs and security holes in software products, another critical piece of the open source process.

The non-negotiated license question begins with the problem that copyright law anticipates the sale of a physical copy of an intellectual product to a purchaser. Once the sale is made, the copyright owner has in effect exhausted the right to control distribution of the work, under the "first sale" rule. The purchaser can then (with a few exceptions) lend, rent, or resell the purchased copy. This is what bookstores and libraries do with books, and it clearly serves the interest of disseminating information more widely. Does the first sale rule apply to digital information, which is often licensed, not sold *per se?* Licenses represent a more limited transfer of rights, to use the product only under stated conditions. Licenses are covered by contract law and thus are typically thought of as representing a meeting of the minds between the parties that agree to the license. This question raises several problems for software licensing that are particularly important for open source.

The first problem is whether non-negotiated licenses have legal standing. The courts have at times questioned the validity of shrink-wrapped mass commerce licenses or the so-called click-through license procedure because each effectively sets the terms of use for an information product on take-it-or-leave-it terms without negotiation and thus presumably without a meeting of the minds between parties to the contract.[41] It is also contentious to what extent contracts of this sort, which are in effect a one-sided amendment to the terms of sale agreed on between buyer and seller at the time of purchase, can legally override public policy considerations that would limit the possible agreed terms. More simply, can a click-through or mass-market license restrict uses that would normally be permitted under fair use and other limits on copyright law?[42] Can a seller offer such terms, and does the buyer have the right to agree to them, particularly under the procedure that use of the software is equivalent to an assent to the terms?

One of the serious problems with UCITA—the Uniform Computer Information Transactions Act, a proposed state contract law that intends to revise the Uniform Commercial Code—is precisely that it could be used by licensors to do things like disavow any liability for flaws in a program, prohibit reverse engineering of code, change the terms of a license retroactively, and prohibit licensees from describing or criticizing what they find to be flaws in the licensed material. Most open source software developers and advocates strongly oppose UCITA, for obvious reasons, particularly the reverse engineering clause. But the GPL has its own issues as a de facto mass market license. Article 6 reads:

> You are not required to accept this license, since you have not signed it. However, nothing else grants you permission to modify or distribute the Program or its derivative works. These actions are prohibited by law if you do not accept this license. Therefore, by modifying or distributing the Program (or any work based on the Program), you indicate

your acceptance of this License to do so, and all its terms and conditions for copying, distributing or modifying the Program or works based on it.

In effect the GPL depends on a contract that trumps the default rules of copyright. The obligation to give back to the open source community comes from the license terms, not general copyright law. Apart from the take-it-or-leave-it issue and the ability of a mass-market license to require these restrictive terms, the GPL is also potentially vulnerable on the issue of warranties. Article 12 explicitly disclaims all warranties for GPL software "to the extent permitted by applicable law" on the grounds that "the program is licensed free of charge." But what is (or ought to be) permitted in this regard is not entirely clear. The open source process relies on the principle that all software is always a beta release. And open source business models often rely on the intuition that if I give away a program for free, I should be able to disclaim any warranties, but then provide support (including warranties) for a fee because that is a separate service. There is the additional problem of who would be responsible for a warranty when the software is a combined product of the work of many volunteers, outside of a corporate structure. Yet public policy considerations have generally favored the idea that there are both express and implied warranties in the act of releasing a product and that licenses (particularly non-negotiated licenses) should not be permitted simply to renounce those warranties.

An equally important issue arises over the binding of third parties. If the GPL passes muster as a valid contract, it can reasonably bind the parties that are contracting with each other to make use of GPL code. But what about third parties, in particular subsequent users of GPL code, who are required by Article 7 of the GPL also to adhere to its conditions?[43] This provision (the viral clause) is a central part of the community's structure—it guarantees, in effect, that a user is free to do whatever he wants with the code with the exception of depriving others of the right to do the same. The binding of third parties to an agreement like this is more like a property right, as I have said, just one configured around distribution rather than exclusion. It is closer to a "covenant running with the land" than it is to a typical contract. But it is not clear if the law provides for such covenants when it comes to information and intellectual products like software.

The general issue of patent law in software is equally fraught. In principle patents cover inventions and new processes, not expressions *per se*. The general standard for patent protection is that an invention must be useful, novel, and nonobvious. Patent law grants a monopoly that is shorter in time than copyright but broader in scope—because a patent protects the underlying idea within the invention, not just the specific invention itself. The basic bargain is that the patent holder publicly discloses the invention and receives in return a temporary exclusive right to make, sell, or license others to make or sell the patented good. Is software a patentable invention? Until the early 1980s, the consensus answer to this question in both the United States and Europe was, "probably not."[44] Over the course of the 1980s, however, the U.S. Court of Appeals for the Federal Court gradually removed limitations on the patenting of software in a set of decisions that culminated in the famous 1998 State Street Bank decision, which overturned the prohibition on the patenting of mathematical algorithms and business methods.[45]

Many theorists and many software companies as well continue to oppose the patentability of software, for reasons that parallel arguments made against software patents in the 1980s. The temporary monopoly that a patent grants is justified as an appropriate reward for the extensive capital and human resources that an inventor must invest in creating, producing, and distributing an invention. The simplest argument against software patents is that the software industry is different—innovations occur rapidly, they can be made without substantial capital investment, and most importantly they tend to be creative combinations of previously known ideas and techniques. Producing and distributing a piece of software is simpler, faster, and much less expensive than the same process for almost any product of a manufacturing industry. And most software patents would in effect protect mathematical techniques or algorithms when there is rarely a substantial leap in capability but rather incremental change based on skillful combinations of many ideas. As Oracle Corporation puts it, "Whether a software program is a good one does not generally depend as much on the newness of a specific technique, but instead depends on the unique combination of known algorithms and methods."[46] There are also practical arguments that question the suitability of the patent process for managing the difficult question of searching prior art and making reasonable judgments about the novelty and nonobviousness of claimed innovations in software.[47]

But if the practice of patenting software poses complications for the strategies of major businesses, it is potentially devastating to the open source process.[48] The question becomes, Is it possible to engineer different ways of implementing an algorithm or protocol in software code; or can the person who wrote the first computer implementation of a particular function own a patent on that function? Will competitive technological implementations be freely allowed (new expressions of ideas, in copyright lingo), or will they be subject to control by the patent holder? Can companies charge royalty fees (even through so-called reasonable and nondiscriminatory processes) when their technologies are used in supposedly open standards for the web?[49] Remember that most software is useful only to the extent that it is interdependent with other software; patented functions can then exert considerable control over the development of other functions.

In a software patent world, large companies have resources to play in what becomes a strategic game of deterrence and cross-licensing between patent holders. Open source could get shut out of this game. Apart from the several largest open source software companies, who could afford to contest patent litigation or to buy licenses from patent holders?[50] The possible costs of patent litigation would be a powerful deterrent to most open source developers. In a peculiar way open source would probably be more vulnerable to litigation—with proprietary (and thus hidden) code, it is more difficult to tell whether a patent is being violated than with free code that is always open to inspection. Within the software industry, it is well known that patents are regularly infringed upon; this opens up the possibility of selective and discriminatory actions against open source developers, perhaps even brought by a consortium of proprietary software companies that band together for that purpose.[51] And ultimately what patent holder would be willing to grant a license to software that is distributed without restrictions?

The open source community is experimenting with a range of partial defenses against patent restrictions, including arguing against software patents *per se*. One kind of defense is inherent in the fully disclosed nature of the open source process—because the code and the mailing lists that discuss the underlying ideas are documented, it may be easier to demonstrate convincingly "prior art" in defense against a patent infringement claim. Bruce Perens suggests the notion that companies should be encouraged to license their patents for free use with open source software.[52] This could be done on a selective basis, restricting free use of patents to GPL software and thus preventing anyone from freely using patented code in other *proprietary* applications. The open source community might consider a defensive strategy of its own—for example, joining the strategic game by creating an organization that would file for patents on behalf of open source developers and by cross-licensing the open source patent pool with companies. Each of these strategies carries risks, and how they will advance depends heavily on the evolution of patent strategies of major software companies and of public policy deliberations.

Questions for the Future

Open source will impact information technology markets in surprising ways. That is certain. As the code develops, so will conceptual frames that give structure to business models and legal issues around it. There are at least three central conceptual questions that characterize these discussions now. The first is about the role of the "customer" in the production process, specifically as it plays out within business models. Open source turns what would have been called free riders into contributors to a collective good. The abstract argument holds for the open source production process overall, but it may look somewhat different from the perspective of a single company trying to make profits with open source software.

Eric Allman, founder of Sendmail, believes that from a business perspective unsophisticated customers are free riding in the classical sense and tend to degrade the value of the software.[53] His view is that these users demand disproportionate amounts of customer service and, because those services tend not to scale, the costs of providing them soon outstrip the marginal contributions that these same people might make to the development process. One obvious response is that some kinds of services are being priced too low. But that is not a trivial problem to solve in the real world, in part because services are paid for over time and thus have an open-ended character from the perspective of the buyer (while shrink-wrapped software is paid for in a single lump up front). What matters from a purely economic perspective is total cost of ownership, and proprietary software requires services as well that end up pushing total cost of ownership to many multiples of the upfront cost. But from a practical business perspective, cash flow in and out (as well as the timing and predictability of that cash flow) is an important variable. This dynamic constrains how services are priced and makes it even more difficult for companies using open source software to prosper by selling services.

There is another way to look at this problem. The service provider is in fact a service provider because that company, through its expertise, experience, and access to information systems, knows something about the software that the end user does not, something that is valuable at that one critical moment. Put simply, the provider has more domain-specific knowledge than does the end user—at least for the one specific domain in question. The user generally has some domain-specific knowledge as well that the service provider does not. The service provider arbitrages the knowledge asymmetry—but traditionally, in only one direction. That is, the company provides its domain-specific knowledge to the end user in return for money. The channels that go in the other direction—that is, where the service provider learns from the end user what she knows—are typically much weaker and are not generally used in the same way. The open source process relies in part on strengthening the same kind of channels in a different setting (the development process). Seen in this light, if the unsophisticated end user is in fact degrading the value of the software, it is mainly because the business model has not yet figured out how effectively to channel the knowledge flowing in the other direction into the software, rather than letting it be dispersed. The practical challenge is to design business models that turn this loss around and make it into an opportunity.

The second and third conceptual questions arise from interlinked uncertainties about the relationship between the business enterprise and the community that develops open source software. The intellectual and practical discourse that surrounds the issue of a commons has left an important and very basic ambiguity about how this relationship ought to be structured. The continuing legal debates about protection of software as intellectual product reflect that ambiguity.

One implicit view holds that open source software is a commons that, like the grazing pasture Garret Hardin analyzed or many environmental commons, is already "out there." Another way to put this is to say that provision of the commons is unproblematic from the perspective of the organization that wants to build a business model around it. Provision is exogenous; the problem a business has to worry about is simply avoiding degradation, and the digital nature of this particular commons makes that problem much less worrisome than the physical (and thus rival) character of Hardin's pasture. A good business model simply is one that succeeds in creating additional value on the edge of the commons.

There is a second perspective that views provision of the commons as endogenous to the larger ecology of business organizations that sit on its edge. In other words, open source software is not a "given" resource that, from the perspective of a business model, is simply there for the taking. Rather, for the business to use the commons in a sustainable fashion, it has to be deeply integrated into the developer community and the process that this community engages in to build software.

That engagement can and does take many forms. Education is an obvious one. Sun Microsystems benefits greatly from its strong connections to university training in computer science. Graduate students who cut their programming teeth on Solaris are a huge resource for Sun when they leave the university; they may come work for Sun, or buy Sun computers in their new jobs, or write applications that run first on Solaris. As Linux becomes an increasingly popular teaching tool in graduate computer science programs, a similar set of opportunities presents for open source business models.

Some of the larger open source business organizations have built relationships with the community by hiring key developers and paying their "day jobs." Other organizations have tried to act as publicity-focusing devices that enhance the reputational payoff for developers who contribute to their particular products. Red Hat took the unusual step of reserving a block of IPO shares for as many open source developers as the company could identify through Internet searches. Each strategy has its complications; for example, the IPO gambit got entangled in complex SEC rules that place strict limits on who is eligible to invest in these risky shares.[54] And even though all the software written by Red Hat employees is released under GPL and is thus freely available to the open source community, there is no doubt that paying day job salaries influences software development in directions that the paymaster values.

These conceptual ambiguities—about the relationship between the customer, the business organization, and the software development community—provide a space for new business models that continue to innovate and experiment. Much of this innovation is happening in the form of new and evolving licensing structures. Escrow agreements for source code are another area of experimentation. Some escrow agreements allow source code to be released after a specific period of time, if certain terms of a contract are broken or if the software vendor goes out of business or otherwise terminates a deal.[55] The Bitkeeper model of commercially crippled software is being worked out in other settings. Companies are testing reputation-enhancing mechanisms, market-based incentives for developers, and fresh ways to encourage the private financing of what will become public works.

One of the interesting ideas is to create a software completion bond market where developers would write free software so long as they keep getting enough money in "donations" to make it worth their while to do so. On the other side of the exchange, customers would fund the software completion bond with the guarantee of getting the money back if the software was not produced and released by a specific date. The business intermediary in this case provides the platform for the bond market—a platform that could be a thin trading function, a place where software developers announce a price structure to add particular functions or features to an open source program, or a mechanism that offers impartial standards of quality and performance that determine whether the bond should be paid off.[56] In a real sense the deflation of stock prices after 2000 has led to a healthy acceleration of this kind of organizational innovation, which is becoming at least as important to the future of the open source production process as is the evolution of the code itself.

The success of open source software clearly will have implications for industry structure and the shape of markets in computing and information processing. Some of these effects are predictable, and already visible to an extent.

At the simplest level, open source undermines the possibilities for lock-in and thus the hold-up problem that comes with proprietary technologies. Free source code removes the ability to restrict unilaterally how software is used in the future. Contrast this with the situation in which a proprietary vendor can choose not to upgrade a particular software package for use on an older or unpopular hardware platform, leaving the person owning that hardware stuck with the choice of using obsolete software or buying new computers. Another kind of holdup happens when a proprietary software vendor merges with or is bought by another company, and some set of products is cannibalized to allow another product to get to market. The economics are straight-forward: When the future of a software product depends on a single entity, that entity has extraordinary pricing power because it is de facto a monopolistic supplier to a customer that may already have huge sunk costs in the relationship. It is as if there were no aftermarket parts suppliers for your particular automobile—once you bought your Saab, you could only buy Saab tires, Saab windshield wipers, even Saab gasoline. And if Saab chose after two years to stop making tires for your particular model, you would have to buy a new car when the tires wore out.

In transaction cost models, the ex post possibility of this kind of holdup would constrain investment ex ante.[57] In "normal" industry set-tings, that effect should hold. But in an industry this fundamental and dynamic, it is just as likely that the "customer" would allow herself to become a de facto prisoner of the proprietary vendor because that is less risky than not making the investment and thus falling behind in critical enabling technologies. It is impossible to estimate the result-ing aggregate inefficiency of the market, but it is certainly significant, and the costs would only become greater as information technologies reach deeply into more sectors of modern economies.

The use of open source software changes the shape of the market by creating the possibility for competitive suppliers to enter and upgrade, customize, service, and otherwise work with existing software invest-ments. Now you can buy a Saab and know that even if Saab goes out of business you will be able to maintain your automobile and even up-grade it. Apart from taking out the deadweight inefficiencies that must be in place in the monopolistic market, it seems certain that the over-all investment in information technologies will expand when open source is available (just as people will buy more cars when there is an active independent service and aftermarket parts sector) because the ex ante disincentives to invest are reduced.

At the same time, it is clear that profit in the system will be distrib-uted away from the pseudomonopolistic software vendor. The balance of power in the market could begin to shift back toward hardware manufacturers, most of whose products have been commoditized over the last decade. If open source software becomes a standard in a segment of the market, hardware manufacturers will be left to distinguish themselves through optimizing the particular configuration of a piece of hardware that integrates with the now-commoditized software in exactly the way that the customer desires. Design and aesthetics (as Apple emphasizes) as well as financing and servicing contracts could become more important distinguishing features—much as they are in the auto and airplane industries. A consolidated mainstream hardware industry could coexist with a set of niche producers who build systems optimized for unusual applications in smaller market segments. Independent system integrators and software customizers could spring up (and die out) in a highly adaptive industrial ecology.

These are only suggestions of what is possible, not predictions. The point is to show that these kinds of market shifts are plausible, and that they would be highly disruptive changes, perhaps as revolutionary as the Internet and the web were for the information and communications industries in the mid-1990s. And no significant reconfiguration of a market comes without risks. At least two important risks can be seen with some clarity right now.

The first is a question of new market dominance: Could a company like Red Hat replace Microsoft as a dominant supplier in the market for operating systems? The deeper question is, What does market dominance imply when the product is open source software? Free source code is a commitment against some kinds of opportunism, because attempts to exploit a dominant position through lock-in won't work in a market in which barriers to entry are kept low by the availability of the code. Red Hat's firm promise to release all its software under the GPL is not only aimed at keeping the developer community on board; it also serves as a commitment mechanism against opportunism later on. Indeed it seems unlikely that Red Hat would have been able to achieve such a large presence in the market without this kind of commitment.

But there is another side to the GPL coin that is worrisome. When Red Hat releases its software under GPL, it creates a situation in which anyone else trying to build something on top of Red Hat software must also release its software under GPL. This means that any valuable innovation by another individual programmer or company can almost immediately be reincorporated into Red Hat software, removing the competitive advantage of a new entrant. That is not a problem from an industry-wide perspective; in fact, it is a core strength of open source because it guarantees the rapid diffusion of improvements.

Where it becomes a potential problem is when a company has first-mover advantages of a huge market share with the accompanying advertising, marketing, and distribution power. The Internet certainly has reduced the importance of these traditional channels to some degree, but hardly to zero. Someone else may innovate; but if Red Hat dominates the conventional marketing and distribution channels, it could be Red Hat that reaps most of the economic benefit. In principle, no one can produce anything new from Red Hat software that Red Hat can't absorb and then market more effectively. This is similar conceptually to one of the antitrust complaints against Microsoft: It integrates valuable but auxiliary functions into its operating system to undermine new entrants. The GPL in an odd way protects Red Hat's ability to do the same. The practical importance of market power concentration is certainly one of the driving forces behind the May 2002 decisions of four other Linux distributions (Caldera, Turbolinux, SuSE, and Conectiva) to develop jointly a single uniform distribution called UnitedLinux.[58]

The practical significance of this problem will depend on the degree to which branding and dominance of traditional marketing and distribution channels remain important. In a world in which so much else will have changed, it is hard to foresee the shape of this trend. But it is possible to envision a scenario in which innovation slows down because of bottlenecks in the distribution channels—bottlenecks that provide excess rents for a single dominant vendor through an odd kind of open source opportunism.

The second risk is financial. Consider the downside consequences of the commoditization of core software functionality, in the context of financial markets that have been expecting something quite different. If in several years we look back on the notion of a proprietary operating system as a quaint relic of an earlier era, then it is obvious that we are today sitting on an intellectual property valuation bubble that will have to burst. The risk becomes significant deflation in the IT sector. There is an obvious analogy to the telecommunications industry in 2001. Incumbent telecom providers and new companies in the 1990s borrowed huge amounts of money (in many cases on twenty- to thirty-year bonds) to build massive amounts of bandwidth and switches. A few years later, technological changes rendered the switches obsolete, the hoped-for demand didn't materialize, and bandwidth became essentially a cheap commodity. Many of these incumbent companies are going bankrupt, some faster than others. The investment is stranded in a world of excess supply and the bonds will not be paid back.

Might some incumbent proprietary software vendors land in the same place if the profitability of their medium- and long-term investments is undermined by the success of open source? And might some of their biggest customers end up having to depreciate large costs for software functionality that their competitors and new entrants will be able to get at much lower expense? A bust in the proprietary software market would likely have less of a wide-ranging effect on financial markets than did the telecom bust, primarily because software as an industry is barely leveraged in comparison to telecom. But it would still be a noteworthy economic event with significant implications for at least the short-term future of information technology.

These are disciplined speculations about the future of business models in open source and the possible consequences. Yet the disruptive effects of the open source production process could be as great or greater outside the information sector, at first because of the increased efficiency of information processing that will affect many other economic activities, and second because of the spread of the model of production itself to other sectors of the economy. These broader possibilities I leave for discussion in the concluding chapter.

CHAPTER 8

The Code That Changed the World?

Like many elements of the Internet economy, the media surrounds open source software with an overblown mix of hype and cynicism. These are short-term distractions from a profound innovation in production processes. Consider an analogy from *The Machine that Changed the World,* a study of the Toyota lean production system for manufacturing autos. That book made two simple and profound points: The Toyota "system" was not a car, and it was not uniquely Japanese. The parallels are obvious. Open source is not a piece of software, and it is not unique to a group of hackers.

Open source is a way of organizing production, of making things jointly. The baseline problem is that it is not easy for human beings to work together and certainly not to produce complex integrated systems. One solution is the familiar economy that depends on a blend of exclusive property rights, divisions of labor, reduction of transaction costs, and the management of principal-agent problems. The success of open source demonstrates the importance of a fundamentally different solution, built on top of an unconventional understanding of property rights configured around distribution. Open source uses that concept to tap into a broad range of human motivations and emotions, beyond the straightforward calculations of salary for labor. And it relies on a set of organizational structures to coordinate behavior around the problem of managing distributed innovation, which is different from division of labor. None of these characteristics is entirely new, unique to open source, or confined to the Internet. But together, they are generic ingredients of a way of making things that has potentially broad consequences for economics and politics.

This book explains the open source process—how it came to be, how it operates, how it is organized. I put forward a compound argument about individual motivations, economic logic, and social structure to account for a process that reframes the character of the collective action problem at play. This argument yields insights into the nature of collaboration in the digital political economy. It also yields insights about how human motivations operate in that setting and the possibilities for conflict management that result. At a minimum, these are pragmatic demonstrations about a production process within, and as a product of, the digital economy that is quite distinct from modes of production characteristic of the predigital era. There are broader possibilities. The key concepts of the argument—user-driven innovation that takes place in a parallel distributed setting, distinct forms and mechanisms of cooperative behavior regulated by norms and governance structures, and the economic logic of "antirival" goods that recasts the "problem" of free riding—are generic enough to suggest that software is not the only place where the open source process could flourish.

There are many things that this book does not try to be. It is not a detailed ethnography of the communities that build open source software. It is not an extended analysis of the practical business and management issues that open source raises. It is not a book about theories of innovation, intellectual property rights, or copyright *per se* (although I touched on each of these). And it is not a claim that open source is necessarily a good thing, a morally desirable thing, or an antidote to undesirable things that are happening in the information economy.[1] The open source story can be mined for insights and arguments as well as normative claims in each of these areas as well as others, and I hope that these disclaimers will be seen as an invitation to others.

For a political economy audience in particular, I need to emphasize that this book also is not an attack on rational choice models of human behavior and organization. There are strong intellectual, disciplinary, and even emotional attachments to rational choice explanations, about which I am frankly agnostic. In my view it is the substantive content of the terms in the explanation that matters, not how it is or can be labeled. I do not see evidence for an explanation based on altruism, which (in some formulations, but of course not all) stands opposed to rational behavior. A minimal and reasonable standard of rational behavior to me means that individuals respond to their environment, compare the costs and benefits of a behavioral choice, and will not choose to do actions that have more costs than benefits.[2] That is simply a way of asking, What are their motivations, how do they make sense of what they are doing, and how does it add up to a choice, individual and social? Clearly, a great deal of human behavior is not motivated by narrow rationality concerns. The vast majority of human behavior is never monetized. Most art is not sold but simply given away. Only a tiny proportion of poetry is ever copyrighted or published. And most software code has never and will never see the inside of a shrink-wrapped box.

At the same time, computing and the creation of software have become deeply embedded in an economic setting. The money stakes are huge. The Free Software Foundation (among others) condemns this fact from a moral perspective, but that does not make it untrue. An uneconomic explanation of open source, if such a thing really were possible, would probably be uninteresting and also probably wrong. The challenge is to add substantive meaning to a rational and economic understanding of why the relevant individuals do what they do, and how they collaborate, in open source.

The perspective I have adopted is limited in these ways, but it does yield some interesting implications. I begin this concluding chapter with a set of ideas about the political economy of the Internet, concentrating particularly on the logic of distributed innovation, and the meaning and function of the commons in economic and social life. I then consider some general lessons about cooperation, how power relates to community structures, and the next phase of information technology–enabled economic growth in both developed and developing economies. The final sections take up two important issues that open source raises for political economy and particularly international politics. The first is about conceptualizing what happens at the interface between the hierarchy and the network. And the second is about hypothesizing the scope of the implications. How generalizable is the open source process and how broad might its repercussions turn out to be?

My answer, to foreshadow, has a mini-max flavor to it. Even if this were simply a story about software, the consequences are significant for the next phase of global economic growth. For international politics, the demonstration of large-scale nonhierarchical cooperation is always important; when it emerges in a leading economic sector that disregards national boundaries, the implications are potentially large. And that is the minimum case. If the open source process is a more generalizable production process that can and will spread, under conditions that I lay out as hypotheses, then the implications will be bigger still.

Rethinking Property

Open source is an experiment in social organization around a distinctive notion of property rights. Property is, of course, a complicated concept in any setting. For the moment, consider a core notion of property in a modern market economy as a benchmark. The most general definition of a property right is an enforceable claim that one individual has, to take actions in relation to other individuals regarding some "thing."[3] Private property rests on the ability of the property holder to "alienate" (that is, trade, sell, lease, or otherwise transfer) the right to manage the "thing" or determine who can access it under what conditions. Put most simply, ownership of property is the right to exclude others from it according to terms that the owner specifies.[4] This is the core entitlement that energizes the act of market exchange, with all of its attendant practices. Most of the time we are inclined to think of property in this sense and the exchange economies through which it flows, as almost a natural form of human interaction. The most obvious applications of this story are to physical widgets, but it is in no sense limited to heavy objects you can drop on your foot. With special (and limited) exceptions for things like fair use of copyrighted material, this same core concept applies to mainstream ideas about intellectual property.

Lawyers know that all of these ideas about property are problematic, but those controversies should not be taken as evidence that the underlying notions are less important in practice and in theorizing about social systems. To some big-picture economic historians like Douglass North, the creation and securing of core property rights enable the development of modern economic growth paths; their presence or absence explains why some societies are wealthy and others are poor.[5] In international relations theory, one of the essential functions of the sovereign state is to secure exclusive property rights. John Ruggie has argued that the extrusion of a universal realm along with overlapping authorities and rights lies at the heart of the historic transformation from the medieval to the modern era.[6] And in contemporary controversies around intellectual property, the notion of exclusion remains like a brick wall that other arguments keep bumping their heads up against. When you clear away all the complexity, isn't it somehow "natural" that property carries with it the right to exclude others from it, or to sell it or trade it to others in a way that transfers that right to them?[7]

Open source radically inverts this core notion of property. Property in open source is configured fundamentally around the right to distribute, not the right to exclude. If that sentence still sounds awkward, it is a testimony to just how deeply embedded within our intuition the exclusion view of property really is. With all its shortcomings, humans have built a workable economy on a foundation of property rights as exclusion. The open source process poses a provocative question: Is it possible to build a working economic system around property rights configured as distribution, and what would such a system look like? Much of this chapter tries to sketch out pieces of an answer to that question.

Recognize that open source–style conceptions of property are not at all unique to the software world. I am not talking here about the notion of gift economies.[8] I am talking about the many parts of human life that are organized around property notions more closely connected to *stewardship* or *guardianship* than to exclusion, and in particular to stewardship combined with distribution. As I said earlier, there is no state of nature in how people own things or what that means. Property is a socially constructed concept that can be and is constructed in different ways. As an example, consider modern religious traditions in the contemporary United States. What does a rabbi own, or more precisely, what is his or her property relationship to a tradition? Religious leaders at one time held essentially exclusionary keys to traditions. The Jerusalem Temple locked up the Torah within a holy of holies; only the highest priests could enter. Blessings, sacraments, and rituals were under Rabbinic control. Excommunication as it was practiced in the Catholic Church is the essence of an exclusionary property right. I am less concerned here with how these rights changed than with the stark differences they exhibit today.[9] Certainly a rabbi no longer owns a tradition in the sense that he or she can exclude you from taking a piece of it, modifying it, and combining it with other traditions in ways that suit your own needs. I have a friend who lights Shabbat candles but on Saturday night, practices Buddhist meditation, and believes very deeply in some of the core teachings of Jesus Christ. That is not exceptional; rather it illustrates the way in which people now treat notions of property around religious traditions. In effect, the property rights regime is much like open source. People take the religious "code," modify it, recombine it with pieces of code from elsewhere, and use the resulting product to scratch their spiritual itch.

It is only one small step from there to redistributing what you have created to others as a "new" religion, which is increasingly a common practice. Many established religious leaders resist these changes—understandably, because the changes profoundly threaten their basis of legitimate authority. But it is probably too late to go backward. There is too much "open code" in circulation. Technology surely enabled this change (it does matter that anyone can access any religious text in an instant on the web). But more profoundly important is the mindset change around what property rights attach to texts and traditions, which are often intricately intertwined. It is this property mindset shift that drives change in what a rabbi is. More generally, there has been a dramatic change in what it means to be a leader in a religious community. Change the foundations of property, and you change the network of relationships that radiate outward from that which is owned, in fundamental and often unexpected ways.

I will come back to this point later when I discuss power and communities; but for the moment, recognize an interesting corollary. In nonauthoritative settings—that is, in relationships primarily characterized as bargaining relationships—power derives in large part from asymmetrical interdependence.[10] Put simply, the less dependent party to the relationship (the one who would be harmed least by a rupture) is the more powerful. In the kinds of modern religious communities I am talking about here, it is the leader who is dependent on the followers more than the other way around. This dependence changes the dynamics of power. Leaders of open source projects understand the consequences intuitively—the primary route to failure for them is to be unresponsive to their followers. In Hirschman's terms, this is a community that empowers and positively legitimates exit while facilitating voice.[11] Understanding how leadership will function in a community like that is a work in progress, for the open source community, religious communities, and—just possibly—other elements of human organization as well.

How far, then, might this technologically enabled, mindset-shifting change in property rights extend? Clearly similar issues are already in play within controversies over copyright and how it is being remade in the digital era.[12] What is at stake here is more fundamental than moving the fuzzy boundaries around the idea-expression distinction or the precise parameters for what constitutes fair use. It is, instead, the logical basis of copyright as an institution. For property fundamentalists, who believe that the right to exclude others ultimately is a moral consequence of having created something, transaction cost–reducing technological innovations may shift the boundaries of fair use (often toward greater constraint), but the core foundations of intellectual property are not at risk.[13] Property fundamentalists are a minority; most theorists see copyright as a social bargain anchored in a pragmatic compromise. Particularly with digital technologies, it is inefficient to limit distribution (because the costs of nonrival distribution essentially are zero) once a digital good has been created. The pragmatic compromise was, How much excludability is needed to generate rents that can incentivize people to create in the first place?

The weights on the terms of that compromise have long been controversial, but really only on the margins (is 25 years long enough? Why not 14 or 154?). The fact is, no one really knows the terms of a creative person's utility function or how to measure the social utility that is gained from easing distribution, so the answer is a form of guesswork—or in the political process, a game of power and vested interests. Now new communities have put the basic terms of the compromise itself up for grabs, and the questions are an order of magnitude more significant. Napster was the most attention-grabbing example. What made Napster important was not its underlying technology, but rather how Napster used technology to experiment with a fundamentally different notion of intellectual property. Rather than incentivizing creativity by limiting distribution, Napster incentivized distribution and assumed that creativity would take care of itself. The record companies feared Napster not because of the technology (it's too late to do anything about that), but because of the mindshift that the experiment represented. The courts cut short the Napster experiment, but there will be others. In a real sense, open source software is a broader and longer-standing experiment in the same kind of logic. And it has worked extremely well, as the early evidence suggested Napster was doing.

These experiences imply something about property that is both simple and profound. The problem is not just that the current regime is conceptually insecure. The problem is that technology has made visible the fact that it does not work very well in practice, and that other things that are not supposed to work, do. If we find out from these kinds of experiments that some core assumptions about formulating the balance between creativity and distribution were wrong—that is, not just the weight of the terms in the bargain, but the structure of the bargain itself—then the debates over copyright extension to 50 or 100 years, or whether fair use means 1 or 20 photocopies, will seem quaint. Property rights could shift dramatically because (fundamentalism and vested interests in the political process aside), from an intellectual standpoint, there is nothing to anchor them where they are except utilitarianism. I will come back to some of the practical consequences of that for cooperation and institutions.

Organizing for Distributed Innovation

Adam Smith was a profound theorist of productivity gains from the division of labor. What then limits the degree of granularity in that division and consequent specialization? For Smith, it was mainly the extent of the market. Smith observed more finely developed divisions of labor in cities than in rural settings, and he reasoned that this was because markets were larger in cities. Since Smith, declining transportation costs have raised the effective size of markets in world trade, thereby making other limiting factors more visible.[14] Gary Becker and Kevin Murphy explicitly summarized some of the costs in a modern economy of combining the efforts of specialized workers: principal-agent problems, the possibilities for free riding, and, most deeply, the problem of coordination among complex pieces of knowledge that no one person can hold in totality.[15]

As I explained in Chapters 5 and 6, the open source process reframes the problem of free riding in fundamental ways. And distributed innovation on the open source model does not depend so heavily on bringing agents' incentives into line with those of principals, mainly because the differentiating lines between agents and principals are made so blurry. The problem of coordinating complex pieces of knowledge then becomes the key rate-limiting factor in productivity. This is not news: Friedrich Hayek understood it to be the essential problem of a "modern" economic order. He believed deeply that the price mechanism was the way to make it work.[16] Since Hayek, knowledge management theorists have raised serious doubts about the robustness of the price mechanism for coordinating complex knowledge systems. The Internet, because of the way in which it organizes intelligence and control, both makes this question of how to coordinate complex distributed knowledge more immediate, and presents partial solutions to it.

The essence of the Internet lies in an engineering principle that reflects a simple design decision by its original architects. David Isenberg calls it "the stupid network"; other terms are "neutral" network or end-to-end network.[17] Because the Internet was configured originally as a network of multiple, diverse networks, and because the architects of the Internet decided not to try to anticipate how their network might be used, they designed the protocols that are today's Internet to be neutral or "stupid." The Internet does not know what it is carrying. The intelligence and the majority of the processing power in the network are pushed out to the edges.[18] This is opposite to the switched telephone network that is made up of relatively stupid edges (your phone) and a smart network (complicated switches at the center) that make the system work by having intelligence at the center.

In networks, intelligence is a source of power and control. The phone companies control the switched telephone networks because they own the switches where the intelligence lies. In the Internet, power follows intelligence out to the edges. Barriers to entry are low and nondiscriminatory. The conduit becomes just a pipe that carries what people on the edges ask it to carry. The stupid network empowers innovators to try out their innovations without having to ask permission or procure a license from the network owner. And it is a network in which feedback moves directly from user to innovator without being filtered through a network-owning intermediary.

The open source process and the Internet share central features of an end-to-end conceptual architecture. Distributing source code and licensing it under GPL ensures low and nondiscriminatory barriers to entry. The decision about when and how to innovate then lies with the user on the edge of the network. The center does not really control the process so much as incorporate pieces of innovation into itself. And if it fails to do so successfully, a new center can always form at what was formally an edge.

Modern communications networks have done what Smith said. By reducing transaction costs and expanding the size of potential markets, they have driven more elaborate and complex divisions of labor in production. With massively reduced transaction costs, you can easily imagine breaking up a product into smaller and smaller modules and assigning each to the most efficient producer anywhere in the world.[19] Speed and efficiency go up, and costs go down. This division of labor could become very elaborate, but it would still be a division of labor in a fundamental sense. A central decision-making structure runs the process, divides and assigns tasks, and puts back together the results. Its major problem is the same as in any division of labor—getting the least efficient link in the chain to deliver.[20]

End-to-end innovation goes a step beyond simply reduced transaction costs. It enables parallel processing of a complex task in a way that is not only geographically dispersed but also functionally dispersed.[21] End-to-end architecture takes away the central decision maker in the sense that no one is telling anyone what to do or what not to do. This is the essence of *distributed innovation,* not just a division of labor. There are no weak links in this chain because there is, in a real sense, no chain. Innovation is incentivized and emerges at the edges; it enters the network independently; and it gets incorporated into more complex systems when and if it improves the performance of the whole.

That is of course an idealized version of the story. An end-to-end technological architecture may indeed be truly neutral, but technology does not exist on its own. The political and organizational interfaces that touch that technology and link it to human action typically are biased. Pricing of the Internet is a political construction, a complex legacy of telecommunications regulation that allowed a form of arbitrage on top of existing infrastructure to favor packet-switched communications. In contrast, legal structures that support large-scale production in corporate hierarchies may be biased against distributed innovation.[22] As open source software becomes increasingly mainstream in corporate applications, people have started companies to customize and service the software, and these companies have to make money, follow corporate law, and otherwise interface with conventional economic and legal systems. These constraints require (and generate) some real organizational innovation, which becomes a necessary piece of sustaining end-to-end innovation systems.

This point may seem obvious, but it is something that technology mavens often sidestep. Eric Raymond famously said about open source, "with enough eyeballs all bugs are shallow." What is clearly missing from that statement, and is ultimately as important, is how those eyeballs are organized. What happens in end-to-end systems (and the characteristics of distributed innovation) depend heavily on organization. An end-to-end network architecture does not lead directly to the social equivalent, an end-to-end organization of the institutions that use networks as tools.

The underlying problem here is to specify general organizational principles for distributed innovation, a problem-solving algorithm that works. The open source process suggests that there are four principles:

- *Empower people to experiment.* This is a familiar concept. To make it work depends on technology (people need easy access to tools) and on socially constructed incentives.
- *Enable bits of information to find each other.* This is an engineering concept. A diverse set of experiments will produce a little signal and lots of noise, and in many different places. The bits of information that are signal need to be able to find each other and to recognize each other as signal.
- *Structure information so it can recombine with other pieces of information.* This is also an engineering concept, an extension of the notion of modularization. Signals need essentially to be in the same "language" so, when they find each other, they can recombine without much loss of information.
- *Create a governance system that sustains this process.* This is a social concept, often (but not necessarily) expressed in rules and law. The GPL prevents private appropriation of a solution, which is an important part of what governance needs to do. Governance of a

distributed innovation system also needs to scale successfully (organized effectively, more eyeballs really are better than fewer). And it needs to do this at relatively low overhead costs.

Looking at this list of principles, you have to be struck by its resemblance to the algorithm represented by the genetic code. DNA "experiments" through easy mutation; pieces of information find each other through chemical bonding; the process of reproduction is exquisitely engineered to enable recombination. And there are elaborate internal governance systems—repair enzymes, immune responses, regulatory genes—that allow the system to scale surprisingly well.[23] I don't want to push this analogy too far. But because I have put more stress on the advantages, I do want to use it to suggest some of the downsides that also come with distributed innovation.

Consider, for example, the well-known problem of how systems subject to path dependency through increasing returns can lock in to suboptimal equilibrium.[24] One way to read the story of Linux is to say that the open source community has found a way to make the jump from the equivalent of QWERTY to DVORAK.[25] On that logic, other operating systems are suboptimal performers but are locked in to markets by increasing returns and high costs of switching. An aggregate jump to a more optimal performer would bring better returns in the long run but is hard to engineer due to the massive upfront investment required that no one has the incentive to provide (and the incumbent has great incentives to block). Coordinating the investment jump among all the people who would have to make it to make it worthwhile is impossibly expensive, even if there were a clear focal point for the alternative equilibrium. The system remains stuck in a suboptimal path.

But Linux is challenging that equilibrium and may overturn it in at least some market segments. If this happens, open source will have demonstrated one way to invest successfully in the jump to a higher performance path. Traditional economic analysis will suggest that this was the outcome of subsidization—after all, Linux is essentially free up front and thus the community of developers heavily subsidizes the jump. That analysis is not wrong, so far as it goes. But we should be careful not to accept typical related assumptions about the reason that subsidy is being offered. These developers are not making standard calculations about longer-term returns nor are they providing subsidies at time t=0 in the interest of later exploiting monopoly power at time t=1. Indeed, the form of the subsidy (giving away the source code) is nearly a binding commitment *not* to do that.

This sounds like good news, but there is a potential downside to this logic as well. Could an operating system market dominated by Linux get stuck over time in its own suboptimal equilibrium? The open source process is very good at debugging, but debugging an increasingly inefficient architecture at some point can become an exercise in futility. Old buildings can be renovated in many different ways, but at some point it really does make economic and aesthetic sense to knock them down and start over.[26] The winner-takes-all positive network externalities of software make this a hard problem, whether we are in a proprietary or open source setting.[27] In principle, it may be harder, not easier, for a nonhierarchical open source community to move to a fundamentally new architecture, and there may come a time when many wish there was a boss who had the authority to order that shift.

Distributed innovation systems like open source will need different organizational means of dealing with that potential trap. Linux developed an interesting mechanism fairly early in its evolution. By 1994 Torvalds recognized that the idea of a developer-user had an inherent, internal contradiction in practice. The developer wants to work on tough new problems and stretch the boundaries of what is possible; the user wants to work with a reasonably stable platform (of course, a single person could be a developer in this sense for part of the day and a user at another time). The answer was a clever organizational innovation—parallel release structures for the code base. The stable code tree is tested, "proven," and optimized for users, while the experimental code tree tries new ideas and experiments with new functionalities. This is a simple idea, but it allows Linux to satisfy two audiences with different and sometimes conflicting needs. And importantly, it also fosters synergy between them because new features are tested in the development tree first and then incorporated into the stable tree as they are proven.

The software lock-in problem is a specific example of a more general phenomenon that was crystallized by James March and later popularized by Clayton Christensen in his book *The Innovator's Dilemma*.[28] Particularly with bounded rationality at play, individuals and organizations alike face a difficult trade-off between the *exploration* of new possibilities and the *exploitation* of old certainties.[29] If you overinvest in exploration, you end up with too many undeveloped new ideas and too few working products. But if you stick with exploitation, refining and improving on the margins of what you already know, you can easily get stuck in a suboptimal trap while someone else creates something truly new. Even in substantively rational models of decision-making, the problem remains because investment in exploration is inherently risky, dependent on developments in other areas that the rational decider cannot control, and often interdependent on the investment decisions of others.

There is no clean solution to this dilemma. Christensen argues that it is the core challenge for successful business strategy; March says, "Maintaining an appropriate balance between exploration and exploitation is a primary factor in system survival and prosperity."[30] Different kinds of organizations create their own distinctive institutions to try to manage the dilemma—businesses have skunk works, academics have sabbaticals and MacArthur fellowships, and so on. Distributed innovation systems like open source have a simple advantage here that helps compensate for the inherent tendency to stick to debugging an existing architecture. Any single open source developer might suffer from individual versions of the innovator's dilemma in her own decision-making about where to invest her time, but the decision as a whole remains disaggregated among the community. Because everyone has access to the source code, anyone can make a different calculation at any time. The story of Samba TNG (Chapter 6) is a good example of this process at work. Ultimately the freedom to fork code distributes much more widely the ability to make different bets on the exploration-exploitation trade-off, and that raises the probability that on aggregate some decisions will pay off. Put simply, end-to-end innovation systems depend on a market logic of disaggregated decisions rather than on a central intelligence to manage the innovator's dilemma.

A second question about end-to-end innovation systems is how well they respond to the diverse needs of users in the many different segments of a complicated community. Placing intelligence at the edges of the network creates demands on users as well as opportunities. Open source software is sometimes criticized as "hackers writing for hackers"—in other words, making too many demands on the kind of end-user who wants technology to be plug-and-play. Clearly open source software today is stronger on the server side than it is in end-user applications; it is a favorite of sophisticated systems administrators more than the home PC user. The standard explanation for this imbalance is the motivations of the producers—hackers do prefer to write for other hackers. The technical aesthetic that the open source process depends on is more focused on solving complex programming problems than it is on engineering for convenient user interfaces and simplicity. It is true that the mainstreaming of open source products in the early twenty-first century has changed the calculus around that issue to some degree. Market challenges can be seen as technical challenges when they get sufficiently complicated. A truly elegant graphical user interface (GUI) is a technological achievement as well as an achievement of understanding the psychology and practicality of users' needs. Projects like KDE and GNOME (two GUIs for Linux) as well as companies like Red Hat and Eazel (now defunct) take on some of these challenges.

But it is possible that end-to-end innovation systems will generally underperform in these specific kinds of user interface settings, for two related reasons.[31] Some programmers believe that understanding direct user experience requires extensive physical interaction—that is, focus groups, not Internet mailing lists. The more general point here is that design for components like user interfaces still rests on the transmission between individuals of a great deal of tacit information. This requirement makes it difficult to modularize and difficult to develop in parallel distributed settings. End-to-end innovation systems lack a good mechanism for getting at the underlying concepts of tasks like this in novel ways. That may change as advances in information processing move more human experiences out of the tacit realm and into communicable forms, but for now this seems a notable constraint.[32]

A third question is how end-to-end innovation systems interact with standard-setting. Open source processes tend to be powerful magnets that attract standards to form around them. The economic logic (antirivalness, increasing returns, de facto subsidization) is part of the reason. Another part is that open source removes intellectual property barriers that create the possibility of competitive advantage for the owner of the standard. The commercialization of Linux suppliers does not change that. If Red Hat innovates and that innovation becomes popular in the market, other Linux suppliers can adopt the innovation as quickly as they wish, because they will always have access to the source code and the right to use it.[33]

In other words, releasing source code is a credible commitment against the possibility of using a standard for technological lock-in and hold up. Proprietary standards cannot make this commitment in the same way. Microsoft is often accused of mixing into so-called open standards "secret" APIs, the hooks on which developers build interacting applications.[34] Another accusation against Microsoft is that the company uses its market power to embrace, extend, and extinguish standards—for example, incorporating a standard into Windows but adding extensions to it that increase its functionality in some way but make it incompatible with other, non-Microsoft implementations. This is precisely what the open source community accuses Microsoft of trying to do with Kerberos, a standard Internet authentication protocol that provides the critical service of allowing two remote users on the Internet to verify each other's identity.[35]

These are not arcane technical issues; they have huge consequences for the evolving shape of a network economy. Consider, for example, the web browser war that erupted between Netscape and Microsoft around 1996. If that had extended into a similar war on the server side, two separate World Wide Webs—an Internet Explorer web and a Netscape web—might have been created, with all the resulting costs of duplication and lost synergies. A big reason this scenario did not happen was Apache—the open source product that came to dominate the server side and that could not be hijacked to favor either the Microsoft or Netscape browser. Companies and governments that buy large software packages for long-term use increasingly value this aspect of open source standards because it inoculates them against later exploitation of lock-in by a dominant supplier.

The market power of open source standards may also infect other kinds of software outside its immediate market. The case of Qt is an interesting example. In 1998, Linux developers were building a new graphical desktop interface for the operating system.[36] Matthias Ettrich was behind one of the most promising GUIs called KDE (K Desktop Environment) that was licensed under GPL. The problem was that Ettrich built KDE using a proprietary graphical library called Qt from a company called Troll Tech. Qt was not fully open source; it could be used freely in some circumstances, but in others Troll Tech required a developer's license at $15,000. Ettrich thought Qt was the best tool for what he wanted to do, and the license allowed him to use it, so he went forward. The promise of an elegant GUI for Linux was sufficiently powerful that some other developers were also willing to look past the problems with Qt licensing or fudge the open source definition in this one case. That temptation met very strong resistance from others in the community, who worried that KDE would succeed and that Linux would then become dependent on nonfree software. At first they tried to convince Troll Tech to change the Qt license; the proposal was that Qt would be GPL code when used in free software but would still be subject to a commercial license if it were used in a commercial product. Troll Tech demurred on the grounds that this would effectively cede control of the code base to the open source community and gut the commercial value of the product.

This looming disagreement set in motion two firm responses from the open source community. The first, led by Miguel de Icaza, was a new GUI project called GNOME that would be built on a fully free graphical library, Gtk+, as an alternative to Qt. The GNOME project immediately attracted a lot of attention and effort from open source developers and notably from Red Hat, which stuck by its strict open source commitment by contributing coders to GNOME.[37] Another set of developers started a project called Harmony, to create a fully open source clone of Qt that could be built into KDE.

As GNOME improved and Harmony demonstrated the promise that it could in fact replace Qt, Troll Tech recognized that Qt risked being surpassed and effectively shut out of the Linux market. In April 1998 Troll Tech set up the KDE Free Qt Foundation, to ensure that a free version of Qt would always be available and to commit itself against later making any claims on Qt-dependent software. Later that year Troll Tech wrote a new license called the Qt public license; in late 2000 the company decided simply to license the code under GPL.

How these dynamics are likely to affect the national and particularly the international politics of standard-setting remains unclear. These politics are typically analyzed around bargaining power between and among firms, national governments, and, to a lesser extent, international institutions. Open source adds an interesting twist. The open source community is clearly not a firm, though firms represent some of the interests of the community. And the community is not represented by a state, nor do its interests align particularly with those of any state. The community was international from the start and remains so; its motivations, economic foundations, and social and political structures bear very little obligation to national governments. We simply do not know how this community will interact with formal standards processes that remain deeply embedded in national and international politics as well as industry dynamics. (There are some relevant and researchable examples—The Linux Standard Base, Internet Engineering Task Force (IETF), and to some extent the Internet Corporation for Assigned Names and Numbers (ICANN)—but that is a subject for another book.) I will return to the question of how national governments may interact on this issue and whether it might be possible to manipulate the dynamic in ways that would yield national advantage.

My fourth point returns to the upside through a relatively narrow perspective—what might end-to-end innovation in software mean for the foundations of the information economy? Quite simply, it could be revolutionary, possibly more so than the rapid expansion of hardware capabilities has been over the last twenty years. As I said earlier, there is no Moore's Law for software. But software is the rate-limiting factor of the information economy and, as hardware capabilities continue to advance, the mismatch becomes increasingly evident.[38] Whether or not open source software will replace Windows on the desktop is irrelevant from this broader technological perspective. At a higher level of abstraction, the question becomes, Can open source software become an enabler of a next generation of information-processing and communications tools, by accelerating the rate of performance improvement in the rate-limiting step?

There are suggestions that it is already having this effect as we move toward ubiquitous computing, the presence of vast information-processing capabilities in everything humans use, from simple household appliances to distributed supercomputers. At the bottom end of this spectrum, open source programs have major advantages: They are highly configurable, cheap, and most important, available for experimentation without restrictions. An inventor who wants to build an intelligent toaster has free access to the source code of an operating system or other programs without royalties or licensing schemes. The home video recorder Tivo runs on an open source operating system built from Linux. IBM and Nokia among others are experimenting with open source operating systems for the next generation of mobile phones and communications devices.[39] In 2000 AOL announced a project to build a mass market Internet appliance on the Transmeta Crusoe chip running a scaled-down Linux and a simple open source browser. There are many such projects; what is significant in this example is that there is no Intel processor and no Microsoft software. At the higher end, the impending move to widespread use of 64-bit processors (Intel's Itanium and AMD's Hammer) puts Linux and Windows essentially on equal starting ground in the competition with Sun's 64-bit Ultrasparc servers that run Solaris (Sun's proprietary Unix).

The most interesting possibilities for acceleration are in the use of open source software in distributed or cluster computing. At the very high performance end of the computing spectrum where supercomputers build simulations of extraordinarily complex phenomena like climate patterns, the often custom-designed hardware is extraordinarily expensive and system software stands out clearly as the weakest link.[40] As early as 1994, researchers began experimenting with open source software tools to tie together large numbers of standard, off-the-shelf personal computers into a de facto supercomputer. This is called Beowulf architecture. In 1998 researchers at Los Alamos built a Beowulf-class supercomputer from 140 Alpha microprocessors running Red Hat Linux. It ran at 47.7 gigaflops, which made it number 113 in the list of the world's 500 fastest computers, and cost $300,000—about one-sixth the cost of a 48-gigaflop supercomputer from Silicon Graphics.[41] IBM's Los Lobos project in 2000 tied together 512 Pentium 3 processors running Linux and achieved 375 gigaflops, making it the world's twenty-fourth fastest supercomputer. In 2001 IBM built similar machines for the U.S. Department of Defense, the National Center for Supercomputing Applications, Royal Dutch/Shell, and others. In 2003 open source cluster computing moved to the forefront of technology for massive multiplayer online gaming, which (despite its recreational purpose) is an extremely demanding set of applications.[42]

These and many other developments in cluster computing are important not just because they reduce the price of supercomputing.

The more significant change is that cluster architecture begins to move high-performance computing into the realm of a commodity—something that can extend to lots of places and can advance much more quickly than single-application, highly customized systems. This could be as disruptive to economic and social practice as was the widespread dissemination of the desktop PC in the late 1980s. The next step, analogous to how the Internet tied together personal computers, is the move toward grid computing, whereby anyone with a simple connection to the next-generation Internet could access the mass of processing power that is distributed throughout the network.[43] Software again is the rate-limiting factor to grid computing. The emerging standard comes from the Globus project, an open source collaboration between national labs, industry, and universities.

It is easy to dream up science fiction–style scenarios about how the grid will bring supercomputing power to anyone, anywhere, and transform the way humans think, communicate, and solve problems. I don't need to indulge in that here simply to point out that the next generation of end-to-end innovation will depend on lots of software code, reliable code, but most importantly compatible code, recombinant code that interfaces straightforwardly with other code. The open source process has shown that it is possible to build this kind of code within its own end-to-end, distributed innovation setting. The next chapter in the story of distributed innovation will probably be an order of magnitude more surprising in its revolutionary implications, and make the consequences of the first-generation Internet seem quaint.

The Commons in Economic and Social Life

More than thirty-five years ago Garrett Hardin introduced the metaphor "tragedy of the commons" into common parlance.[44] He argued that resources that are rival and held in common (for example, a grazing pasture) tend to be depleted by overuse because each user passes some of the costs of use onto others. If the resources cannot be depleted (for example, a digitally encoded symphony) but need to be provided by voluntary human action in the first place, a related tragedy can develop if nonexcludability means that no one has an incentive to provide the commons good to start. Diverse theoretical and empirical critiques of Hardin's argument have chipped away at the edges, but the core insight remains powerful and central to law and economics debates about intellectual property in the digital era. Technology has brought this debate to a crossroads. It is now, or soon will be, possible efficiently to "privatize" or "enclose" all intellectual products. CDs can be copy-protected; books can have embedded chips that charge you every time you copy a page, or go back and read a page more than once; and a law like the DMCA makes it illegal to build tools that circumvent these systems regardless of how those tools are used.

It is not hard to make an economic efficiency argument that would support this kind of regime. After all, when I spend $48 for a book, I am actually buying a package of rights to use that book in a variety of ways, only some of which I might really want (for example, I might want to read only a few chapters, photocopy a particular chart, and quote one paragraph). Disaggregate these uses, charge separately for each, and a deadweight loss of efficiency can be extruded from the package. At this very stark level, there is no conceptual room left for an intellectual commons. Fair use of copyrighted materials, on this logic, exists today only because the transaction costs of making a diverse set of contracts for the limited use of the material in different ways would be prohibitively high.[45]

But this version of the efficiency argument is too monochromatic. Legal scholars have argued eloquently for the particular importance of a distinct commons in communications and intellectual property as a whole.[46] These arguments often invoke the open source phenomenon as an example of how core common infrastructures can be provided and maintained in ways that contribute to welfare while remaining outside the boundaries of what James Boyle called the "second enclosure movement."[47]

Open source code indeed mimics a commons along lines of an early FSF insight: nondiscrimination matters more than market price *per se*. The distinctiveness of the commons lies in freedom to "use" the commons without restriction, and forever. Embedded here are at least two discrete claims about the functions of a commons and why it plays a valuable, even essential role in economic and social life. These claims need to be separated cleanly so they can be developed, evaluated, and aligned against the narrow efficiency story, now that technology has made it a realistic alternative.

The first and most familiar argument is that a commons functions as a feedstock for economic innovation and creative activity. Put simply, this is the stuff that you can use to "build on the shoulders of giants" without having to ask their permission or pay them a restrictive license fee. I am not here going to take on the huge literature debating the parameters around that argument as well as the practicalities of how it could and should be implemented. I want simply to separate out and emphasize the economic logic behind the core insight, which leads to a commons producing an increase in innovation and aggregate welfare (instead of a tragedy). Think of a commons simply as a set of inputs to a production process. Now imagine privatizing some of those inputs. This would change their price and availability on the market, acting much like a tariff does in trade theory. This then changes the behavior of producers, who make substitutions. Choices about what inputs to use become biased systematically toward inputs that the producer itself owns or can easily assemble the rights to use (in other words, those without the tariff). In a world of perfect information and costless transactions, people could trade these rights and scramble their way back toward an optimal allocation of resources. In this world, the costs of inputs go up, availability becomes selectively biased, and aggregate welfare suffers.

Heller and Eisenberg call this "the tragedy of the anticommons" to distinguish it from the routine underuse that is a part of any functioning intellectual property rights system (and is justified as a bargain for incentivizing production in the first place).[48] This is not just theory; it is an increasingly visible problem—for example, in pharmacogenomics research in which complex and overlapping patent claims on genetic code make it difficult to assemble the package of rights needed to produce a drug. Benkler makes a convincing case that creative industries would tend to substitute inputs from intrafirm sources and owned inventory because they can use those inputs at marginal cost, while they would have to pay additional fees (as well as pay the extra costs of searching for and assembling rights) to the owners of other information inputs.[49] This story is clearly and powerfully applicable to software code as well.[50]

Recognize that in none of these cases is it really possible to quantify the deadweight loss of an anticommons tragedy. More importantly, it is not possible to precisely compare those costs to the incentives that might be lost (or gained) by moving the parameters of intellectual property protection. Each term in the equation is uncertain, which means that the arguments tend to corrode into rhetoric or theology.[51] Prescriptive arguments about what the law should do depend heavily on counterfactuals that are plausible but no more than that. I am not saying that public policy can be made without these kinds of arguments; clearly it is all we have to go on. I am pointing out that the innovation and aggregate welfare argument for the commons will not by itself secure its intellectual foundation against the challenge of technological change.

There is a second argument about the function of a commons that is less frequently made explicit. This argument points to the importance of participation in creative activity by individuals, simply for the sake of participation itself. In other words, creative action is an individual good regardless of whether it contributes to measurable aggregate creativity, innovation, or social welfare. We think it is important and valuable that children draw pictures of clouds even though not a single one is as good as those drawn by Van Gogh. We value the explosion of individual creativity facilitated by the web even though the vast majority of what is "published" there adds little that is measurable to society's stock of knowledge. And we value these things for their own sake, not because they can be interpreted as investments in an educational process that may later yield unspecified innovation.

These may sound like fuzzy notions in the middle of what feels primarily like an economic discourse; but they of course have a long pedigree in many different fields of thought, from developmental psychology to theories of participatory democracy, and increasingly within studies of human-computer interaction.[52] And so it is important to point out how the open source software process fits within this argument. Consider the case in favor of constitutionally protected speech, which (apart from its social value as an error-correcting mechanism) lies in part with the enhanced autonomy it confers on individuals. Speech demands a nondiscriminatory infrastructure. Software code is not precisely speech, but it is coming close in some sense to being the infrastructure for communication. Certain bodies of code are essential tools of expression, in the same way that pens and paper were for an earlier technological era. It enhances personal autonomy to own those tools, or at least to be sure that no one else owns them in a restrictive way. Would it be good for democracy if newsprint were engineered to dissolve when someone tried to photocopy it? Or if you could only write on it in particular languages?

Consider also the value of how open source facilitates competence development. I am not saying that people using Linux will become skilled programmers or that they should. I am saying that systems administrators, students, hobbyists, and the occasional end-user will be incentivized, enticed, or tempted to develop a slightly higher level of competence with their tools. At a minimum they will have the opportunity to use knowledge and resources they have at hand to try to solve a problem, a kind of personal efficacy that many people feel technology has progressively taken away from them. This too may sound romantic. But the nature of the relationship between individuals and their tools of production—a core component of political identity—does change with technology and custom, and it is not locked in by human nature. Let me go out on a limb and suggest that those who see hints of a new class ideology developing around information technology are not necessarily wild-eyed.[53] "Bit-twiddlers" are neither exactly proletariat nor bourgeoisie. They may not own the means of production in the sense that Marx argued, but they certainly do have significant control over those means, in a more profound way than the term "symbols analysts" or "knowledge workers" captures.[54] As a rough generalization, they value science and technological problem-solving elegance equally at least with profit. Technocracy rather than a hierarchy of money is their route to authority and respect. Is this the kind of "class" that Piore and Sabel, for example, believed might emerge from the second industrial divide, emerging instead from the divide between industrial and information era production? It is far too soon to say, and the prospect at least for some is far too attractive not to be skeptical of premature claims, so I simply leave this as a question.

These claims about the social and economic importance of the commons are not to say that Hardin was mistaken—rather, that he saw only part of the picture. And I am not making the argument that current intellectual property thought is "wrong." It is not wrong, but neither is it right. It simply modulates incentives to produce and distribute things in particular ways. A great deal of critical thinking has gone into sketching out the downside implications of extending the realm, scope, and time frame of exclusive intellectual property protections to digital goods. The open source process and the analytics of the commons that follows from it help to illuminate some of the upside implications of a different property rights regime. Neither regime necessarily drives out the other; they have coexisted for some time and will probably continue to do so, even though the boundaries may shift.[55] Move the boundaries and some things will not be produced. Some incentives will unravel. Something will be lost. On the other hand, something will be gained as well. It is harder in some sense to label and name those gains because we are still in the midst of developing a language to talk about them and a set of arguments to categorize and evaluate them. Discussing in explicit terms the value of a commons, including but also outside of its contributions as a feedstock for innovation, is an important part of that process.

Development and International Economic Geography

The digital divide between developed and developing countries is now a central feature of international politics and the global economy. The slogan captures a fundamental disparity in access to and the ability to use new technologies, a reflection of long-standing divides of poverty, education, and freedom to make choices. What impact might the open source process have on this set of issues?

The question is embedded in a defensible worry that digital technologies may be set to exacerbate global inequality. In fact it is easy to write a lock-out scenario in which developing economies risk falling further behind the leading edge of a digitizing world economy. The combination of Moore's Law (rapid increases in processing power at declining prices) and Metcalfe's Law (positive network externalities, meaning that the value of the network increases disproportionately as it grows) suggests that markets can grow intensively and dramatically *within* the developed world, without necessarily having to expand geographically at the same pace. As developed economies create networked purchasing and production systems that depend on advanced digital technologies, countries that are not connected on favorable terms (and firms within those countries) are deeply disadvantaged. International organizations and nongovernmental organizations are increasingly computer-enabled as well, which means they will favor interaction with countries and organizations in the developing world that are similarly enabled and can interact effectively with their information systems.

The point is that sophisticated information technology capabilities are becoming a prerequisite to effective interaction with the world economy. And while the prerequisites have grown, so have the potential downsides of lacking them. The industrial economy may have had inherent limits to growth, implying that exclusion of much of the world's population was actually necessary in some sense (it is impossible to imagine a world in which every family in China burns gasoline in an internal combustion engine). There are no such inherent limits to the information economy that we can now see. From an efficiency perspective, the possible exclusion of 4 billion people from the next era of wealth creation makes no sense. From an ethical standpoint, it is even more problematic than was the exclusion of previous eras, because there is no intrinsic environmental or resource-based reason for it.

In practice a lockout of emerging markets from the global information economy is unlikely. For developing countries that do participate, the key issue will be the terms of interconnection, much as were terms of trade in the post–World War II global economy. That experience provides cautionary tales. Dependency theorists in the 1970s identified perverse patterns of development whereby some emerging economies were incorporated into multinational production networks primarily for extractive purposes, either via exploitation of raw materials or low-cost labor. In either case there was insufficient productive investment and little potential for the emerging economy to upgrade its position over time. The resulting patterns of development were skewed definitively in favor of the developed world, while the dependent economies suffered deteriorating terms of trade and increased vulnerability to business cycle fluctuations. Or they found themselves with "enclaves" that were connected to the global economy but almost completely separate from the local economy, offering few benefits to the developing country as a whole. In both cases, the hoped-for second-order development effects spreading to the broader economy were limited at best. Contemporary arguments about "body-shopping" for low value–added data entry and simple programming in India, Malaysia, and other developing countries reflect a logic that is very similar to the insights of dependency theory.

If you accept the proposition that software is an enabler of the next phase of economic growth and development, it makes sense to overlay what we know about the open source process onto this kind of story and put forward some hypotheses about how it might change. Start with the simple notion that software is a tool for manipulating information. If the tool is essentially free to anyone who wants to use it, and freely modifiable to make it useful in whatever way the user can manage, then lots of people will grab the tool and experiment with it. The argument about end-to-end architecture is just as valid across countries as it is within countries. The open source community has been international from the start, and it remains so. That is more than simply noting that open source developers live all over the world. It is important that developers in China, Indonesia, and other developing countries contribute to open source software; but what is more important is that they all have access to the tool, and on equal terms. The open source community transcends national boundaries in a profound way because its interests (as well as its product) are not tied to or dependent on any government.

The degree to which a software tool can be used and expanded is limited in practice. But with open source software, it is limited only by the knowledge and learning of the potential users, not by exclusionary property rights, prices, or the power of rich countries and corporations. I remain cautious in thinking about what this means: Knowledge and learning are real constraints, but they are a different kind of constraint than are exclusionary rights and power. The free diffusion of tools will not create a profound leveling phenomenon. Even when everyone has equal access to tools, some people can and will use those tools to create more value than others. Consider an analogy to an imaginary world in which everyone had access to as many steam engines as they wanted, all at the same time, at nearly no cost, and with an open ability to disassemble, customize, and reassemble the components. Economic development would still have been uneven, but it might have been *less drastically uneven* than it is today.

If extrapolating this thought experiment to the information economy sounds outlandish even as a hypothesis, take a step backward toward more familiar discussions within developmental economics about the question of "appropriate technology" for poor countries. For most of the second half of the twentieth century, rich country governments and international development institutions were the ones making the most important decisions about "appropriate technology." Open source software shifts the decision-making prerogative into the hands of people in the developing countries. In one sense the provision of a freely available technological infrastructure represents by itself a form of wealth transfer to poor countries, but it is a wealth transfer that developing countries can maneuver to their particular advantage. To provide real products and services on top of the infrastructure requires an investment of local labor. India, China, and many other developing countries have a surplus of inexpensive technical manpower. Combining this with free software tools creates the possibility of an interesting kind of competitive advantage that would certainly matter in local markets and in some cases might be important in global markets as well.[56] One of the advantages of the GPL is that it then prevents a dysfunctional enclosure of mobilized "southern" resources into "northern" properties protected by patents that are offered for resale to the "south" at exploitative prices, a depressingly common pattern for knowledge-intensive products as diverse as music, plant varieties, and pharmaceuticals.

The potential to invigorate information productivity in developing economies is real. One of the consequences of the extraordinarily rapid growth of raw processing power over the last decades is that leading-edge users and the innovative applications that they develop for their own practical purposes have actually been the drivers and shapers of technological change, because they are the creators of meaningful demand for better, faster, and cheaper computing. It's well known that military demand played a major role in the first generations of computer technology. Census bureaus, banks, and insurance companies drove a second generation through the use of huge databases. The web drove innovation in the 1990s. It is likely that the process of annotating and processing the information released in the human genome project will be an important driver of the next generation of innovation.

Recognize that each of these "lead-use" applications came from the developed world, principally from the United States. Some years ago development theory posited that emerging economies were simply less sophisticated and less advanced versions of developed economies and that they would transit the same stages to arrive at essentially the same place some years later. This so-called stage theory is now discredited. Emerging markets have their own autonomous development logics. This will be just as true for economies transiting the information revolution as it was for those transiting the industrial revolution. The promise inherent in this argument is that software innovations can and should come from everywhere. Emerging markets are not implicitly stuck relying on commoditized, hand-me-down innovation from the developed world. They can have their own lead users who pull technology development toward applications that fit specifically the indigenous needs and demands of emerging markets. Indeed, because information technology is more easily customized than were many industrial-era technologies, the opportunity for autonomous lead users in emerging markets to deeply influence the direction of technology development is considerable. Open source software helps to tap this potential. For indigenous demand to be expressed, users really have to understand the menu of possibilities they face and the ways in which a digital infrastructure could contribute to their lives. When those possibilities are evolving as quickly as they are today, it seems certain that users generate demand primarily through a process of learning by doing.[57] Only over time and with increasing familiarity do users gradually come to understand and then to imagine what the technologies can do for them. The empowerment that comes with free access to source code is not then simply a gratifying emotional experience; it is a necessary economic prerequisite of evolving demand.

In many cases the "killer apps" for developing economies, which are the applications that find widespread acceptance and drive technology forward, will almost certainly come from *within* those economies. In other words, many design principles developed in the United States for American users are not going to be directly transferable to the developing world. The same is true of the granular peculiarities of payment systems and even more so of e-governance applications. The Simputer project, a $250 portable computer (running Linux) designed and built by a consortium from the Indian Institute of Science and the Bangalore-based software company Encore, is an illustrative example of how this process can work. This remarkable machine provides connectivity to the Internet, allows sharing among multiple users, supports text-to-speech capability for illiterate persons, and provides voice feedback in local languages.[58] In other words, it is a leading-edge experiment in a mass-market information appliance, not a cheapened or dumbed-down version of the Palm Pilot.

It is also the case that many countries have distinct political and security incentives to avoid lock-in to proprietary software products. Cities in Brazil have been at the forefront of legislation mandating government offices to use free software when possible; similar laws have been proposed in France, Argentina, Italy, Spain, and others. In spring 2002 a Peruvian congressman defended a similar bill brought up in Lima with these arguments: "To guarantee national security or the security of the State, it is indispensable to be able to rely on systems without elements which allow control from a distance or the undesired transmission of information to third parties. Systems with source code freely accessible to the public are required to allow their inspection by the State itself, by the citizens, and by a large number of independent experts throughout the world. Our proposal brings further security, since the knowledge of the source code will eliminate the growing number of programs with 'spy code.'"[59]

I quote at length because the letter demonstrates vividly that the issue is more than cost-savings. There is nationalist ideology here but also concrete interests. It is no surprise to industrial organization theorists that governments (like any customer) want to avoid locking themselves into a single private provider for crucial tools. And it is no surprise to international relations theorists that states want to avoid becoming dependent on software whose export is under U.S. legal jurisdiction and whose development is controlled by America's dominant software industry. Communications networks, e-government applications, and of course just about everything that makes up a modern military force increasingly run on sophisticated software. No national government, if it had alternatives, would have chosen during the twentieth century to accept dependence for steel or petroleum on a single supplier or a small number of suppliers based in a potential rival nation. And so it is no surprise that the Chinese government in particular has supported the development of Red Flag Linux and other open source packages as a distinct alternative to proprietary software—in part as a development tool, and in part as a lever to reduce potential dependence on a company that just happens to be based in Redmond, Washington, USA.[60] The emerging global security environment after September 11, 2001, will likely accelerate these trends, as the United

States capitalizes on its advantages in information processing to contribute to its new doctrine of preemptive security.

Of course information technology and open source in particular is not a silver bullet for long-standing development issues; nothing is. But the transformative potential of computing does create new opportunities to make progress on development problems that have been intransigent. In the broadest sense, the potential leverage on development comes not from software itself, but from the broad organizational changes that the open source process as a way of making software will drive. I am not arguing that developing countries can use the open source process to make up for lack of sufficient legal and economic infrastructure, or replace institutions by installing Internet connections. I am saying that there are interesting possibilities for building systems of distributed innovation within emerging economies that lead to autonomous innovation. This could have a significant impact on development prospects.

Power, Transaction Costs, and Community

In 1968 two of the most influential figures behind Arpanet argued that computer networks would have radical transformative effects on human thought and society.[61] Particularly since the Internet became popularized in the late 1990s, there has been an outpouring of literature on "virtual communities," the social life of people and information within networks, as well as organizational and business implications. There is far too much rich imagination, critical theory, and (increasingly) empirics within this literature for me to summarize it here. My point is to lay out a core analytic that has close ties to a governance argument in the similarly unstructured space of international politics, overlay the open source process on top of that analytic, and explore some implications for thinking about the governance of communities. The core analytic is made up of two parts, relational power and transaction costs.

The concept of relational power is simply that power is an attribute of relationships rather than of actors *per se*. Bundles of capabilities do not by themselves give anyone or any organization the capacity to get others to do what they otherwise would not do, or set the terms for cooperation and conflict. Power instead takes shape within complex relationships in which bargaining happens on many different levels, and lots of stuff (both material and symbolic) is exchanged.

Modern theories of international politics grappled with relational power under the heading of "complex interdependence."[62] A key puzzle that needed to be solved in that setting was to explain the development of stable cooperative relationships, "regimes" made up of norms, principles, rules, and decision-making procedures that were (surprisingly) durable despite their nonauthoritative basis.[63] Regime theory built on the fundamental insight of the Coase theorem to propose a solution. With firm property rights and sufficiently low transaction costs so the actors involved could readily make contracts, markets could handle externalities reasonably well—in fact, at the limit, markets would produce an efficient outcome without any need for authoritative regulation. As long as the international system remained anarchic, or lacking an authoritative governance structure capable of enforcing contracts, this seemed a vital mechanism for sustaining decentralized cooperation between autonomous states. The trick was to find a way to bring down the relatively high transaction costs that seemed to characterize much of international politics. That then was the core function of international regimes—to reduce transaction costs so international politics as a whole could move somewhat closer to a Coase-style equilibrium.[64]

A great deal of recent thought about e-commerce and Internet community tracks this logic of relational power and transaction costs. The ability to move information around the world without friction has been deeply associated with a market metaphor, even more deeply a market-based ontology as a way of seeing the world. Two related things point in this direction: decisions being pushed down either to the individual or to the machine on a case-by-case basis, and the massive reduction of transaction costs enabling those individuals (or machines) to find each other and agree to an exchange. And so the Internet has often been portrayed as a "perfecter" of markets, bringing a vision of efficiency ordered through "perfect" information (as economists say) and Coasian equilibrium arrived at in relationships outside of authority.

This story is most clearly expressed in the business literature, of course. But it is also an important part of the stories that people tell about affinity communities facilitated by communications technology.

The worldwide community of stamp collectors existed long before the Internet, but the Internet has made it possible to "fix" many of the "market failures" that the community must have suffered (for example, imperfect price and availability information for particular artifacts, individuals in remote places who did not trade as much as they wanted to, and so on). People suffering from rare diseases presumably would have liked to communicate with each other to exchange information, support, and so on before the Internet, but the transaction costs of finding each other around the world were prohibitively high.

In this kind of discourse, the failure of a community to take shape because of high transaction costs is just as much a market failure as is the nonevent of a contract to exchange money for widgets that would make both sides better off but does not happen because the widget owner can't find the buyer. The perfection of markets and the realization of potential communities are theoretically identical.

Let me take this argument one step further before I break it open. *Wired* magazine's former editor Kevin Kelly talks about a vision of a world made up of "smart" objects—a world in which everything has an embedded microprocessor and its own Internet address. He once excitedly explained, "This chair I'm sitting in will have a price in real-time, if you want to sit in it you will know exactly how many resources you will have to trade to do that."[65]

That would be efficient. But multiply that kind of interaction many times over into a social system and ask yourself if it is the kind of world you want to live in. There is a more profound point that I want to make explicit, about the way in which the metaphor and the accepted ontology of markets constrains how people think about the possibilities that technology is spawning.

Imagine a smart chair, connected to a lot of other smart things, with huge bandwidth between them, bringing transaction costs effectively to zero. Now ask yourself, With all that processing power and all that connectivity, why would a smart chair (or a smart car or a smart person) choose to exchange information with other smart things through the incredibly small aperture of a "price"? A price is a single, mono-layered piece of data that carries extraordinarily little information in and of itself. (Of course it is a compressed form of lots of other information, but an awful lot is lost in the process of compression.) The question for the perfect market that I've envisioned above is, Why compress? My point is that even a perfect market exchange is an incredibly thin kind of interaction, whether it happens between chairs or between people, whether it is an exchange of goods, ideas, or political bargains. I want to emphasize that communities, regimes, and other public spheres can come in many different shapes and forms. The "marketized" version is only one, and it is in many ways an extraordinarily narrow one that barely makes use of the technology at hand.

One way to open up this story is to go back and reexamine its roots in the Coase theorem. Changes in transactions costs (like any other costs) are phenomena that happen at the margin (in the economic not pejorative sense). But of course low transaction costs are only one ingredient in the Coase equilibrium. The other is secure, well-defined property rights; and as I have said, these property rights are now in play in a new way. My argument here simply is that shifting property rights can and will likely destabilize the foundations of existing cooperative arrangements and institutions, and possibly in more radical ways than do changing transaction costs. According to Coase, the transition to a new set of "stable" property rights would be the trickiest part for institutions to navigate. And it seems almost certain to me that we will be living through such a transition for at least the next decade.

One important aspect of institutional innovation happening within that transition can be seen within new manifestations of networks. More specifically, a variety of networks are emerging around different answers to two questions that lie at the core of governance (even in a network): What are the major resources of power and control, and what are the ordering principles? Consider a schema that captures a slice of that variety (see Figure 5).[66] The axes are self-explanatory and are meant simply to capture three distinct kinds of variance in network interactions. Connectivity is the technological enabler that pushes experimentation with all three kinds of networks out on their distinctive trajectories. And three very different kinds of networks emerge.

eBay is an example of a massive, low-transaction-cost, one-to-one electronic flea market where buyers and sellers are empowered to find each other and contract through a modified auction process. eBay itself provides the trading platform and a reputation management system that facilitates single-shot interactions between nearly anonymous parties.[67] Power in this self-described "community" lies with the provider of the trading platform, because eBay itself writes the rules for

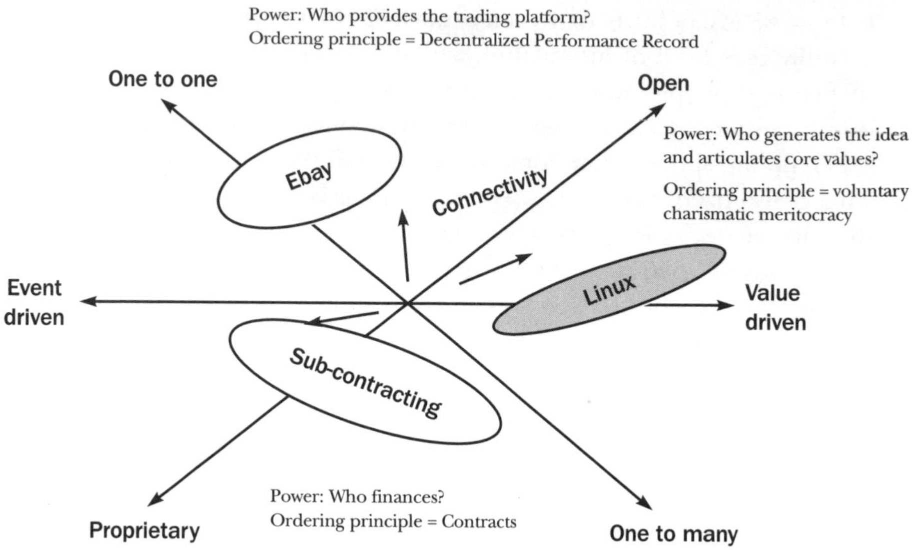

Power: Who provides the trading platform?
Ordering principle = Decentralized Performance Record

One to one

Open

Power: Who generates the idea
and articulates core values?

Ordering principle = voluntary
charismatic meritocracy

Ebay

Connectivity

Event
driven

Value
driven

Linux

Sub-contracting

Power: Who finances?
Ordering principle = Contracts

Proprietary

One to many

Figure 5 Varieties of networks.

transactions and the operation of the reputation system. Governance is decentralized to the participants and focused on assuring the performance over time of the trader, rather than the quality of the underlying asset that is being traded.

The subcontracting or Hollywood model is a very different kind of network. The organizing principle is simply a highly disaggregated or outsourced division of labor. If I want to make a movie, I search for and assemble the specific inputs I need—a director, some actors, a lighting designer, a sound producer, and many more—around the task of creating the film. These inputs will work together for several months and then (just as quickly as I brought them together) disband, to later reassemble with other inputs in some new configuration for another movie. This is the exemplar of a virtual organization, but there is really nothing particularly virtual about it, other than the fact that technology reduces the costs of identifying and assembling the optimal inputs for my particular project. Power in this community is closely tied to finance, because it is the investment that acts as glue to pull together a temporary coalition of skilled inputs. The individual or organization that invests in bringing together the virtual organization also holds the reins of governance because that player writes the contracts that set the terms of interaction.

The open source model occupies the third niche in this scheme. The community is formally as open as eBay, and more open in the sense that opportunities for voice are greater. But rather than a single-shot contract or even a series of them, the community is connected by a shared goal of creating a common product. Like the Hollywood model, collaboration requires an individual to hold many (not just one) other individuals in working relationships. Power in this community, at least to start, belongs to the person who generates the idea and articulates the core values behind the project. But as the community takes shape, its very openness moves power away from the leader and toward the followers, as I discussed. Governance remains voluntary throughout, in large part because of this odd trajectory of power. A rough meritocracy coexists with charismatic personalities, a charisma that has the distinctive characteristics that I explained in Chapter 6.

Connectivity will drive each of these kinds of networks further along their respective trajectories.[68] The eBay model will move toward an increasingly perfect market, through more efficient management of reputations, better price discovery, more liquidity. The Hollywood model will move toward more elaborate specialization, extend its geographical scope, and so on. One of the things the open source model will do is to show the limits of some basic notions about the functions of large-scale governance. Principal-agent problems are not the big "problem" that governance mechanisms have to solve in this setting. As I explained, distributed innovation on the open source model does not depend on bringing agents' incentives into line with those of principals. The distinction itself looks arbitrary—who exactly is the principal and who is the agent in this environment? Another and related thing the open source model will do is challenge more broadly some of the tenets of how we think about pluralism within organizations, and how pluralism scales. Many organizations, including some international organizations, today claim a special normative status because of their pluralist composition.[69] The challenge is that the distinctiveness is going away. Pluralism at many different levels is being enabled by communications technologies and by experimentation with property; together, these are reducing the marginal cost of adding voices toward an asymptote of zero. Open source demonstrates how it is then possible for an increasingly large number of actors, public and private, to enter the contest for control over the channels by which technical expertise (or claims of expertise) flow. Neither international nor any other politics is heading all the way to one big pluralist society in which anyone can be part of any organization. But the default position is, indeed, changing—as the active choice becomes a matter of whom to *exclude* rather than whom to *include*. As more inclusive and pluralist organizations grow up in the space of international politics and economics, organizations like today's international organizations will come to look less special and the legitimacy they have drawn from that special status will dissipate. I think about this ongoing process as a kind of "disaggregation" of legitimacy, and I think the spreading of claims on legitimacy to a variety of unexpected and unlikely actors is set to continue, in international politics as much as elsewhere.[70]

Networks, Hierarchies, and the Interface

As Secretary of State in the Nixon Administration, Henry Kissinger famously asked, "When I call Europe who answers the phone?" Behind this glib comment lies a profound theoretical issue and a very practical set of questions for governments, corporations, and other organizations. What Kissinger really was asking is, How does a hierarchically structured government (the United States) deal effectively (communicate, cooperate, or compete with) a powerful institution structured in a fundamentally different way? Take this one step of generalization further and the question becomes what are the dynamics of increasingly dense relationships between hierarchies and networks.

Microsoft is asking parallel questions about open source. In 2001 Microsoft essentially declared war on open source software.[71] Remember that Microsoft (for better or worse) is one of the most profoundly successful organizations on earth when it comes to strategy. It has an extraordinarily well-honed system for managing its relationships with other corporations (too successful by some accounts). It is just as expert and nearly as successful in managing its relationships with governments. But Microsoft has no strategy template for managing a relationship, even a hostile one, with the open source community. You can't buy that community; you can't drive it out of business; you can't hire away the talent; and you can't really tie it up in the courts (although

Microsoft has tried each of these tactics).[72] Imagine someone asking, "When Microsoft calls Linux who answers the phone?" The question makes no sense. It presupposes a structural configuration of an organization that is not true of many networks and certainly not of the open source community.[73]

National governments face similar problems. For many years the United States has been fighting an undeclared war against terrorist networks like al-Qaeda. After September 11 the U.S. government made that a de facto declared war. But modern war is a social convention that evolved between national governments. One state declares war on another and the other declares war back. Each makes demands on the other; their ambassadors meet; they try to negotiate an end to violence; they bargain and fight in some evolving mix and then perhaps sign a treaty. It is a gruesome repertoire, but both sides understand what their roles are and how the game is played. The war against terrorism is different. A national government, perhaps the largest and most hierarchical national government on earth, has declared war on a transnational network. That network has certainly committed acts that we call war against the United States, but it has made no explicit demands on the United States. In fact it does not even announce itself as the attacker. How do you bargain with an enemy that hides and doesn't tell you what it wants? Who do you bargain with? It is a comforting fiction, but still a fiction, that Osama Bin Laden is the political equivalent of a president or king. Loosely coupled cell-like network structures act sometimes in coordination and sometimes not.

The underlying analytic that portrays war as a bargaining game between two discrete and similarly structured actors that differ primarily in terms of power and preferences was a convenience for international relations scholarship that helped people think about large-scale international conflict during the Cold War. But more important differences now lie in how organizations are structured and how those structures complicate setting the terms of their interaction, even in war. Complex networks have at least five characteristics that complicate how they relate to hierarchies:[74]

- Structural complexity: The "wiring diagram" can be extraordinarily intricate.
- Network evolution: The wiring diagram can change quickly.

- Connection diversity: The links between nodes vary in strength, direction, and even sign of influence (+ or -, excitatory or inhibitory).
- Dynamical complexity: The state of each node can vary rapidly.
- Node diversity: There are many different kinds of nodes.

And finally there is the notion of meta-complication: Each of these complexities can influence and exacerbate each other.

There is a huge literature evolving across the social sciences looking at the structure and functioning of networks. I focus here on the related but different question, What happens at the interface, between networks and hierarchies, where they meet? The interface between differently structured systems is typically a very creative place where new forms of order, organization, and even life arise. In physics it has been called the edge of chaos, where order meets disorder and where phase changes take place. In evolutionary theory, it is a source of new species, not just marginal variation. In organization theory, boundary spanners are a major creative force behind new kinds of organizations.[75] This is also the place where the relationship between the open source process and more traditional forms of organization for production are being worked out. The general point is that one of the key social science challenges at present is to conceptualize more clearly how hierarchically structured organizations (like large governments and corporations) develop and manage relationships with network organizations. I have found no good comprehensive model, but there are analytic suggestions about the kinds of problems arising at the interface that need to be solved. One set of problems involves communication. Information flows among differently structured channels in hierarchies and networks. It may be encoded in different protocols, perhaps even what amount to different languages. Another set of problems falls around coordination. A de facto division of labor between the network and the hierarchy (even in a conflictual relationship) needs a coordination mechanism, but neither price nor authority will cross the interface successfully.

A literature in business and foreign policy as well as a more theory-oriented literature in international politics is beginning to grapple with these problems. The first two seem to take their cue from the important arguments of sociologists like Dimaggio and Powell, who developed a powerful argument about isomorphism, detailing some of the pressures driving organizations that are connected to each other in highly dense relationships to change so they come to look more like each other structurally.[76] And so it is common to read how formerly hierarchical organizations, particularly large businesses, are in the process of transforming themselves into networks. In the foreign policy and security field, David Rondfeldt and John Arquilla have for almost ten years been making prescient arguments about the rise of networks in international conflict and the implications for what they call "netwar."[77] Their policy propositions—"hierarchies have a difficult time fighting networks, it takes networks to fight networks, and whoever masters the network form first and best will gain major advantages"—track the institutional isomorphism literature by encouraging hierarchical governments to remake their security organizations as networks to interface successfully with their networked adversaries.

These arguments and the policy strategies they carry will likely prove themselves quite useful in the longer term. But in the medium term, isomorphic pressures on institutions are just that—pressures, not outcomes. It is important to resist the fiction that national governments and large corporations are all going to become networked organizations in the foreseeable future, because they won't. And terrorist organizations are not soon going to become hierarchical structures with clear lines of command, ambassadors, and physical capitals. The reality is more complicated: Both forms will coexist and have to find ways to relate to each other.

In international relations theory, Margaret Keck and Kathryn Sikkink have asked similar questions about relationships between transnational "advocacy networks" and national governments.[78] Other studies of global social movements talk about the emergence of "complex multilateralism" to describe a form of governance that emerges in the interaction between international organizations and transnational networks.[79] These are valuable perspectives so far as they go. But they still suffer from an unfortunate "bracketing" of the hierarchal structures as that which is somehow "real" or concrete, while trying to prove that networks "matter" vis-à-vis more traditional structures.[80] The next question they naturally ask, "Under what conditions do networks matter?" is premature unless the answer can be well structured in terms of necessary and sufficient conditions. To get to that point requires a good conceptual articulation of the space in which the game of influence is being played out. And that is still lacking.

The open source story as I have told it here points to a different way forward. Two distinct but equally real organizational forms exist in parallel to each other. The dynamic relationship between hierarchies and networks over time determines both the nature of the transition and the endpoint. One form may defeat the other through competition. Both may coexist by settling into nearly separate niches where they are particularly advantaged. Most interesting will be the new forms of organization that emerge to manage the interface between them, and the process by which those boundary spanners influence the internal structure and function of the networks and the hierarchies that they link together.

If my generic point about creativity at the interface is correct, it is then my strong presumption that this is a problem suited for inductive theorizing through comparative case study research. The war against terrorism, the relationship between open source and proprietary models of software production, and the politics among transnational NGO networks and international organizations share characteristics that make them diverse cases of a similarly structured political space. I am certain that some of the most interesting processes in international politics and economics over the next decade are going to take place in this space, at the interface between hierarchies and networks (rather than solely within either one). Comparing what evolves in diverse instantiations of that space is one way forward.[81]

Generalizing Open Source

The success of open source is a story about software. If it were only that, it would still be important for social scientists thinking about cooperation problems. And it would still have significant implications for economic growth and development.[82] That is the minimum case. If the open source process has more general characteristics, if it is a generic production process for knowledge that can and will spread beyond software *per se,* then the implications might be considerably larger. My purpose here is not to take a definitive position on this question, but rather to lay out some of the conditions that embed it.

Markets and hierarchies are reasonably good at coordinating some kinds of human behavior and not very good at others. Creative intellectual effort, for example, is highly individuated, variable in its transparency, often tough to measure objectively, and thus very difficult to specify in contracts. Another way to make the same point is to say that firms and markets only tap into a piece of human motivation—an important piece certainly, but for many individuals only a small part of what makes them create. This should sound obvious to anyone who is or has worked with artists, musicians, craftspeople, authors, dancers, and so on. There is nothing unique to the Information Age here.

Many of these creative endeavors are practiced by single individuals or by small groups. When you put them together into a large group, the dynamics of cooperation change. Orchestras have conductors, who struggle with finding a balance between individual creativity and the joint product that a symphony represents. Companies that rely heavily on knowledge and creativity spend enormous effort trying to strike a similar balance. Leaders of organizations like these will often say they feel like they are tapping into 25 or 30 percent of what their employees have within them, and if only they could find a way to access some of that unused 70 percent. This, I think, is the reason why the open source phenomenon attracts such curiosity outside the software world. If this experiment in organization has found a way to tap a greater percentage of human creative motivation (if only 10 percent extra), then the question of how to generalize and expand the scope of that experiment becomes a very interesting one to a much broader group of people.

One important direction in which the open source experiment points is toward moving beyond the discussion of transaction costs as a key determinant of institutional design. Make no mistake: Transaction costs are important. The elegant analytics of transaction cost economics do very interesting work in explaining how divisions of labor evolve through outsourcing of particular functions (the decision to buy rather than make something). But the open source process adds another element. The notion of open-sourcing as a strategic organizational decision can be seen as an efficiency choice around distributed innovation, just as outsourcing was an efficiency choice around transaction costs.

The simple logic of open-sourcing would be a choice to pursue ad hoc distributed development of solutions for a problem that (1) exists within an organization, (2) is likely to exist elsewhere as well, and (3) is not the key source of competitive advantage or differentiation for the organization. Consider, for example, financial companies that, when merging with other financial companies, need to build a software bridge that links different types of legacy databases and computer systems. This is a notoriously difficult problem that financial companies typically outsource to specialist consulting firms. That decision creates a useful division of labor for the financial company in question, but it is extremely inefficient for the industry as a whole, which has to start almost from scratch and recreate solutions to this kind of problem every time a major merger goes through.

An alternative strategy would be to open source a solution to the problem. Dresdner Kleinwort Wasserstein did something like this with the help of Collab.net to stimulate the creation of a developer community around a base of source code. The idea was to find people in other places sharing a similar problem, involve them in a common developer effort, spread the development cost around the organizations, and increase the mobilized talent pool. If measuring the parameters were easy, the strategic choice to open source would be a function of comparing benefits you gain from the distributed development effort to costs you incur getting it started along with savings you will bring to your competitors by giving them free access to the same tools that you have. Because no one can measure those parameters in advance (and often not even after the fact), the decision becomes an experiment in organizational innovation. We are seeing many such experiments now and will likely see more of them as the success of open source becomes more widely understood. But there is no inherent reason this experiment will be bounded within information technology.

Consider this scenario. A petrochemicals company owns the intellectual property rights to a specific refining technique that it has developed at considerable cost in its own labs. But because the problem that this technique solves is generic and well known, an international network of graduate students is collaborating in an open source–style process to try to solve the same problem. The open source process is advancing rapidly and generating a lot of attention. Some of the engineers who work for the petrochemical company are contributing to the open source process in their spare time—it seems to be a more creative endeavor through which they can play with ideas more freely than they can at work. At some point, the engineers and the executives at the company realize that the open source process has produced a refining technique as good as or better than their proprietary technique. And now they face a major decision. They could try to fight the open source alternative in the market or in the courts. They could try to hire the graduate students who built the code and attempt to enclose the knowledge within their organization. Or they could embrace the new process and encourage their engineers to engage with it so they could understand it better and customize it to the company's advantage. They could build the plants that use the new process, improve it as they learn by doing, manage the production, marketing, and regulatory issues for the product, and so on.[83]

I think it likely that this scenario will come to pass in various economic sectors and that there will be experiments in managing it from each of these angles (and others). One of the next steps in research on open source should be to build analytic models that try to specify conditions that favor or hinder these experiments. I do not have a fullfledged model to propose at this point, but I suspect any model will have to focus on at least two factors that transaction cost economics does not emphasize. The first is the relationship between problemsolving innovation and the location of tacit information, information that is not easily translated into communicable form.[84] As information about what users want and need to do becomes more fine-grained, individually differentiated, and hard to communicate, the incentives grow to shift the locus of innovation closer to them by empowering them with freely modifiable tools. The second is the importance of principles and values, in contrast to efficiency as an organizing concept. This goes back to the example of the smart chairs and the eBaystyle community. Increasingly efficient economic exchange has its own decreasing marginal returns, both as an organizing principle and as an explanatory variable for looking at Linux-style communities and the conditions under which they will form.

A note of caution: As open source has begun to attract broad public attention over the last few years, the term itself has been overused as a metaphor. There are now experiments with an open-cola alternative to Coke and Pepsi, an "openmusic" registry, an "openlaw" project at Harvard Law School, and any number of "open content" projects to build mass encyclopedias, for example. Many of these are simply "open" forums in the sense that anyone can contribute anything they wish to a mass database. Others are essentially barn-raising volunteer projects that look for interested people around the world to make a donation to a common pool. Many of these projects gain their ideological inspiration from the open source process and tap into some of the same motivations. Many are interesting experiments in using Internet technologies to organize volunteer efforts and affinity groups. But in many instances these projects are not organized around the property regime that makes the open source process distinctive. That is not any kind of criticism; it is simply an identification of a difference, but it is an important difference that needs attention at this early stage of building models that specify conditions under which the open source process will be favored.

Experimenting with open source production in different knowledge domains will involve a lot of learning by doing. Consider, for example, the structure of medical knowledge in a common family practice type setting, which is interestingly parallel to the structure of knowledge for in-house software development. My doctor in Berkeley has a hard problem to solve. I present myself to her with an atypical sinus infection, low-grade fever, aching muscles, and a family history of heart disease. The bad news is that I represent to her a highly customized configuration and a finely grained problem. The good news is that there almost certainly is a similarly configured patient presenting somewhere else at the same time. At the very least, other doctors are solving pieces of my problem in other settings.

The second piece of bad news, though, is that she will find it extremely difficult to access that distributed knowledge and thus will most likely have to figure out my problem without much help. In fact doctors have very cumbersome means of upgrading the common medical knowledge that they draw on to support their work (it takes a long time to publish papers in journals; these papers are not configured for easy recombination; and so most doctors facing an unfamiliar problem will call friends to see whether they have faced a similar problem recently, or know someone who has). Certainly bandwidth has been a limiting factor in the effective use of knowledge (a typical CAT scan picture is a huge data file). But as the bandwidth comes on line, the key issue will be the social organization of knowledge-sharing and upgrading. From the perspective of the medical care system as a whole, there is enormous wasted effort when the doctor in New York ends up going through a problem-solving process that a doctor in Berkeley has already figured out in a very similar case, simply because she has no way to search for and access that knowledge efficiently—even though the California doctor has no reason not to share it (and could very much benefit from diffuse reciprocity in a future reverse "trade"). In software development the open source process is a way of sharing precisely information of this character in an effective way. As I have explained it in this book, the process depends on culture, technology, organization, and to some extent the nature of the knowledge that is being shared.

Primary care medicine has similar cultural characteristics and a parallel organization of practice; what seems to be missing is the intersection between the technology and the nature of the knowledge to be shared. Many doctors would today claim that much problem-solving knowledge in medicine cannot really be put into communicable form. An X-ray picture surely is knowledge that can be digitized, while the skill of how to make a diagnosis by palpating a patient's chest is a tacit form of knowledge that each practitioner has to recreate for himself. But is the difference with software source code really a difference of kind? At one time source code was also difficult to communicate—before the Internet, people had to carry large tapes and disks around from place to place. When bandwidth increases, the parameters change. The distinction between tacit and digitizable knowledge may be less severe than practitioners in any particular field of endeavor tend to think. After all, source code is not easy to read; there is tacit knowledge embedded in the structure of an elegant solution to a programming problem that experts have and novices don't. Would a massive expansion of bandwidth show that "tacit" knowledge in medical practice has similar characteristics?[85] I pose that as an honest, not rhetorical, question, with the caveat that a positive answer would make certain aspects of medical practice an obvious place to experiment with open source style knowledge production.

A second and in some sense obvious application of the open source process might be in genomics.[86] The human genome sequence published by the National Institutes of Health and Celera in 2001 is at best in fact a rough draft. The next decade (at least) of genomic science will be spent correcting and "annotating" the sequence, separating signal from noise, interpreting what information is being used by human cells and in what ways, essentially debugging an enormous body of code.

This is the most ambitious and probably the most important knowledge production task of the first half of the new century. It is increasingly taking place *in silico* (on a computer) rather than *in vitro* (in a test-tube). The barriers to entry are getting lower as the DNA sequencing and manipulation technologies become cheap and available, which is the same kind of transition that happened to computing with the creation of the PC. Ten thousand dollars, a fast Internet connection, and a couple graduate courses in biochemistry are all you need to become a "bio-hacker." And much of the basic source code to hack is freely available (in both senses of the word "free"). Viable economic structures could be built up around open source genomics. For example, the farmer might not buy prepackaged seeds from a distributor. Instead he would buy a conveniently packaged genetic sequence, which he would then be free to modify for his own particular setup and conditions, and then synthesize ("compile") the DNA into a functioning genome for his corn crop. He might offer his sequence customizations to others under a license like the GPL, while companies spring up to provide auxiliary services for a fee (such as helping farmers to organize the crop options that would be available to them and make them work together well on a particular piece of land).

There are at least two important cross-cutting pressures against this kind of evolution. The culture of the genomics community is simply not as open as is the culture of the computer science community. The same underlying norms of sharing that software engineers built up in the early years of computing and are part of the history of that community are not available for the genomics community in the same way, at least not in its recent history. Rather than recapturing a version of the Unix-style past for the basis of a different narrative, the genomics community would probably have to import these ideas about alternative ways of organizing from outside, or be "invaded" by a new set of players who carry those ideas. The second pressure is external, the force of government regulation. Government action facilitated the development of the open source software process (even if not intentionally). In contrast, the liberal patent rules for genetic data allowed a much more restrictive intellectual property regime to evolve quite early around genomics. September 11 and its aftermath—particularly the doctrine of preemptive security applied to bioterrorism—reinforces that regime. It is far too early to tell how these conflicting pressures will balance out, but there is no doubt they form an interesting (if not very well controlled) experiment for generalizing open source.

The open source community itself has been circumspect about trying to generalize a set of conditions under which the model could spread. Some of this caution is tactical—Eric Raymond has said more than once that he wants to see open source win the "battle of ideas" in the software world and consolidate its home base before too much energy gets expended anywhere else. But the software world is not likely unique, and successful models of production do not always behave in politically expedient ways. The arguments in this book point to a set of general hypotheses that I have presented over the course of the narrative and analysis, and I summarize them here in conclusion. They fall into two broad categories, the nature of the task and the motivations of the agents.

The open source process is more likely to work effectively in tasks that have these characteristics:

- Disaggregated contributions can be derived from knowledge that is accessible under clear, nondiscriminatory conditions, not proprietary or locked up.
- The product is perceived as important and valuable to a critical mass of users.
- The product benefits from widespread peer attention and review, and can improve through creative challenge and error correction (that is, the rate of error correction exceeds the rate of error introduction).
- There are strong positive network effects to use of the product.
- An individual or a small group can take the lead and generate a substantive core that promises to evolve into something truly useful.
- A voluntary community of iterated interaction can develop around the process of building the product.

Some of these hypotheses shade off into arguments about the motivations and capabilities of the agents. To be more precise, the open source process is likely to work effectively when agents have these characteristics:

- Potential contributors can judge with relative ease the viability of the evolving product.
- The agents have the information they need to make an informed bet that contributed efforts will actually generate a joint good, not simply be dissipated.
- The agents are driven by motives beyond simple economic gain and have a "shadow of the future" for rewards (symbolic and otherwise) that is not extremely short.
- The agents learn by doing and gain personally valuable knowledge in the process.
- Agents hold a positive normative or ethical valence toward the process.

These are expansive hypotheses; the parameters in many instances would be hard to measure and specify *a priori*. As is the case for many such hypotheses about social processes, they are broadly indicative of the kinds of conditions that matter. They tell you where to look, and even more so where not to look, for answers. That may not be fully satisfying, but it's not a bad place to start when you are looking at something so intriguing and at the same time unfamiliar.

NOTES

INDEX

Notes

1. Property and the Problem of Software

1. Mitchell Stoltz, a software engineer at Netscape, suggested this analogy to me.
2. More precisely, programmers write programs in source code. Computers execute instructions in machine language. A separate program called a compiler transforms source code to object code that is either directly executable or undergoes another step into machine language.
3. Free Software Foundation, "The Free Software Definition," Boston: Free Software Foundation 1996, at *www.fsf.org/philosophy/free-sw.html.*
4. See the full definition at *www.opensource.org/docs/definition.php* (Open Source Initiative, "The Open Source Definition, Version 1.9," 2002).
5. The open source software repository SourceForge *(www.sourceforge.net)* held over 67,402 hosted projects as of September 2, 2003.
6. See the monthly web server survey run by Netcraft, an Internet services company based in Bath, England, at *news.netcraft.com/archives/web_server_survey.html.*
7. Jim Kerstetter with Steve Hamm, Spencer E. Ante, and Jay Greene, "The Linux Uprising," *BusinessWeek,* March 3, 2003.
8. If you use a Macintosh, you are already there: OS X is built on open source code.
9. Lawrence Lessig, *Code and Other Laws of Cyberspace.* New York: Basic Books, 2000; and Lessig, "Open Code and Open Societies: Values of Internet Governance," *Chicago-Kent Law Review* 74, 1999, pp. 101–116.
10. See, for example, David Bollier, *Silent Theft: The Private Plunder of Our Common Wealth.* New York: Routledge, 2002. Bollier has consistently made the most sophisticated and eloquent arguments on this point.

11. Peter Schwartz, Peter Leyden, and Joel Hyatt, *The Long Boom: A Vision for the Coming Age of Prosperity*. Cambridge, Mass.: Perseus Publishing, 1999.

12. Marc A. Smith and Peter Kollock, eds., *Communities in Cyberspace*. London: Routledge, 1999, p. 230.

13. Of course organization theorists know that a lot of management goes on informally within the interstices of this structure, but the structure is still there to make it possible.

14. Eric S. Raymond, "The Cathedral and the Bazaar," in *The Cathedral and the Bazaar: Musings on Linux and Open Source by an Accidental Revolutionary*. Sebastopol, Calif.: O'Reilly & Associates, 1999, p. 30.

15. Raymond, "The Cathedral and the Bazaar," p. 30.

16. Frederick P. Brooks, *The Mythical Man-Month: Essays on Software Engineering*. Reading, Mass.: Addison-Wesley, 1975.

17. In *The Hacker Ethic and the Spirit of the Information Age* (New York: Random House, 2001), Pekka Himanen explores these three characteristics as central to the "hacker ethic." I agree with this portrayal, but I don't share the notion that these are somehow distinctive to Information Age work. In my view, they have characterized human motivation for a very long time (think of cave paintings).

18. Chapter 8 discusses in detail the notion of a neutral network and its implications.

19. Gary S. Becker and Kevin M. Murphy, "The Division of Labor, Coordination Costs, and Knowledge," *The Quarterly Journal of Economics* 57(4), November 1992, pp. 1137–1160.

20. Stewart Brand, *How Buildings Learn: What Happens after They're Built*. New York: Viking Press, 1994.

21. A good review is Paul Dourish, *Where the Action Is: The Foundations of Embodied Interaction*. Cambridge, Mass.: MIT Press, 2001.

22. Joseph Schumpeter, *Capitalism, Socialism, and Democracy*. New York: Harper and Row, 1942. You can find a related argument in Mark A. Lemley, "Place and Cyberspace," UC Berkeley Public Law and Legal Theory Research Paper No. 102, 2002.

23. John Ruggie, "'Finding Our Feet' in Territoriality: Problematizing Modernity in International Relations," *International Organization* 47(1), Winter 1992, pp. 139–175.

24. Francois Bar, "The Construction of Marketplace Architecture," in The BRIE-IGCC E-conomy Project, *Tracking a Transformation: E-Commerce and the Terms of Competition in Industries*. Washington, D.C.: The Brookings Institution Press, 2001.

2. The Early History of Open Source

1. Neal Stephenson, *In the Beginning . . . Was the Command Line.* New York: Avon Books, 1999.
2. Paul N. Edwards, *The Closed World: Computers and the Politics of Discourse in Cold War America.* Cambridge, Mass.: MIT Press, 1996, p. 124.
3. Peter H. Salus, *A Quarter Century of UNIX.* Reading, Mass.: Addison-Wesley, 1994, p. 26.
4. Pekka Himanen, *The Hacker Ethic and the Spirit of the Information Age.* New York: Random House, 2001. See also Charles Sabel, *Work and Politics: The Division of Labor in Industry.* New York: Cambridge University Press, 1982.
5. Joan M. Greenbaum, *Windows on the Workplace: Computers, Jobs, and the Organization of Office Work in the Late Twentieth Century.* New York: Cornerstone Books/Monthly Review Press, 1995, p. 45. See also Joan M. Greenbaum, *In the Name of Efficiency: Management Theory and Shopfloor Practice in Data Processing Work.* Philadelphia: Temple University Press, 1979.
6. Quoted in Salus, *A Quarter Century,* p. 11.
7. Eric S. Raymond, "Philosophy," ch. 1, *The Art of Unix Programming* at *www.catb.org/~esr/writings/taoup/html/philosophychapter.html.*
8. Salus, *A Quarter Century,* p. 36.
9. Ibid., p. 39.
10. Marshall Kirk McKusick, "Twenty Years of Berkeley Unix: From AT&T-Owned to Freely Redistributable," in Chris DiBona, Sam Ockman, and Mark Stone, eds., *Open Sources: Voices from the Open Source Revolution.* Sebastopol, Calif.: O'Reilly & Associates, 1999, p. 32.
11. Salus, *A Quarter Century,* p. 151.
12. TCP/IP stands for Transfer Control Protocol/Internet Protocol. It is a set of rules for communication among computers on the Internet. In a real sense these protocols "are" the Internet.
13. Andrew Leonard, *Bots: The Origin of a New Species.* San Francisco: Hardwired, 1997. See Chap. 1, in which Leonard's source is Duane Adams, the DARPA contract monitor who administered the Berkeley Unix contracts.
14. Kirk McKusick, quoted in Salus, *A Quarter Century,* p. 160.
15. "Stack" is a technical term for a set of network protocol layers that work together. Stack is also used to refer to the software that implements the protocols—hence, the TCP/IP stack "implements" TCP/IP in Unix.
16. Salus, *A Quarter Century,* p. 164.

17. Steven Levy, *Hackers: Heroes of the Computer Revolution* (Garden City, N.Y.: Anchor Press/Doubleday, 1984) is still the best and most enjoyable account of these clubs.

18. Charles F. Sabel, *Work and Politics: The Division of Labor in Industry.* New York: Cambridge University Press, 1982.

19. Andrew S. Tanenbaum, *Operating Systems: Design and Implementation.* Englewood Cliffs, N.J.: Prentice Hall, 1987, p. 13.

20. Peter Temin and Louis Galambos, *The Fall of the Bell System.* Cambridge, England: Cambridge University Press, 1987; W. Brooke Tunstall, *Disconnecting Parties: Managing the Bell System Breakup: An Inside View.* New York: McGraw-Hill, 1985.

21. McKusick, "Twenty Years of Berkeley Unix," p. 39.

22. In fact several licensees almost immediately made the software available for anonymous FTP (file transfer protocol). This meant that anyone with an Internet connection could download the software for free and without restrictions.

23. See Marshall Kirk McKusick, Keith Bostic, and Michael J. Karels, eds., *The Design and Implementation of the 4.4BSD Operating System.* Reading, Mass: Addison-Wesley, 1996; and the account in Peter Wayner, *Free for All: How Linux and the Free Software Movement Undercut the High-Tech Titans.* New York: HarperBusiness, 2000, pp. 44–46.

24. Leonard, *Bots.* Joy remains relatively skeptical about open source processes because he believes that good code ultimately is written by a very few talented people.

25. Salus, *A Quarter Century,* p. 216.

26. Steven Weber, "International Political Economy 'After' the Business Cycle," *Journal of Social, Political, and Economic Studies* 21(3), Fall 1996; and "The End of the Business Cycle?" *Foreign Affairs* 76(4), July/August 1997.

27. Richard Stallman, "The GNU Operating System and the Free Software Movement," in DiBona, Ockman, and Stone, *Open Sources.*

28. Andrew Leonard interview with Richard Stallman. See Leonard, *Bots.*

29. See *www.gnu.org/philosophy/why-free.html* for a basic statement of Stallman's position.

30. Stallman, "The GNU Operating System," p. 56.

31. See "What Is Copyleft?" at *www.gnu.org/copyleft/copyleft.html;* and GNU General Public License at *www.gnu.org/copyleft/gpl.html.*

32. Quoted in Salus, *A Quarter Century,* p. 223.

33. McKusick, "Twenty Years of Berkeley Unix," p. 45. The Berkeley lawyers wanted the case heard close to home and not in New Jersey, the home of AT&T and Unix Systems Laboratories.

34. Some legal wrangling continues. In the winter of 2003, the SCO group

launched a legal initiative claiming exclusive rights on Unix shared libraries and threatened to sue some Linux distributors, including IBM, for misappropriation of trade secrets, tortious interference, unfair competition, and breach of contract. (Through a series of corporate buyouts, SCO (formerly called Caldera International) may own legal rights to the original development work done on Unix during the 1970s and 1980s by Bell Labs.)

35. Wayner, *Free for All,* p. 96.

3. What Is Open Source and How Does It Work?

1. Linus Torvalds, <torvalds@klaava.Helsinki.FI> Free minix-like kernel sources for 386-AT Article <1991Oct5.054106.4647@klaava.Helsinki .FI> in Usenet newsgroup comp.os.minix, 5 May 1991. Also at *groups .google.com/groups?selm=1991Oct5.054106.4647%40klaava.Helsinki.FI& oe=UTF8&output=gplain.*

2. Eric Raymond, *The Cathedral and the Bazaar.* Cambridge, Mass: O'Reilly & Associates, 1999, pp. 22–23.

3. See Hans C. Girth and C. Wright Mills, trans. and eds., *From Max Weber: Essays in Sociology.* New York: Galaxy Books, 1946.

4. Frederick Brooks, *The Mythical Man-Month.* Reading, Mass.: Addison-Wesley, 1975, p. 4.

5. Reprinted as Chapter 16 in *The Mythical Man-Month,* 2nd ed. Reading, Mass.: Addison-Wesley, 1995.

6. Ibid., p. 183.

7. Ibid., p. 184.

8. For other interesting examples, see William C. Wake, *Extreme Programming Explored.* Reading, Mass.: Addison-Wesley, 2001.

9. Brooks, *The Mythical Man-Month,* p. 32.

10. Ibid., p. 44.

11. Raymond, *The Cathedral and the Bazaar.*

12. See *www.sourceforge.net.*

13. See *www.counter.li.org/estimates.php.*

14. See, for example, the work by Ilka Tuomi, including "Internet, Innovation, and Open Source: Actors in the Network," *First Monday* 6(1), January 8, 2001; the Kiel Linux Survey (results at *www.psychologie.uni-kiel.de/linux-study/*); the Orbiten Free Software Survey, at *orbiten.org/ofss/01.html;* and the FLOSS survey of the International Institute of Infonomics, University of Maastricht, at *www.infonomics.nl/FLOSS/report/.*

15. Rishab Ghosh and Vipul Ved Prakash, "The Orbiten Free Software

Survey," *First Monday* 5(7), July 2000, at *firstmonday.org/issues/issue5_7/ghosh/index.html.*

16. CODD goes through files line by line looking for developer attribution patterns. Details at *orbiten.org/codd/.*

17. Red Hat Linux v. 6.1, Linux kernel v. 2.2.14, projects at an archive for cryptography and security programs (*www.munitions.vipul.net*), and about 50 percent of the code available on *www.freshmeat.net.*

18. Ilka Tuomi, "Learning from Linux: Internet, Innovation, and the New Economy," working paper, April 15, 2000.

19. Gwendolyn K. Lee and Robert E. Cole, "Demystifying Open Source Software Development: The Mobilization, Organization, and Process of the Linux Kernel Development," working paper, UC Berkeley Haas School of Business, December 31, 2001, p. 12.

20. One possibly major problem is that students and other "private" contributors would show up as ".com" if they sent code from their yahoo.com or hotmail.com email addresses, as many do. And contrary to public perception, .org does not always mean nonprofit.

21. See *www.linux.org/info/index.html.*

22. *www.unc.metalab.edu.* The assessment is reported in Bert J. Dempsey, Debra Weiss, Paul Jones, and Jane Greenberg, "A Quantitative Profile of a Community of Open Source Linux Developers," School of Information and Library Science, University of North Carolina at Chapel Hill, N.C., October 1999, at *ibiblio.org.*

23. Metadata is simply "data about data," in this case describing how, when, and by whom a particular set of data was collected, and how the data was formatted.

24. See Dempsey et al, "A Quantitative Profile of a Community of Open Source Linux Developers," School of Information and Library Science at the University of North Carolina at Chapel Hill, N.C., at *www.ibiblio.org/osrt/develpro.html.* See also Bruce Kogut and Anca Metiu, "Open Source Software Development and Distributed Innovation," *Oxford Review of Economic Policy* 17(2), 2001, pp. 248–264.

25. GNOME is the GNU Network Object Model Environment. The study is Stefan Koch and Georg Schneider, "Results from Software Engineering Research into Open Source Development Projects Using Public Data," *Diskussionspapiere zum Tatigkeitsfeld Informationsverarbeitung und Informationswirtschaft,* Nr. 22, Wirtschaftsuniversitat Wien, 2000.

26. See *www.opensource.org/open-jobs.html.*

27. Oliver Williamson, *The Economic Institutions of Capitalism: Firms, Markets, Relational Contracting.* New York: Free Press, 1985.

28. Hillis, a well-known computer scientist and an early innovator in massively parallel processing, made this comment in private communication.

29. Paul Vixie, "Software Engineering," in Chris DiBona, Sam Ockman, and Mark Stone, eds., *Open Sources*, p. 98, emphasis added.

30. Mark Granovetter, "Strength of Weak Ties," *American Journal of Sociology* 78, 1973, pp. 1360–1380.

31. Peter Wayner, *Free for All: How Linux and the Free Software Movement Undercut the High-Tech Titans*. New York: Harper Collins, 2000), p. 118.

32. See *www.slashdot.org, www.kuro5hin.org, www.freshmeat.net*, for examples.

33. This debate is reprinted in DiBona, *Open Sources*, pp. 221–251.

34. John Seely Brown and Paul Duguid, *The Social Life of Information*. Boston: Harvard Business School Press, 2000.

35. Metalab estimates that less than 3 percent of free software is in public domain. *www.ibiblio.org/pub/licenses/theory.html*.

36. See *www.debian.org*; the social contract is at *www.debian.org/social_contract.html*.

37. Melvin E. Conway, "How Do Committees Invent?" *Datamation* 14(4), April 1968, pp. 28–31.

38. See, for example, *www.bell-labs.com/user/cope/Patterns/Process/index.html*.

39. See, for example, James D. Herbsleb and Rebecca E. Grinter, "Architectures, Coordination, and Distance: Conway's Law and Beyond," *IEEE Software*, September/October 1999, pp. 63–70.

40. Ibid., p. 67.

41. Ibid., p. 68.

42. More details on these alternative arguments in Chapter 5.

43. Eric Raymond, "Homesteading the Noosphere," in *The Cathedral and the Bazaar*, pp. 79–137.

44. Similarly for Marcello Tosatti, to whom Cox handed off the primary maintainer role (after agreeing with Torvalds) for the 2.4 kernel in 2002.

45. Perl is a programming language that is widely used for system administration tasks and for complex e-commerce applications that depend on interactivity and the ability to "glue" data and interfaces together.

46. Glyn Moody, *Rebel Code*. Cambridge, Mass.: Perseus Publishing, 2001, p. 137, quoting Wall.

47. Roy T. Fielding, "Shared Leadership in the Apache Project," *Communications of the ACM* 42(4), April 1999, pp. 42–43.

4. A Maturing Model of Production

1. Benedict Anderson, *Imagined Communities: Reflections on the Origin and Spread of Nationalism*. London: Verso, 1983.

2. For a detailed history with greater emphasis on the individuals in the story, see Glynn Moody, *Rebel Code*. Cambridge, Mass.: Perseus Pub-

lishing, 2001; and Linus Torvalds and David Diamond, *Just for Fun: The Story of an Accidental Revolutionary.* New York: HarperBusiness, 2001.

3. Michael J. Piore and Charles F. Sabel, *The Second Industrial Divide: Possibilities for Prosperity.* New York: Basic Books, 1984.

4. See, for example, Peter Wayner, *Free for All: How LINUX and the Free Software Movement Undercut the High-Tech Titans.* New York: HarperBusiness, 2000; James Howard, "The BSD Family Tree," *Daemon News* at *www .daemonnews.org/200104/bsd_family.html,* April 2001; and Jordan Hubbard's history at *www.freebsd.org/doc/en_US.ISO8859-1/books/handbook/ history.html.*

5. *www.freebsd.org/doc/en_US.ISO8859-1/books/handbook/history.html;* also see Wayner, *Free for All,* p. 210.

6. *www.netbsd.org/Ports/.*

7. James Howard, "The BSD Family Tree," *Daemon News* at *www.daemon news.org/200104/bsd_family.html,* April 2001.

8. Adam Glass to NetBSD users list, December 23, 1994, *mail-index .netbsd.org/netbsd-users/1994/12/23/0000.html.*

9. Theo de Raadt, mail archive between de Raadt and the NetBSD core, December 20, 1994, to October 5, 1995, at *www.theos.com/deraadt/core mail.*

10. Larry McVoy, "The Sourceware Operating System Proposal," November 9, 1993, at *www.bitmover.com/lm/papers/srcos.html.*

11. A mirror site is a replica of an existing site. It is used to improve the availability of a site that is getting congested or is geographically far away from the users. FTP (file transfer protocol) is a standard format for sending data between computers.

12. Torvalds, quoted in Moody, *Rebel Code,* p. 48.

13. Selected excerpts from this debate can be found in Appendix A, "The Tanenbaum-Torvalds Debate," in Chris DiBona, Sam Ockman, and Mark Stone, eds., *Open Sources: Voices from the Open Source Revolution.* Sebastopol, Calif.: O'Reilly & Associates, 1999.

14. Author's interviews with a variety of sources.

15. Peter Wayner, *Free for All,* p. 66.

16. The growing literature on communities of practice is inspired by John Seely Brown and Paul Duguid, "Organizational Learning and Communities of Practice: Toward a Unified View of Working, Learning, and Innovation," *Organization Science* 2(1), February 1991, pp. 40–57.

17. *www.opensource.org/licenses/mit-license.php.*

18. See Joshua Drake, "Linux NetworkingHOWTO," at *www.tldp.org/ HOWTO/Net-HOWTO/,* 2000.

19. This made sense at the time because in 1992 it was not yet clear that TCP/IP would come to dominate the network.

20. Joshua Drake, "Linux NetworkingHOWTO," at *www.tldp.org/HOWTO/ Net-HOWTO/*, 2000.

21. Alternatively he would sometimes ask the developer who wrote the code to send it to Cox.

22. Web servers now take on much more complicated tasks, including security, authentication, and providing sophisticated gateways to vast databases.

23. Moody, *Rebel Code,* p. 127.

24. Alan Cox led the effort to build this capability into Linux, reinforcing his position as the key lieutenant to Torvalds.

25. Torvalds later told Glyn Moody that he did not want to favor any commercial Linux venture over another.

26. Not only specialist magazines (*Computerworld*) but also mainstream business magazines (*Forbes*) and general interest newsmagazines (*Times*) carried special features on Linux and Linus Torvalds in the summer and fall of 1998. Amy Harmon, "Rebel Code," *The New York Times Magazine,* February 21, 1999; Josh McHugh, "For the Love of Hacking," *Forbes .com,* August 10, 1998, at *www.forbes.com/global/1998/0810/0109044a .html.*

27. Raymond, quoted in Moody, *Rebel Code,* p. 181.

28. The Red Hat IPO took place on Wednesday, August 11, 1999. The IPO price was $14, and the stock finished the day at $52.06. The VA Linux IPO took place on December 10, 1999. The IPO price was $30, and the stock finished the day at $239.25.

29. Moody, *Rebel Code,* p. 215.

30. Netscape's browser cost $39 for commercial use; it was free for use at universities and in many other settings. The important revenues for both Microsoft and Netscape lay in selling server software; the browser acted as a loss leader.

31. Between April and June 1998, activity on the three main Mozilla mailing lists declined by between 60 and 70 percent.

32. Annotated by Eric S. Raymond, "Halloween Document 1 (Version 1.14)," 31 October–1 November, 1998, at *www.opensource.org/halloween/ halloween1.html.*

33. "Fear, Uncertainty, and Doubt" (FUD) is a term that critics of Microsoft (and occasionally Microsoft itself, internally) use to describe one style of the company's competitive tactics.

5. Explaining Open Source: Microfoundations

1. The title of Torvalds's book has, unfortunately, reinforced that perception. See Linus Torvalds and David Diamond, *Just For Fun: The Story of*

an Accidental Revolutionary. New York: HarperBusiness, 2001. See also "After the Microsoft Verdict," *The Economist,* April 8, 2000.

2. Popular media often portray the open source community in this light, but fail to account for the fact that many "beneficiaries" of this altruism (apart from the developers themselves) are major corporations that use Linux software.

3. See Eytan Adar and Bernardo A. Huberman, "Free Riding on Gnutella," *First Monday* 5(10), October 2000, at *firstmonday.org/issues/ issue5_10/adar/index.html.*

4. Of course this is not always the case, for example, in evolutionary theory in which one way of solving the problem has been to redefine the unit of analysis away from the individual organism that is or is not acting "altruistically."

5. Lawrence Lessig, *Code and Other Laws of Cyberspace.* New York: Basic Books, 1999.

6. Another unfortunate characteristic of the data is that it is heavily weighted (about two-thirds) toward people who characterized themselves as "users" or "interested observers" with only one-third self-identifying as core developers.

7. Full results at *www.psychologie.uni-kiel.de/linux-study/.* The three most important gains (all scoring 4.6 on a scale of 1 (very unimportant) to 5 (very important)) were "having fun programming," "improving my programming skills," and "facilitating my daily work due to better software." "Lack of payment" was much less important (2.2); "time lost due to my involvement in Linux" was a bit more important (2.6).

8. The Boston Consulting Group Hacker Survey, Release 0.3. Presented at LinuxWorld, January 31, 2002, at *www.bcg.com/opensource/BCG HACKERSURVEY.pdf.* BCG surveyed a random selection of developers from SourceForge; the results were based on 526 respondents (a 34.2 percent response rate).

9. Another important survey, carried out under EU auspices, is Free/Libre and Open Source Software: Survey and Study. See FLOSS Final Report, International Institute of Infonomics, University of Maastricht, The Netherlands, June 2002, at *www.infonomics.nl/FLOSS/report/.*

10. Mike Gancarz, *The Unix Philosophy.* Boston: Butterworth-Heinemann, 1995.

11. Allison made this comment at the conference "Rethinking Business in Light of Open Source," cosponsored by OSDN and BRIE, San Francisco, April 2001.

12. Salinger is believed to have written a large number of manuscripts that are not to be published but remain locked up.

13. In an interview, one developer made the evocative analogy that opening your source code is a little like sitting around Central Park in your underwear.
14. Pekka Himanen, *The Hacker Ethic and the Spirit of the Information Age.* New York: Random House, 2001.
15. Eric von Hippel, *The Sources of Innovation.* New York: Oxford University Press, 1988. See also von Hippel, "Sticky Information and the Locus of Problem Solving: Implications for Innovation," *Management Science* 40(4), April 1994, pp. 429–439.
16. The obvious analogy is to arguments about the markets for broadcast television.
17. Von Hippel, *The Sources of Innovation,* Chapter 8.
18. See The Boston Consulting Group Hacker Survey, presented at LinuxWorld, January 31, 2002, at *www.bcg.com/opensource/BCGHACKER SURVEY.pdf* (downloaded July 12, 2002). The sample here is a 10 percent random selection among developers on SourceForge; of the 1,648 developers identified, the BCG group received a response rate of 34.2 percent.
19. Interview with Linus Torvalds, *First Monday* 3(3), March 1998, at *www.firstmonday.dk/issues/issue3_3/torvalds/index.html.*
20. David Constant, Lee Sproul, and Sara Kiesler, "The Kindness of Strangers: The Usefulness of Electronic Weak Ties for Technical Advice," *Organization Science* 7, March–April 1996, pp. 119–135.
21. The classic discussion of institutional norms and reward systems/incentives in the "scientific community" is Robert Merton, *The Sociology of Science: Theoretical and Empirical Investigations.* Chicago: University of Chicago Press, 1973.
22. Mark Stone, "Chivalry," at *www.digitalpilgrim.com/personal/chivalry.html.*
23. This is one way in which the norms of the open source community and the norms of modern academic communities, at least those in the United States, are different.
24. Josh Lerner and Jean Tirole, "The Simple Economics of Open Source," NBER, February 25, 2000. This is an important paper that draws on others' analyses while recognizing its own limitations as a "preliminary exploration" that invites further research.
25. In the BCG survey only 11.5 percent of respondents chose "reputation" as a key motivating factor. In interviews programmers often talk about the importance of reputation within their community, but rarely connect it directly to monetizable outcomes.
26. Paul Duguid, personal communication, March 2002. Duguid goes on to suggest that working code does not get widely read "unless you are one

of the famed names"—that is, an already famous coder. This inverts the reputational argument to suggest that if you have a strong reputation your code gets read, rather than you get a strong reputation because people read your code.

27. Ilkka Tuomi uses this phrase in "Learning from Linux: Internet, Innovation, and the New Economy," an important working paper of April 15, 2000.

28. Again, that does not mean it is wrong; it simply places reputonics in perspective as one among several microfoundational motivations.

29. Steven Levy, *Hackers: Heroes of the Computer Revolution.* Garden City, N.Y.: Doubleday, 1984. It is worth noting how these beliefs are interestingly distinct from the norms of academic scientific research, from which this community arose (and to which, of course, it still has very strong ties).

30. Eric S. Raymond, "How to Ask Questions the Smart Way," *www.tuxedo.org/~esr/faqs/smart-questions.html,* p. 1.

31. Ibid., p. 9, emphasis in original.

32. For a simple formal model, see Robert Axelrod, "An Evolutionary Approach to Norms," *The American Political Science Review* 80(4), December 1986, pp. 1095–1111.

33. Jutta Allmendinger, J. Richard Hackman, and Erin V. Lehman, "Life and Work in Symphony Orchestras: An Interim Report of Research Findings," Report No. 7, Cross-National Study of Symphony Orchestras. Cambridge, Mass.: Harvard University, 1994. This paper was later published as "American Music: Life and Work in Symphony Orchestras," *The Music Quarterly* 80(2), Summer 1996, pp. 194–219.

34. Mark S. Granovetter, "The Strength of Weak Ties," *American Journal of Sociology* 78(6), 1973, pp. 1360–1380; David Constant, Sara Kiesler, and Lee Sproull, "The Kindness of Strangers: On the Usefulness of Weak Ties for Technical Advice," *Organizational Science* 7, 1996, 119–135.

35. George Akerlof, "The Market for Lemons: Quality Uncertainty and the Market Mechanism," *Quarterly Journal of Economics* 89, 1970, pp. 488–500.

36. Eric S. Raymond, "Homesteading the Noosphere," in *The Cathedral and the Bazaar: Musings on Linux and Open Source by an Accidental Revolutionary.* Sebastopol, Calif.: O'Reilly & Associates, 1999, pp. 79–136; a more general application to the Internet is Richard Barbrook, "The Hi-Tech Gift Economy," *First Monday* 3, 1998, pp. 1–13.

37. This is not entirely good news, of course. Nietzsche characterized gift-giving as part of a "lust to rule"; Levi-Strauss saw gift cultures as having the potential to be highly oppressive because of the escalating and imprecise obligations they create. See Frederick Nietzsche, "On the Gift-

Giving Virtue," in *Thus Spoke Zarathustra* in *The Portable Nietzsche*, trans. W. Kaufmann. New York: Penguin Books, 1982, p. 301. Claude Levi-Strauss, *The Elementary Structures of Kinship*, trans. J. H. Bell, J. R von Sturmer, and R. Needham. Boston: Beacon Press, 1969.

38. Ralph Waldo Emerson, *Essays*, 2nd series. Boston: Houghton Mifflin, 1876, p. 161.

39. Lewis Hyde, *The Gift: Imagination and the Erotic Life of Property*. New York: Vintage Books, 1983.

40. For example, see Davis Baird, "Scientific Instrument Making, Epistemology, and the Conflict between Gift and Commodity Economies," *Philosophy and Technology* 2(3–4), Spring/Summer 1997, pp. 25–45; Andrew Leyshon, "Scary Monsters? Free Software, Peer to Peer Networks, and the Spectre of the Gift," *Environment and Planning D: Society and Space* 21, 2004.

41. Eric S. Raymond, "Homesteading the Noosphere," *First Monday* 3(10), 1998, p. 99.

42. Mancur Olsen, *The Logic of Collective Action; Public Goods and the Theory of Groups*. Cambridge, Mass.: Harvard University Press, 1971; also see the summary and clever (but highly polemical) critique by Eben Moglen, "Anarchism Triumphant: Free Software and the Death of Copyright," *First Monday* 4(8), August 1999, at *www.firstmonday.dk/issues/issue4_8/moglen/*. Smith and Kollock use this conventional frame to label Linux an "impossible public good." Marc Smith and Peter Kollock, eds., *Communities in Cyberspace*. New York: Routledge, 1999.

43. The classic articulation is Paul A. Samuelson, "The Pure Theory of Public Expenditure," *The Review of Economics and Statistics* 36, 1954, pp. 387–389.

44. See Elinor Ostrom, *Governing the Commons: The Evolution of Institutions for Collective Action*. Cambridge, Mass.: Cambridge University Press, 1990; see particularly the distinction between appropriation and provision problems in Chapter 2.

45. Rishab Aiyer Ghosh, "Cooking Pot Markets: An Economic Model for the Trade in Free Goods and Services on the Internet," *First Monday* 3(3), March 1998, at *www.firstmonday.dk/issues/issue3_3/ghosh/index .html*.

46. Ghosh, "Cooking Pot Markets," p. 16.

47. See Russell Hardin, *Collective Action*. Baltimore: Johns Hopkins University Press, 1982, pp. 67–89; Gerald Marwell and Pamela Oliver, *The Critical Mass in Collective Action: A Micro-social Theory*. New York: Cambridge University Press, 1993, particularly Chapter 3.

48. Olsen, *The Logic of Collective Action*.

6. Explaining Open Source: Macro-Organization

1. Recognize that the precise definition and boundary of a species is sometimes ambiguous (as is true of a code fork).
2. Robert Young and Wendy Goldman Rohm offer an interesting industry perspective in *Under the Radar: How Red Hat Changed the Software Business and Took Microsoft by Surprise.* Scottsdale, Ariz.: Coriolis, 1999, p. 181.
3. Albert O. Hirschman, *Exit, Voice, and Loyalty: Responses to Decline in Firms, Organizations, and States.* Cambridge, Mass.: Harvard University Press, 1970.
4. Robert Axelrod, *The Evolution of Cooperation.* New York: Basic Books, 1984.
5. Robert Young and Wendy Goldman Rohm, *Under the Radar,* pp. 179–183.
6. That is, the overall pie would be smaller. Clearly there are parameters within which this argument is true. Outside those parameters (in other words, if the pie were not *too* much smaller and the distributional scheme were *much* more favorable), it would be false. It would be possible to construct a simple model to capture the logic of that last sentence, but it is hard to know—other than by observing the behavior of developers—how to attach meaningful values to the important parameters in the model.
7. Robert C. Ellickson, *Order without Law: How Neighbors Settle Disputes.* Cambridge, Mass.: Harvard University Press, 1991, p. 270.
8. Eric S. Raymond, "Homesteading the Noosphere," *First Monday* 3(10), October 1998, pp. 90–91, at *www.firstmonday.dk/issues/issue3_10/raymond/index.html.*
9. See, for example, the exposition in James Tully, *A Discourse on Property: John Locke and His Adversaries.* Cambridge, Mass.: Cambridge University Press, 1980.
10. Raymond, "Homesteading the Noosphere," p. 127. These norms obviously leave lots of wiggle room for disagreement.
11. Thanks to Mark Stone for discussions about this point.
12. See, for example, Mike Gancarz, *The Unix Philosophy.* Boston: Digital Press, 1995.
13. Eric S. Raymond, "Philosophy," ch. 1, *The Art of Unix Programming* at *www.catb.org/~esr/writings/taoup/html/philosophychapter.html,* p. 4.
14. See *www.opensource.org/advocacy/faq.html.*
15. Raymond, "Philosophy," p. 7.
16. "What Motivates Free Software Developers," interview with Linus Torvalds, *First Monday* 3(3), March 1998, at *www.firstmonday.dk/issues/*

issue3_3/torvalds/index.html; and Linus Torvalds and David Diamond, *Just for Fun: The Story of an Accidental Revolutionary.* New York: HarperBusiness, 2001.

17. Donald K. Rosenberg, *Open Source: The Unauthorized White Papers.* New York: John Wiley & Sons, 2000, p. 109.

18. Andrew Tridgell, "Samba-TNG Fork," October 2000, at *us1.samba.org/ samba/tng.html.*

19. John Maynard Smith, ed., *Evolution Now: A Century after Darwin.* San Francisco: Freeman, 1982.

20. Clayton M. Christensen, *The Innovator's Dilemma: When New Technologies Cause Great Firms to Fail.* Boston: Harvard Business School Press, 1997.

21. One detailed estimate is by David A. Wheeler, "More Than a Gigabuck: Estimating GNU/Linux's Size," June 29, 2002 manuscript, at *www .dwheeler.com/sloc/redhat71-v1/redhat71sloc.html.*

22. For different approaches, see Henry Mintzberg, *The Structuring of Organizations: A Synthesis of the Research.* Upper Saddle River, N.J.: Prentice Hall, 1979; James G. March and Herbert A. Simon, *Administrative Behavior.* New York: Macmillan, 1957; Oliver E. Williamson, *The Mechanisms of Governance.* New York: Oxford University Press, 1996.

23. For example, see Kevin Kelly, *New Rules for the New Economy: Ten Radical Strategies for a Connected World.* New York: Viking Press, 1998; Donald Tapscott, "Business Models in the New Economy," 2000, at *www.agile brain.com/tapscott.html.*

24. For a recent survey, see The BRIE-IGCC E-conomy Project, *Tracking a Transformation: E-Commerce and the Terms of Competition in Industries.* Washington, D.C.: Brookings Institution Press, 2001.

25. See W. Richard Scott, *Organizations: Rational, Natural and Open Systems.* Upper Saddle River, N.J.: Prentice Hall, 1981; S. Brusconi and A. Prencipe, "Managing Knowledge in Loosely Coupled Networks," *Journal of Management Studies* 38(3), November 2001.

26. Linus Torvalds, "The Linux Edge," in Chris DiBona, Sam Ockman, and Mark Stone, eds., *Open Sources: Voices from the Open Source Revolution.* Sebastopol, Calif.: O'Reilly & Associates, 1999, p. 108.

27. Thanks to Jed Harris for a very helpful discussion on this issue.

28. In symmetrical multiprocessing, any idle processor can be assigned any task, and additional processes can be added to improve performance and handle increased loads.

29. See Melvin E. Conway, "How Do Committees Invent," *Datamation* 14(4), April 1968, pp. 28–31; David L. Parnas, "On the Criteria to Be Used in Decomposing Systems into Modules," *Communications ACM* 31(11), 1988, pp. 1268–1287.

30. Communication with Jed Harris, February 2002. This paragraph relies heavily on his arguments.

31. Background on OpenSSH at *www.openssh.com/*.

32. Text at *www.debian.org/social_contract.html*. As I explained in Chapter 4, the Debian Free Software Guidelines later were modified slightly to become the Open Source Definition of the Open Source Initiative and thus the core statement of the general constitutional principles behind open source licenses. See *www.opensource.org/docs/definition_plain.html*; the major change is that Debian-specific references were removed.

33. See the discussion in Frank Hecker, "Setting Up Shop: The Business of Open-Source Software," at *www.hecker.org/writings/setting-up-shop.html*.

34. See BSD license "template" at *www.ibiblio.org/pub/Linux/LICENSES/bsd.license*.

35. *www.gnu.org/licenses/gpl.html*.

36. Dynamic linking takes place when two programs make "calls" on each other's resources, but do not compile together as if they were one program.

37. See Richard Stallman, "Why You Shouldn't Use the Library GPL for Your Next Library," February 1999, at *www.gnu.org/licenses/why-not-lgpl.html*.

38. Richard P. Gabriel and William Joy, "Sun Community Source License Principles," 2001, at *www.sun.com/981208/scsl/principles.html*.

39. Ibid., p. 5.

40. Interviews. Note that part of the response (as was the case with SSH) has been to work around Sun by building a pure open source implementation of Java, called Kaffe (www.kaffe.org).

41. Gabriel and Joy, "Sun Community Source License Principles," at *www.sun.com/981208/scsl/SCSLPrinciplesPublic.pdf*, p. 6.

42. Interview with Apache Group members; Roy T. Fielding, "Shared Leadership in the Apache Project," *Communications of the ACM* 42(2), April 1999, pp. 42–43.

43. *www.apache.org*.

44. See the general discussion in James G. March, "Exploration and Exploitation in Organizational Learning," *Organization Science* 2(1), 1991, pp. 71–87; and the specific discussion in Jae Yun Moon and Lee Sproul, "Essence of Distributed Work: The Case of the Linux Kernel," *First Monday* 5(11), 2000, at *firstmonday.org/issues/issue5_11/moon/index.html*.

45. See the thread "A Modest Proposal: We Need a Patch Penguin" on the Linux kernel mailing list, Rob Landley, January 28, 2002, mirrored at *old.lwn.net/2002/0131/a/patch-penguin.php3*.

46. Quoted by Joe Barr, "Linus Tries to Make Himself Scale," on

Linuxworld.com, February 11, 2002, at *www.linuxworld.com/site-stories/2002/0211.scale.html.*

47. Ibid.

7. Business Models and the Law

1. For a detailed discussion of versioning, see Hal Varian and Carl Shapiro, *Information Rules: A Strategic Guide to the Network Economy.* Boston: Harvard Business School Press, 1998.
2. Frank Hecker, "Setting Up Shop: The Business of Open-Source Software," June 20, 2000 (revision 0.8), at *www.hecker.org/writings/setting-up-shop.html.*
3. This is what Microsoft has done with its "shared source" initiative. For details, see *www.microsoft.com/resources/sharedsource/Licensing/default.mspx.*
4. Oliver E. Williamson, *The Mechanisms of Governance.* New York: Oxford University Press, 1996.
5. For example, see the RealNetworks justification of the decision to release much of its source code in October 2002. "RealNetworks Releases Helix DNA Producer Source Code to Helix Community," press release on December 9, 2002, at *www.realnetworks.com/company/press/releases/2002/helixprod_sourcecode.html.*
6. Torvalds acknowledges this, but he would be unlikely to use the term "competitive advantage" to describe it.
7. Yochai Benkler, "Coase's Penguin, or Linux and the Nature of the Firm," *Yale Law Journal* 112, Winter 2002–2003, p. 23.
8. This story is not only parsimonious; it also provides a better explanation of salary differentials in the academic world.
9. Robert Young and Wendy Goldman Rohm, *Under the Radar: How Red Hat Changed the Software Business and Took Microsoft by Surprise.* Scottsdale, Ariz.: Coriolis, 1999; Hecker, "Setting Up Shop." Of course these lists are not logically exhaustive.
10. John Landry and Rajiv Gupta, "Profiting from Open Source," *Harvard Business Review,* September–October 2000, p. 22. HP gives this example: If you wanted to build an online relocation service, e-speak would help you set up the relationships among the key partners (shipping, insurance, real estate, health insurance, and so on).
11. See *www.bitkeeper.com/bk19.html.*
12. This licensing provision stands outside the bounds of the "official" open source initiative guidelines at *www.opensource.org/.*
13. "Not Quite Open Source," *Linux Weekly News,* 1999, at *www.lwn.net/1999/features/bitkeeper.phtml.*

14. Young and Rohm, *Under the Radar,* p. 40.

15. Apple's decision to concentrate first on an open source Unix-style operating system for the desktop PC rather than for servers and mainframes reverses what most other companies (including Dell and IBM) have chosen to do.

16. See Apple Public Source License, *www.publicsource.apple.com/apsl.*

17. Protected memory is a feature that allows a single program to crash without crashing the entire operating system. Preemptive multitasking is a procedure that lets the operating system decide when to switch resources from one application program to another. This replaces the more primitive procedure of cooperative multitasking, whereby the programs have to cooperate and decide how to allocate resources among themselves.

18. Interviews with current and former Apple employees.

19. See *developer.apple.com/darwin/projects/darwin/faq.html.*

20. Jordan Hubbard, "Open-Sourcing the Apple," *Salon.com,* November 17, 2000, at *dir.salon.com/tech/review/2000/11/17/hubbard_osx/index.html.*

21. See, for example, *www.globus.org.* See also Ian Foster and Clark Kesselman, eds., *The Grid: Blueprint for a New Computing Infrastructure.* New York: Morgan Kaufmann Publishers, 1998. For an interesting application to protein structure mapping (a task that demands huge processing power) with a philanthropic twist, see "Platform Computing Teams with IBM and AFM to Build European Grid for the French Telethon 2001: Internet Users to Donate Unused PC Processing Power to Create Virtual Supercomputer to Analyze Proteins, Genetic Diseases," at *www .platform.com/newsevents/pressreleases/2001/telethon_29_11_01.asp.*

22. See *www.eclipse.org.*

23. See *www.osdl.org.*

24. John Markoff, "Sun Microsystems Is Moving to an 'Open Source' Model," *The New York Times,* December 8, 1998, p. C6.

25. Likely reflecting Bill Joy's overall perspective on the quality of most code "checked in" through open source processes. See also Dan Gillmor's column "Sun Could Learn a Lesson on Java from Netscape," in *San Jose Mercury News,* September 18, 1998, p. 1C.

26. With the exception of Sun's decision to release the Staroffice program, a competitor to Microsoft's Office productivity suite, as "full" open source under the GPL. Sun acquired Staroffice in the summer of 1999 and released it under GPL in October 2000, setting up the Openoffice.org source project in conjunction with Collab.net. See *www.openoffice.org.*

27. Robert Lemos, "Progeny Reborn in Linux Services," *ZDNet News,* October 16, 2001, at *zdnet.com.com/2100-1103-530903.html.*

28. Another major source of revenue for MySQL is, of course, support contracts for GPL version installations.

29. See "A Closer Look at Linux," at *www.sun.com/2002–0319/feature/;* "Sun Stroke," *The Economist,* March 16, 2002, p. 5; Mark Boslet, "Sun Microsystems Offers Concession to Open-Source Developers on Java," *The Wall Street Journal,* March 27, 2002, p. 7.

30. In fact 2002 saw major shifts in this direction by large firms including AOL, Google, Amazon, and the New York Stock Exchange. The other alternative to Sun systems was, of course, Windows.

31. Siva Vaidhyanathan makes this point forcefully in *Copyrights and Copywrongs: The Rise of Intellectual Property and How It Threatens Creativity.* New York: NYU Press, 2001.

32. Trademark is another important branch of intellectual property law that has (at least until now) been less controversial in its application to open source.

33. This example comes from the famous suit brought by Apple against Microsoft. The courts decided that the overlapping window design was unprotectable due to the narrow range of expression possible for ideas about user interface windows. Apple Computer, Inc. v. Microsoft Corp., 799 F. Supp. 1006 (N.D. Cal. 1992), aff'd, 35 F.3d 1435 (9th Circuit 1994).

34. Eben Moglen, "Anarchism Triumphant: Free Software and the Death of the Copyright," *First Monday* 4(8), August 2, 1999 at *www.firstmonday.dk/issues/issue4_8/moglen/index.html.*

35. The first substantial court case, in early 2002, pits MySQL AB against Progress Software Corporation. Interestingly, by the time the lawyers filed for an injunction against Progress, the company had come into compliance with the GPL by releasing the source code for its product. The suit continued in part because of other perceived slights by the company, including a questionable move to register the domain name mysql.org, that have caused considerable bad blood in the relationship. David Lancashire, "The MySQL.org Controversy," unpublished manuscript, UC Berkeley, May 2002.

36. Brodi Kemp, "Copyright's Digital Reformulation," unpublished manuscript, Yale Law School, 2002.

37. Another important case that I do not consider here is the dispute between Princeton Professor Edward Felten and the Recording Industry Association of America, over the publication of methods for cracking digital watermarks of the Secure Digital Music Initiative.

38. Johansen apparently did not write the tool, but helped to polish it and circulate it on the Internet.

39. An earlier lawsuit brought by the DVD Copyright Control Association claimed that websites linking to DeCSS violate trade secret law. This

case became embroiled in the question of whether source code can be protected as speech under the first amendment, and appeals are pending before the California Supreme Court.

40. Further complicating matters, in early 2002 Norwegian prosecutors indicted Jon Johansen for his role in contributing to DeCSS code, under a Norwegian law that prohibits the breaking of a protective device in a way that unlawfully obtains access to the data. Johansen was found innocent in January 2003; but as I write this, the case is being appealed. As of August 25, 2003, the California Supreme Court ruled that the Court of Appeals needed to reexamine evidence regarding whether banning publication of DeCSS is unconstitutional, a position the Court of Appeals had previously supported (per the Electronic Frontier Foundation, August 25, 2003, at *blogs.eff.org/IP/Video/DVDCCA_case/20030825 _eff_bunner_pr.php*).

41. Case law is mixed on this question; some argue that the contract requires a meeting of the minds on terms, and others argue that use constitutes agreement to terms after notice.

42. See, for example, Mark A. Lemley, "Beyond Preemption: The Law and Policy of Intellectual Policy Licensing," 87 *California Law Review* 111, January 1999.

43. Article 7 states, "Each time you redistribute the Program (or any work based on the Program), the recipient automatically receives a license from the original licensor to copy, distribute, or modify the Program *subject to these terms and conditions.* You may not impose any further restrictions on the recipient's exercise of the rights granted herein" (italics added).

44. The 1966 Report of the President's Commission on the Patent System recommended against patents on computer programs; a 1973 Supreme Court decision ruled against patents on mathematical algorithms. See *Gottschalk v. Benson,* 409 US 63 (1973).

45. The decision is at *www.law.emory.edu/fedcircuit/july98/96–1327.wpd.html.*

46. Oracle Corporation Patent Policy Statement, available at *www.base.com/ software-patents/statements/oracle.statement.html.*

47. An excellent overview is Brian Kahin, "Policy Development for Information Patents in the United States and Europe," presented at "Frontiers of Ownership in the Digital Economy," Institut Francais des Relations Internationales, Paris, June 10, 2002, and available at *cip.umd.edu/ kahinifri.doc.*

48. Many large software companies have chosen a defensive strategy, selectively applying for patents and building up a patent portfolio that can be used to deter or respond to potential infringement lawsuits—for example, by offering to settle with cross-licensing of patents.

49. I refer here to the (continuing) controversy over the World Wide Web Consortium's Patent Policy Framework; see *www.w3.org/2001/ppwg/*.

50. In May 2002, Red Hat filed several software patent applications as part of a self-proclaimed defensive strategy.

51. If this seems implausible, consider an analogy to the way in which record companies collaborate within groups like the RIIA against Internet broadcasters.

52. Bruce Perens, "Preparing for the Intellectual-Property Offensive: Patents May Be the Ground on Which the Open Source Battle Is Won or Lost," *Linuxworld.com,* November 10, 1998, available at *www.linuxworld .com/linuxworld/lw-1998–11/lw-11-thesource.html.*

53. Allman is CEO of Sendmail and wrote the original Sendmail program while he was a graduate student at CSRG. He made this argument during a presentation at the BRIE-OSDN conference, "Rethinking Business in Light of Open Source," San Francisco, California, April 2001.

54. For example, non-U.S. taxpayers and "inexperienced investors" according to SEC rules are not eligible. Of the approximately 5,000 developers that Red Hat identified as possible investors, only around one thousand were interested, eligible, and able to participate. Young and Rohm, *Under the Radar,* p. 157.

55. Here is an example. The source code for Ex Libris software, which runs the SUNY library system, is under escrow for the five-year term of the deal with the vendor. SUNY can access the source code at any time; if the deal terminates, SUNY takes ownership of the source. "SUNY's Library Software Contract Includes 'Ultimate Protection': Software Code," *Chronicle of Higher Education,* November 21, 2000.

56. Harold Demsetz, "The Private Production of Public Goods," *Journal of Law and Economics* 13, October 2, 1970, pp. 293–306. See also John Kelsey and Bruce Schneier, "The Street Performer Protocol and Digital Copyrights," *First Monday* 4(6), June 1999, at *www.firstmonday.dk/issues/ issue4_6/Kelsey/index.html.*

57. Oliver E. Williamson, *The Mechanisms of Governance.* New York: Oxford University Press, 1999.

58. Matthew Fordahl, "Linux Vendors Unite to Create Common Distribution System," *The Associated Press,* May 31, 2002. See also *www.united linux.com.*

8. The Code That Changed the World?

1. For example, Lawrence Lessig, "Open Code and Open Societies: Values of Internet Governance," *Chicago-Kent Law Review* 74, 1999, pp. 101–116. See also Lawrence Lessig, "The Limits in Open Code: Regulatory

Standards and the Future of the Net," *Berkeley Technology Law Review* 14(2), Spring 1999, pp. 759–769.

2. An interesting analysis is Christopher Cherniak, *Minimal Rationality*. Cambridge, Mass.: MIT Press, 1986.

3. See John R. Commons, *Legal Foundations of Capitalism*. Madison, Wisc.: University of Wisconsin Press, 1968.

4. Another way to put this is to say that the core of a property right is the exclusive right to choose whether and on what terms the property is made available to others. See, for example, Guido Calabresi and Douglas Melamed, "Property Rules, Liability Rules, and Inalienability: One View of the Cathedral," *Harvard Law Review* 85(6), 1972, pp. 1080–1128. Different packages of rights may include access rights, extraction rights, management rights, and so on, but each is made meaningful by the ability to exclude under defined conditions. A useful analysis is Edella Schlager and Elinor Ostrom, "Property Rights Regimes and Natural Resources: A Conceptual Analysis," *Land Economics* 68(3), 1992, pp. 249–262.

5. Douglass C. North, *Institutions, Institutional Change, and Economic Performance*. New York: Cambridge University Press, 1990.

6. John G. Ruggie, *Constructing the World Polity: Essays on International Institutionalization*. New York: Routledge, 1998.

7. I am not endorsing this "property fundamentalist" perspective; rather, I am simply pointing out that it has an attractive intuition attached to it that probably explains its pull.

8. See Chapter 6 and also Lewis Hyde, *The Gift: Imagination and the Erotic Life of Property*. New York: Vintage Books, 1983; Claude Levi-Strauss, *The Elementary Structures of Kinship,* Boston: Beacon Press, 1969.

9. Thanks to Shari Cohen and Brad Hirshfeld for discussions on this topic.

10. See, for example, S. Bachrach and E. Lawler, "Power Dependence and Power Paradoxes in Bargaining," *Negotiation Journal* 2(2), 1986, pp. 167–184; Robert O. Keohane and Joseph S. Nye, *Power and Interdependence*. New York: Harper Collins, 1989.

11. Albert O. Hirschman, *Exit Voice and Loyalty: Responses to Decline in Firms, Organizations, and States*. Cambridge, Mass.: Harvard University Press, 1972.

12. See, for example, Siva Vaidhyanathan, *Copyrights and Copywrongs: The Rise of Intellectual Property and How It Threatens Creativity*. New York: New York University Press, 2001; Lawrence Lessig, *The Future of Ideas: The Fate of the Commons in a Connected World*. New York: Random House, 2001.

13. In some civil law traditions, there remain elements of fundamentalism in the sense that authors' rights are considered personal or human

rights as well as economic rights. For example, see M. Moller, "Author's Right or Copyright," in F. Gotzen, ed., *Copyright and the European Community: The Green Paper on Copyright and the Challenge of New Technology.* Brussels: E. Story-Scientia, 1989; M. Holderness, "Moral Rights and Author's Rights: The Keys to the Information Age," *The Journal of Information, Law and Technology* 1, 1998, at *elj.warwick.ac.uk/jilt/issue/1998_1.*

14. Paul Krugman, "The Narrow Moving Band, the Dutch Disease, and the Consequences of Mrs. Thatcher: Notes on Trade in the Presence of Dynamic Scale Economies," *Journal of Development Economics* 27(1-2), 1987, pp. 41–55.

15. Gary S. Becker and Kevin M. Murphy, "The Division of Labor, Coordination Costs, and Knowledge," *The Quarterly Journal of Economics,* 107(4), November 1992, pp. 1137–1160.

16. F. A. Hayek, "The Use of Knowledge in Society," *American Economic Review* 35, September 1945, pp. 519–530.

17. David Isenberg, "Rise of the Stupid Network," 1997, at *www.hyperorg.com/misc/stupidnet.html.*

18. For example, transmission control protocol, the TCP in TCP/IP, is an error-checking protocol that could have been implemented in the middle of the network, but was pushed out to the edges instead. See, for example, Jerome H. Saltzer, David P. Reed, and David D. Clark, "End-to-End Arguments in System Design," *ACM Transactions in Computer Systems* 2(4), November 1984, pp. 277–288.

19. With caveats (for example, with regard to communicable knowledge), see Harold Demsetz, "The Theory of the Firm Revisited," *Journal of Law, Economics & Organization* 4(1), 1988, pp. 141–161.

20. Gary Becker and Kevin Murphy, "The Division of Labor, Coordination Costs, and Knowledge," *Quarterly Journal of Economics* 107(4), November 1992, pp. 1137–1160.

21. Bruce Kogut and Anca Turcana, "Global Software Development and the Emergence of E-innovation," Carnegie Bosch Institute, October 1999.

22. Yochai Benkler, "The Battle over the Institutional Ecosystem in the Digital Environment," *Communications of the ACM* 44(2), February 2001, pp. 84–90.

23. Although the overhead costs to this system are actually rather high, probably higher than a consciously engineered system would want to accept.

24. For example, W. Brian Arthur, "Competing Technologies, Increasing Returns, and Lock-In by Historical Events," *Economic Journal* 99(394), March 1989, pp. 116–131.

25. The allusion here is to the configuration of a typewriter keyboard; see

Paul David, "Clio and the Economics of QWERTY," *American Economics Review* 75, May 1985, pp. 332–337. This particular example has been criticized—for example, see S. J. Liebowitz and Stephen E. Margolis, "The Fable of the Keys," *Journal of Law and Economics* 33, April 1990, pp. 1–25.

26. Stewart Brand, *How Buildings Learn*. New York: Viking Press, 1994.

27. General discussion in J. Bradford DeLong and A. Michael Froomkin, "Speculative Microeconomics for Tomorrow's Economy," *First Monday* 5(2), February 2000, at *firstmonday.org/issues/issue5_2/Delong/index.html*.

28. Clayton M. Christensen, *The Innovator's Dilemma: When New Technologies Cause Great Firms to Fail*. Cambridge, Mass.: Harvard Business School Press, 1997.

29. James G. March, "Exploration and Exploitation in Organizational Learning," *Organization Science* 2(1), February 1991, pp. 71–87.

30. Ibid., p. 71.

31. This section benefits from discussions with Elizabeth Churchill of Xerox PARC.

32. But see the work of people like Paul Dourish for the view that this constraint will not change very much. Paul Dourish, *Where The Action Is: The Foundations of Embodied Interaction*. Cambridge, Mass.: MIT Press, 2001.

33. The 1997 move to glibc libraries is a good example; see Robert Young and Wendy Goldman Rohm, *Under the Radar: How Red Hat Changed the Software Business and Took Microsoft by Surprise*. Scottsdale, Ariz.: Coriolis, 1999.

34. An API is an application programming interface. A "secret" API might be used to give a performance advantage to an application sold by the same company that owns the standard. Microsoft is often accused of doing this with Windows and Microsoft Office, for example.

35. Microsoft's extension to Kerberos merged authentication and authorization processes in an efficient way, but also attempted to tie the desktop to the server in the sense that Unix systems could not interact with services offered on Windows 2000 servers. This spawned a complex battle over the open source community's efforts to reverse-engineer the additions for Samba and undermine Microsoft's effort.

36. One of the roadblocks to widespread acceptance of Unix-style systems in the mid-1990s was the relative paucity of graphical user interfaces. The main graphics toolkit for Unix, MOTIF, was not open source, so open source programmers had to build GUIs mostly from scratch. In 1996 there were several different GUI programs running on Linux using different toolkits with idiosyncratic and inconsistent implementations.

37. Glyn Moody, *Rebel Code: Linux and the Open Source Revolution.* Cambridge, Mass.: Perseus Publishing, 2001, p. 263.

38. To some degree, very powerful hardware can compensate for not very sophisticated software (instead of using "smart" algorithms, you throw increasing amounts of brute processing power at a problem), but there are limits to this substitution, as artificial intelligence researchers have so vividly encountered.

39. See, for example, "IBM Develops Prototype of Wrist Watch Running Linux," Reuters, August 7, 2000.

40. Pete Beckman and Rod Oldehoeft explain why in "The Case for Open Source Software Development for Scalable High-Performance Computing," Los Alamos National Laboratory, February 17, 2000, LANL publication LA-UR-00643.

41. Gigaflops (quantity of floating point operations per second) is of course a crude measure of overall performance, but is indicative of what is possible with massively parallel supercomputing.

42. See *www.butterfly.net.*

43. SETI@home is a familiar early and simple example of grid computing.

44. Garrett Hardin, "The Tragedy of the Commons," *Science* 162, 1968, pp. 1243–1248.

45. Jessica Litman, *Digital Copyright.* Amherst, N.Y.: Prometheus Books, 2001.

46. See, for example, Lawrence Lessig, *The Future of Ideas: The Fate of the Commons in a Connected World.* New York: Random House, 2001; David Bollier, *Silent Theft: The Private Plunder of Our Common Wealth.* New York: Routledge, 2002; and the work of Public Knowledge at *www.publicknowledge.org.*

47. James Boyle, "The Second Enclosure Movement and the Construction of the Public Domain," 2001, at *www.law.duke.edu/pd/papers/boyle.pdf.*

48. Michael A. Heller and Rebecca S. Eisenberg, "Can Patents Deter Innovation? The Anticommons in Biomedical Research," *Science* 280(5364), May 1998, pp. 698–701.

49. Yochai Benkler, "Intellectual Property and the Organization of Information Production," *International Review of Law and Economics* 22(1), July 2002, pp. 81–107.

50. Perhaps the effect is even stronger in software when a copyright "owner" does not need to reveal the source code to attain copyright protection, and thus can in some circumstances plausibly keep some elements of the underlying ideas to herself even while protecting the expression.

51. This is certainly true in anticipation of actual behavior; it may be quite

difficult as well to measure the actual effects of particular regimes after some time. See, for example, Brian Kahin, "Information Process Patents in the US and Europe: Policy Avoidance and Policy Divergence," *First Monday* 8(3), March 2003, at *firstmonday.org/issues/issue8_3/kahin/index.html.*

52. For, example, see J. Flanagan, T. Huang, P. Jones, and S. Kasif, *National Science Foundation Workshop on Human-Centered Systems: Information, Interactivity, and Intelligence.* Final Report. University of Illinois, 1997; L. G. Terveen, "An Overview of Human-Computer Collaboration," *Knowledge-Based Systems Journal* 8(2–3), 1995, pp. 67–81.

53. For example, Pekka Himmanen, *The Hacker Ethic and the Spirit of the Information Age.* New York: Random House, 2001.

54. See Robert B. Reich, *The Work of Nations: Preparing Ourselves for 21st-Century Capitalism.* New York: Vintage Press, 1992.

55. Eben Moglen makes this point nicely about cultural production in "The Encryption Wars," interview from *Cabinet* 1, Winter 2000. Also available at *www.immaterial.net/page.php/44/.*

56. IBM as well as Red Hat and Caldera have placed significant bets on this proposition.

57. See Francois Bar and Michael Borrus, "The Path Not Yet Taken: User-Driven Innovation and U.S. Telecommunications Policy," Fourth Annual CRTPS Conference, University of Michigan Business School, Ann Arbor, Michigan, June 5–6, 1998.

58. The Simputer is being used in pilot projects in microbanking, distance education, rural information access, health care, and other applications driven by the demands of local users. See *www.Simputer.org* and particularly the hardware-licensing scheme that is derived from the GPL.

59. Letter from Congressman Dr. Edgar David Villaneuva Nunez to Microsoft Peru, May 2002, at *linuxtoday.com/developer/20020506012260 SSMLL.* See also Ariana Cha, "Europe's Microsoft Alternative: Region in Spain Abandons Windows, Embraces Linux," *Washington Post,* November 3, 2002, p. A1.

60. *www.redflag-linux.com.* Microsoft in late 2002 came to understand the importance of this particular motivation and agreed to show Windows source code to some governments, under extremely restrictive conditions, to reassure them on security issues.

61. J. C. R. Licklider and R. W. Taylor, "The Computer As Communication Device," *Science and Technology,* April 1968, pp. 21–31.

62. Robert O. Keohane and Joseph S. Nye, *Power and Interdependence.* New York: Harper Collins, 1989.

63. Stephen D. Krasner, ed., *International Regimes*. Ithaca, N.Y.: Cornell University Press, 1983.

64. Robert O. Keohane, *After Hegemony: Cooperation and Discord in the World Political Economy*. Princeton, N.J.: Princeton University Press, 1984.

65. Presentation at the Global Business Network meeting, Sonoma, California, June 1999.

66. Thanks to Daniel McGrath and Chris Caine for help with this idea.

67. Steven Weber and John Zysman, "E-Finance and the Politics of Transitions," in *Electronic Finance: A New Perspective and Challenges*. Bank of International Settlements (BIS) Paper No. 7, November 2001.

68. It will likely also create new kinds of networks; I am not claiming that this scheme is in any way comprehensive.

69. See Ernst B. Haas, "Words Can Hurt You, or Who Said What to Whom about Regimes," *International Organization* 36(2), Spring 1982, pp. 207–243.

70. I have developed these arguments in more detail in "International Organizations and the Pursuit of Justice in the World Economy," *Ethics and International Affairs* 14, Winter 2000, pp. 99–117.

71. See, for example, the Prepared Text of Remarks by Craig Mundie, Microsoft Senior Vice President, May 3, 2001, at *www.microsoft.com/press pass/exec/craig/05–03sharedsource.asp*.

72. For examples, see William Bulkeley and Rebecca Buckman, "Microsoft Wages Campaign Against Using Free Software," *The Wall Street Journal*, December 9, 2002, p. 7.

73. As a result, Microsoft has aimed most of its effort at familiar organizations—other companies and governments in particular. Rather than attack the open source community directly, the company has tried to undermine its relationships with customers.

74. A good summary is in Steven Strogatz, "Exploring Complex Networks," *Nature* 410(8), March 2001, pp. 268–276.

75. Stuart Kauffman, *The Origins of Order: Self-Organization and Selection in Evolution*. New York: Oxford University Press, 1993; Donald Chisholm, *Coordination Without Hierarchy: Informal Structures in Multiorganizational Systems*. Berkeley, Calif.: University of California Press, 1992.

76. Paul J. DiMaggio and Walter W. Powell, "The Iron Cage Revisited: Institutional Isomorphism and Collective Rationality in Organizational Fields," in Paul J. DiMaggio and Walter W. Powell, eds., *The New Institutionalism in Organizational Analysis*. Chicago: University of Chicago Press, 1991, pp. 63–82.

77. John Arquilla and David Ronfeldt, "Cyberwar Is Coming," *Comparative Strategy* 12(2), Summer 1993, pp. 141–165; Arquilla and Ronfeldt, eds.,

Networks and Netwars: The Future of Terror, Crime, and Militancy. Santa Monica, Calif.: RAND, 2001, MR-1382-OSD.

78. Margaret E. Keck and Kathryn Sikkink, *Activists Beyond Borders: Advocacy Networks in International Politics.* Ithaca, N.Y.: Cornell University Press, 1998.

79. See, for example, Robert O'Brien, Anne Marie Goetz, Jan Aart Scholte, and Marc Williams, *Contesting Global Governance: Multilateral Economic Institutions and Global Social Movements.* Cambridge, England: Cambridge University Press, 2000.

80. There is really no reason, other than theoretical convenience, to presuppose an ontology of hierarchical actors as the important ones. Dropping this presupposition allows a more differentiated view of the nature of an evolving political space, regardless of whether you call it global civil society.

81. And will be the subject of my next book.

82. Stephen S. Cohen, J. Bradford DeLong, Steven Weber, and John Zysman, "Tools: The Drivers of E-Commerce," in The BRIE-IGCC Economy Project, *Tracking a Transformation: E-Commerce and the Terms of Competition in Industries.* Washington, D.C.: Brookings Institution Press, 2001, pp. 3–27.

83. Which approach or approaches are economically viable will depend on some exogenous variables, including how broadly the law protects things like reverse-engineering of proprietary protocols.

84. Eric von Hippel has sketched out a story about industrial organization that is driven by a strong tendency to carry out problem-solving innovation at the locus of "sticky" information. Eric von Hippel, "Sticky Information and the Locus of Problem Solving: Implications for Innovation." *Management Science* 40(4), April 1994, pp. 429–439.

85. This is obviously not a new question for medical informatics and people who study and design medical decision-making tools; I am simply posing it in a different context.

86. An early example is the ensembl project; see *www.ensembl.org.* See also the advocacy group Bioinformatics at *www.Bioinformatics.org.*

Index

Advanced Research Projects Agency (ARPA), 24, 29, 33–35, 52
Allen, Paul, 36
Allison, Jeremy, 136, 199
Allman, Eric, 216
Alpha processor, 105–106
AMD, 242
AOL, 242
Apache, 2, 90, 125; popularity of, 6; participants in, 65; Internet and, 109–111, 121; IBM and, 178; business logic and, 207; end-to-end innovation and, 239
Apache Group, 92, 110–111; IBM and, 125; governance structures and, 186–187
Apache Software Foundation, 187
Apple Computers, 32, 201–202
Architecture. *See* Software design
Arquilla, John, 263
Artificial intelligence (AI), 46, 83
AT&T, 22; Unix and, 28–29, 31–33, 39–46, 49–53, 98; System V, 35; antitrust suit of, 38–39; licensing and, 39–40; BSDI and, 49–52, 102, 104
Augustin, Larry, 114

Baker, Mitchell, 122
Barksdale, Jim, 122
Barry, James, 124–126
BASH, 103
BASIC, 36
Becker, Gary, 231
Behlendorf, Brian, 90, 110, 206

Bell Telephone Laboratories (BTL), 22, 24; Unix and, 26–27, 29–31, 39; antitrust suit of, 38; networking and, 83. *See also* AT&T
Benkler, Yochai, 194, 245
Berkeley Software Design Incorporated (BSDI), 43; AT&T and, 49–52
Berkeley Software Distribution (BSD), 6, 32; second release (2BSD), 31, 35; third release (3BSD), 33–34; fourth release (4BSD), 34–35, 39; development of, 39–43; licensing issues and, 39–43, 52–53, 62–63, 85, 96–97, 110–112, 114–115, 181, 201–202; x86 chip and, 42–43; developer community and, 91–92; forking of, 95–99; AT&T and, 102, 104; leadership practices and, 168; meritocracy and, 181; Apple and, 201–202; Sun Microsystems and, 203–204
BIND, 6, 121
Bitkeeper, 118–119, 219
Bolt, Beranek, and Newman (BBN), 35, 39
Bostic, Keith, 40–41
Boston Consulting Group, 135, 139–140
Boyle, James, 244
Branding, 193, 197, 200
Brooks, Frederick, 76; Law of, 12, 61–62, 64–65, 171; complexity issues and, 57–59; organization approach of, 59–61
Business: patents and, 4, 18, 22, 32–33, 213–215; hierarchical structure and, 10–12; individual motivation and, 11;

303